In Search of Captain Zero

ALSO BY ALLAN C. WEISBECKER

Cosmic Banditos

In Search of

A Surfer's Road Trip Beyond
the End of the Road

Captain Zero

Ø

Allan C. Weisbecker

JEREMY P. TARCHER/PUTNAM
a member of penguin putnam inc.
new york

Most Tarcher/Putnam books are available at special quantity discounts for bulk purchases for sales promotions, premiums, fund-raising, and educational needs. Special books or book excerpts also can be created to fit specific needs. For details, write Putnam Special Markets, 375 Hudson Street, New York, NY 10014.

Jeremy P. Tarcher/Putnam
a member of
Penguin Putnam Inc.
375 Hudson Street
New York, NY 10014
www.penguinputnam.com

First trade paperback edition 2002
Copyright © 2001 by Allan C. Weisbecker

The Library of Congress cataloged the hardback edition as follows:

Weisbecker, A. C. (Allan C.)
In search of Captain Zero: a surfer's road trip beyond
the end of the road/by Allan C. Weisbecker.
p. cm.
ISBN 1-58542-069-7
1. Mexico—Description and travel. 2. Central
America—Description and travel. 3. Conner, Christopher.
4. Weisbecker, A. C. (Allan C.)—Journeys—Mexico.
5. Weisbecker, A. C. (Allan C.)—Journeys—Central America.
I. Title.
F1216.5.W55 2001
972'.0009'0490922—dc21   00-062895
[B]
ISBN 1-58542-177-4 (Paperback edition)

Printed in the United States of America
9   10

BOOK DESIGN BY AMANDA DEWEY
MAP ON PAGES X–XI BY JEFFREY L. WARD

For Mom

Contents

California

San Miguel (Campground)

30°N

UNITED

MEXICO

25°N

Punta Lobo

20°N

Puerto Vallarta

Nexpa

15°N

Puerto Escondido

Pacific Ocean

10°N

© 2000 Jeffrey L. Ward

110°W   105°W   100°W

STATES
Atlantic Ocean
35°N
30°N
25°N
20°N
15°N
10°N
Gulf of Mexico
Tropic of Cancer
BAHAMAS
CUBA
JAMAICA
Caribbean Sea
BELIZE
GUATEMALA
HONDURAS
EL SALVADOR
NICARAGUA
COSTA RICA
PANAMA
COLOMBIA
Tilapa
La Libertad
San Juan del Sur
Puerto Viejo
95°W
90°W
85°W
80°W
75°W

A Dispatch from Down South

I used to be easy to find. Lived on the last left on Long Island, New York, United States of America. First house on that winding, rural cul de sac. In search of me, if worse came to worst, you could've traveled east on Long Island until you ran out of road at the lighthouse at land's end, then turned around, headed back west and made your first right. There I was, first house.

Long Island. Last left. First house.

Someone in, say, Jakarta, Indonesia, which is about as far as you can get from where I lived on the planet before you start coming back closer again, could have easily been directed to me with those six words.

One time I was in New York City, some 120 miles west of that house, and decided to try an experiment. I bought a postcard at a Grand Central Station kiosk, wrote on it just my name, plus "11954," and mailed it. When I returned to my home a couple days later, it was waiting for me in my mailbox.

That's how small the town is where I used to live. And how easy I was to find when I lived there.

—Somewhere in Central America

Still the waves weep for us evermore
They are but Neptune's tears upon the shore.

FROM A POEM BY MY FATHER

ALLAN CHARLES WEISBECKER, SR.
1921–2000

Big Blue

My last night at the town at which I used to live was spent camped within sight of the lighthouse that marks its eastern limit. I'd given up my house and was all packed up for the road life to come, the possessions I'd deemed irrelevant having been sold, chucked or stored in a friend's basement. Although I was little more than a mile from my former home on the last left before the light, as I turned in the sensation was that I'd already begun an adventure.

There was a personal significance in my choice of campsites: It was only a few yards from where I'd spent my first night on coming to the eastern tip of Long Island some 40 years before, when I was nine years old.

My father had brought me to the end-of-the-road place called Montauk (named for the extinct Montauket Indian tribe) from our home in a New York City suburb to camp out and learn something of the natural world. To this day much of Montauk remains relatively unspoiled, but back in the late 1950s it had a frontier feel. To a nine-year-old boy with an active imagination and whose adventuring had been limited to the writings of Jack London and Robert Louis Stevenson, Montauk's towering, saw-toothed crags, desolate rock-strewn shores and densely impenetrable woods seemed preternaturally wild and remote, an untamed territory where fearsome beasts surely lurked.

The morning after our arrival was a special one, for it was to be my first open-ocean excursion with mask, fins, snorkel and spear gun. I'd learned to dive the previous winter in a YMCA pool, but my wild water experiences had taken me no farther than an upstate lake and the shallow, murky confines of suburban Long Island Sound.

Imagine a young boy, basically a city boy, squatting on his haunches by a fire on the edge of the world. As he shakes off sleep, he gazes out from on high across a seamless expanse of blue vastness broken only by a far distant ship, forlorn and apparently inert, its crew no doubt consumed by a serpent or kraken from below. Picture how the boy's hands are shaking as the tools of the coming sea hunt are unpacked, his father smiling in anticipation of the kill, of blood in the water. Imagine the shivering in the boy's gut as his fear of night monsters is overwhelmingly supplanted by the utterly human fear of a very real unknown. Imagine him so desperately wanting to be back home where his mother will hold him and reassure him that he is even now searching in his mind for a make-believe ailment that will keep him on shore and away from that awful blue vastness.

Now picture the boy an hour or so later, standing on this same promontory, seawater-wet and breathless from the climb back up the cliff, diving knife strapped to his waist, and, dangling from a stringer, a small blackfish slain by his own hand. Imagine him gazing at that now familiar blue vastness and wanting to be out there again, right away.

There are crossroads in one's life, decisions made or not made, acts of will reflecting general directions one is already disposed toward, or in some cases specifically and irrevocably determining those directions—the latter being a true moment of truth, a genuine crossroads. Knowing all that has happened since, it's clear to me that my life would have turned out very differently had I not conquered my fear and entered the water that day.

Forty years later, standing by my rig on the cliff watching the lofty beacon at land's end sweep the silent reach of Big Blue, I found myself dwelling upon my long history with that light. Hundreds of waves ridden on the rocky reefs below it, exploratory dives under the restlessness it surveys, women romanced under its sardonic gaze, safe havens found in its towering lee. After decades of travel to the fairest coastlines on the planet, the stunning panorama before me at that moment was still my unequivocal favorite, and I could not help but wonder if I was seeing it now for the last time. Was I making some awful, irrevocable mistake in my decision to move on?

I slept little that last night. The October air was crisp and very clear, the wind light and from the north. Far out at sea to the southeast the running lights of a single vessel twinkled faintly like a star fallen upon the water. I wondered if it was a local dragger ponderously towing her groundfish net, maybe one of the several boats whose crew I knew and often surfed with.

I worry about my fishermen friends when wind and sea turn brutal and fear reigns on deck. From a total of less than a hundred Montauk commercialmen, on average one is lost every year: a career fisherman who goes offshore for 30 years faces a one-in-three chance of dying on the job. I myself have had three vessels go down under me—one within sight of Montauk Light—and I deeply, viscerally understand that although the sea is a giver of profound joy, it is the source of great fear and sorrow as well.

It was still dark next morning when I turned my rig's nose inland and jounced down a rutted service road to the highway. I was not prepared for the feeling of oppressive sadness, loneliness and sense of failure that accompanied me on my slow, furtive glide through the town that had been my home for so long. There was guilt, too. I had broken most of the promises I'd made to visit friends before my departure. How do you say good-bye when in your heart you believe the parting is final?

Needing to distract myself, I concentrated on my old friend Christopher, and how he himself had so suddenly (but I cannot say unexpectedly) vanished in 1992; how the idea of finding him in some far-flung paradise far to the south was the focus my future so desperately needed. Imagining the inimitable Christopher grin he no doubt sported as he traveled that very road out of town eased the ache as my heavily burdened rig lumbered up that last rise then accelerated westward, just ahead of the gathering dawn.

Still, mine was a fugitive's exit, under cover of darkness.

PART I

South, Baja California

Yes, I shall go into Mexico with a pretty definite purpose, which, however, is not at present disclosable. You must try to forgive me for not "perishing" where I am.

AMBROSE BIERCE

Surfing's a trip—you better have your bags packed.

HERBIE FLETCHER, surfer

1.

At first light this morning, I put some water in the kettle, fired up the stove, then stepped out of La Casita Viajera (the little house that travels) and looked seaward to see what the surf had done overnight. In the gloaming opposite the shoreside loom of the city of Ensenada I could see that the head-high west swell that had been running for the last five days had dropped to a couple feet. I squinted at Todos Santos Island some ten miles out in the bay, thinking that there were probably still sizable waves below the lighthouse near the rock reef break known as Killers. Thought briefly about hiring a local fisherman for a run out there, then decided to spend the day getting my rig—La Casita and the bruiser of an F350 Ford 4 × 4 diesel-powered pickup upon which it sits—ready for the rude ride down the Baja peninsula.

Five days at the San Miguel campground were more than I'd planned, a result of my long-standing traveling rule that dictates that one should never drive away from good surf. Now, with the deterioration of lineup conditions and a worsening crowd factor, I was itching to get on with it. Ensenada, being little more than an hour's drive south of San Diego, is in many ways an extension of the United States, a place and a state of mind I have decided to put behind me.

Odds are Christopher passed this way, may have in fact camped at this very spot overlooking the break. It depends mainly on surf conditions the

5

day he made the Tijuana crossing just to the north—the San Miguel point is in clear view of the highway southbound; at shoulder high or better it's a toughie to pass by.

There's a longtime expat here who lives in a cottage overlooking the point, a guy named Tony, Big Tony. He looked at the photo of Christopher I carry and said Christopher looked familiar, although not from any recent encounter. Which made sense. Christopher had south on his mind back in February of '92, that much I know. South being the natural direction of vanishment, a compass course of no return for the seriously committed.

I'll tell you what: Things are tough up north, and getting tougher.

Mornings toward the end back at Montauk, I'd wake up maybe with a bad feeling about the day's loomings, and go down to the beach, to *my* beach, to ponder what the ocean had to offer, a surf check.

There's a wave, let's say, chest high and glassy, nothing epic but a head-clearer, a gift from a deep low pressure system bouncing along the Carolinas. It's not even a weekend and what am I confronted with? Investment bankers and corporate lawyers with surfboards, another noxious trend of the trendy and an overall sign of deteriorating times. The sun's barely cracked the rim and there they are, a cadre of eastbound Hamptons émigrés, cell-phones-with-modems plugged into surf-racked Beemers and Rovers, uplinking and downloading in the parking lot, blights on the seascape and a last straw of sorts.

And now—after 3,000 hard-driven miles, and having weathered two mechanical breakdowns, an anxiety attack while camped at a defunct railroad station in Pumpville, west Texas (POPULATION 0, the sign said, plus WELCOME); a dissipated hoodang with some unbalanced rodeo cowboys in the border town of Del Rio, Texas; a nocturnal molar explosion and subsequent emergency root canal outside Tempe, Arizona—after having coped with all that, I'm now a foreign country and a new life removed and still the bullshit continues, in the form of certain overly aggressive SoCal types who come down through Tijuana on day trips and weekends to litter the surf lineup and provoke aggravation.

The afternoon of my arrival, for example, I was involved in an extended session in some shoulder-high zippers in front of my campsite, a form of "seahabilitation," as my commercial fishermen friends refer to time offshore, its cure-all therapeutic effects. I was still shaky from the weeklong cross-country road trip, plus the residual effects of my Pumpville anxiety attack; a sweeping rush of unreality that came out of nowhere while I was slopping together a sandwich in La Casita.

For an already edgy, landlocked waterhead, the endless purple mountain majesties and amber waves of grain of the heartland I'd spent interminable days traversing amounted to little more than claustrophobic time and distance between two oceans. By my arrival at that crumbling relic of the old New West, my yearning to gaze upon the infinite, calming perspective of the sea horizon—to reconnect with Big Blue—had become a desperate need. White line fever and too much thinking had taken a severe psychological toll.

I always find the surf lineup a good vantage point from which to objectively review my situation and options. The enlightening perspective out there is partly a result of the inviolate solitude (interlopers are obvious on approach), and partly the effects of an aqueous environment womblike in its security, its easy, pacifying motion, its gently calmative murmur; circumstances that I believe put you in closer touch with the wisdom of the subconscious. And so it is with sadness, depression, angst, call a lowness of spirit what you will. When I hit the water with a surfstick, a lift is in the offing, along with a clarification of my thought processes.

The seahab effect of that marathon surf session was just kicking in when this newly arrived West Coast itinerant stroked on out and immediately proceeded to take off on a wave to which I was already deeply committed. He appeared out of nowhere right on my projected track and an instinctive effort to avoid headlong collision resulted in my going assbackward into a rocky shallows where the San Miguel inside section tends to freight train at low water. I let this unacceptable behavior slide, but when he did exactly the same thing two waves later, I paddled over and, using the still-serviceable Spanish left over from my pot-smuggling days, rambled something to the extent that if my riding waves behind him in the faster and hollower and altogether more interesting part of the wave was a problem, maybe a shore-side discussion on the matter was in order.

As I'd already suspected, the fellow spoke no Spanish, so when he said something surly to that effect, I replied in obviously mock surprise that I assumed he was Mexican since he behaved as if the wave here was his property. Just as the situation was on the verge of deteriorating completely, Big Tony paddled over and hastily introduced me to the guy; Harry or George or Dickhead, who knows, or cares, what the asshole's name was. Tony had been observing the developing confrontation and was seeking to defuse it before it got physical. A former real estate executive in his mid-forties, Tony had experienced his own up-and-bolt epiphany after losing his job for refusing to participate in the selling of a toxic waste landfill to unwitting housing developers. His longstanding surfing residency in the area plus his strapping 6-foot-something frame has made him a sort of de facto keeper of the point break. Although the tension subsided with the cool-your-jets-boys subtext of Tony's intro, a measure of residual disgust lingered, augmented by a cantina brawl I witnessed in Ensenada two nights later, precipitated by an incident in the water.

This morning's coffee in hand, I glanced down at my dog, Shiner, sacked out in her usual spot under the right rear corner of the rig, where my spare Goodyear All Terrain is secured under La Casita's overhang. One eye, the one with the black patch, was open and she acknowledged me with a feeble vibration of her tail—a combination "good morning" and indication that in spite of appearances she was on top of things—then the eye shut down and she was back asleep.

Three new rigs had arrived during the night, beefy pickups with full off-road kits and surf racks affixed to their roll bars. Classic southern Baja cruisers traveling together, the safety-in-numbers theory. They were covered nose to toes with a thick layer of red Baja dust, meaning the fleet was northbound from deeper down the peninsula. Surfboards and sleeping-bagged bodies were scattered across the scree-strewn coal-black beach between an old stone-and-chain wall and the wrack line; as soon as the crew was coherent I'd inquire about surf and road conditions to the south, as well as the prevalence and moods of both *bandidos* and *federales.* Although the two are opposite numbers, an encounter with either can have the same result: an up-close gander at a large-bore orifice followed by a lightening of your resources, or worse.

I'd also ask about Christopher, whether they'd run across him in their travels, although my working theory is that his love of warm water, plus the affinity for the rain forest he developed as an infantry grunt in Vietnam, will have sent him into the far southern latitudes, to Central America.

Christopher had seen heavy combat and returned wounded, but rather than dwell on the horror of Nam he'd reminisce about the Edenic beauty of the jungles there, describing with a beatific smile how artillery and mortar fire would light up the rain forest at night in dazzling and surreal displays, like a fireworks celebration.

This is a key to Christopher Conner, to understanding him. It is both his strength and his weakness that he will somehow find a positive aspect in some appallingly untenable situation. He had had his face shattered in a mortar barrage, but in looking back on that ghastly experience he tightly tunnels his vision to exclude all but the tiny aspect that pleases him. The drawback is that while he's dwelling on some preposterous silver lining in an outright horrific cloud, a means of extrication from the situation may get overlooked. I know this to be the case from unnerving personal experience.

My friendship with Christopher goes back to my discovery of surfing in the summer of 1966. I'd made a Manhattan run from the landlocked suburbs to see a documentary movie called *The Endless Summer,* the tale of two young California surfers who circle the globe looking for the perfect wave. The movie so astounded me that I stayed and watched it again, then returned a couple days later for another double viewing. Up until that time, my only exposure to surfing was through Hollywood's ditzy takes on the early '60s California beach scene and the surf music of the era, the goofball totality of which left this East Coast boy profoundly unimpressed. (I've since grown fond of it all as nostalgia.)

But this . . . this was altogether something else.

The activity itself was mesmerizing in its surreal beauty, the speedy grace and unbridled joy of the wave riders, the delicate power and dreamy elegance of the medium; the latter's kaleidoscopic mutability. I also sensed that there was more to the life of it than the vagabond travelers in the flick were letting on. There was something truly amazing happening here and I wanted in.

By walking into the Kips Bay Theatre on Second Avenue, downtown Manhattan, the die of my life was cast. I'd known since the day I'd followed my father into the water to spear a fish off land's end on Long Island that the sea would somehow play a central role in my life. Suddenly, I knew specifically what that role would be. I scraped together enough money for a used surfboard and returned to Montauk Point.

Christopher, like virtually all the local Montauk surfers, had come from somewhere else to the little fishing village, drawn not only by its unspoiled physical beauty, but its unique geographical circumstances. Thrust out onto the continental shelf with deep water just offshore, the tip of Long Island is ideally situated to pick up incoming groundswells from late summer hurricanes roaring up from the Caribbean, as well as wave-generating low-pressure systems spiraling off the continent. Unlike the straight sand beaches of the rest of the East Coast from western Long Island to New Jersey and on south to Florida, Montauk is blessed with rock bottom points and reefs, irregularities of coastal topography that sculpt incoming waves into rideable form. The pristine stretch of coastline between the town and the point at land's end some five miles to the east is capable of producing waves of similar quality to those of the West Coast. And the seasonal tourism economic base of the area afforded 1960s-era immigrant wave riders night employment at restaurants and bars, leaving days free to pursue that object of great desire rolling in from offshore—surf. Others found berths in the town's fishing fleet; a natural vocation for those with an ingrained affinity for, and knowledge of, the sea.

Being a newcomer not only to the area but to the activity of surfing itself, I found it rough going in the beginning. The muscling I was subjected to in the water and hostile vibes on the beach were my introduction to the territoriality that is so deeply ingrained in surfing's tribal mind-set. At 20, Christopher was three years my senior. We hit it off, and under his tutelage, by mid-summer I'd been accepted as one of the crew. And by God, I was actually surfing.

Along with a cadre of hardcore cohorts, Christopher and I bivouacked at the public campground just east of the village that summer, and off and on for the summers to come. I came to respect him for his intellect, his wry, irreverent, often wacko wit and his love for the sea. Generous to a fault and forgiving of the imperfections of his fellows, he was at once action-oriented and of deeply philosophical inclinations, a rare combination.

People of disparate worldviews and walks of life were drawn to Christopher. A favorite drinking buddy of the town rowdies, he was also popular with intellectual types like Dick Cavett, whose home overlooked the next cove east of the campground. He and Cavett had many an extended beach gab over the years. Christopher became close enough to notorious photographer/artist/adventurer/bon vivant Peter Beard that in the early 1980s he was invited to stay at Beard's Kenya retreat. In Africa, Christopher also holed up for several weeks as the sole companion to hermetic conservationist/writer George Adamson (of *Born Free* fame) at Adamson's remote compound. Christopher's 1982 photographs were likely the last taken of Adamson before he was murdered by terrorist/poachers.

Christopher's philosophical leanings and beguiling good humor were all the more impressive considering his sparse formal education and the traumas of a childhood spent in orphanages, foster homes and reform schools. It was surfing that saved him, he avowed, and we all smiled and nodded and said amen. It was so clear to us what he'd meant. Surfing indeed was a lifestyle. No, more than that: a *life*. It deeply influenced every aspect of our existences, from where we lived to the cars we drove to who our friends were to the temperament of a prospective mate to our career goals, if any managed to surface through the turbulence of our single-minded passion for the water. But more than anything, surfing forged our perception of ourselves and of our relationship to the world around us.

One time in 1970, Christopher and I were in Tetuán, Morocco, looking to score some kilos of hashish to smuggle back to the United States. (An exploratory surf trip to Europe and Africa had evolved into a criminal enterprise.) We'd gotten separated in the confusion of the souk and I wound up in its labyrinthine bowels. Suddenly from nowhere there loomed these three burly, turbaned thugs—leathery skin bedecked with tattoos and self-inflicted scars, silver-handled daggers hanging around their necks—bearing a sheepskin bag filled with hashish slabs. I warily checked the product, then informed them that the deal was not going to go down. Christopher and I were looking for primo blonde and their stuff was low-grade green.

During the stony silence that followed, a nervous little interior voice piped up, pointing out that these goons knew I had money in my boot; I'd had to show it to the shifty-eyed street connection who'd brought me there. Since it therefore followed (continued the little voice) that they might be inclined to simply cut my throat and take it, perhaps the prudent move would be to cordially agree to the deal then get the hell out of there.

But I'd spent the past two years surfing serious waves in Hawaii and another voice, loutish and arrogant and brashly overruling, spoke up. "Those bastards can't do anything to you," boomed the voice. "They never rode big Sunset Beach." I stuck firm in my demurral. The upshot was that they'd nodded and produced the blonde they'd been holding back; the deal went down.

And so it went. My introduction to the wave-riding mind-set that seminal summer on eastern Long Island amounted to a rite of passage; its aftereffects would be far-reaching indeed. But as the summers since '66 rolled on, the years, then the decades, gradually, for most of our crew, things changed: interests, obligations, lifestyles, commitments, attitudes, loyalties. Of the dozen or so of us from that era, and there wasn't a one who didn't swear on his very soul he'd remain among the surfing faithful, the devoutly committed, it was only Christopher and I who were truly left, living the life.

Since Christopher's bolt from Montauk, there were at first sporadic postcards from Down South. Rambling, arcane, disjointed but ultimately insightful, his missives, like his life, contained flashes of brilliance but no discernible structure. Then came that last one, three years ago, with a faded tropical seascape on front, smudged, undated and illegible scrawl on back (postmark likewise indecipherable), the signature in Christopher's hand: "Capitán Cero"—Spanish for "Captain Zero."

Then, nothing. Poof, Christopher was gone, a *desaparecido,* one who "is disappeared."

Unlikely as it was that Christopher is this far north, I'd ask these Baja boys about him, as I will all the picaroons I meet along the way. Because if I've learned one thing over the years, over the decades, it's that with Christopher, with Captain Zero, you just flat never know.

SOUTH

You fly past flats where water has arisen from the deep earth and, guided by the toil of men, fashioned the desert into flowering and prosperous rows of beans and peppers. A lorry-load of farmhands blurs by, northbound to those labors, shoulders hunched against the hot wind in back, sombreros doffed, bandannas shrouding swarthy, sunburnt faces.

2.

"When in doubt stop, get out and walk on up ahead to see just what sort of fresh off-road hell you're in for" is a rule to live by—or at least drive by—when you're south of Ensenada and, in search of the beach, have abandoned Mexico 1, the narrow two-lane blacktop strip that meanders from Tijuana a thousand miles through the Sonoran Desert down to the bottom of the Baja peninsula.

I'm in severe doubt at the moment. When I turned off Mex 1 a couple hours ago this rutted, serpentine dirt track was wide, flat and pointed dead west to seaward. Now I'm hiking eastward down a switchback on the side of a precipitous arroyo to see how serious a mistake I made by bearing right at that last fork . . . and this descending side hill curve is making me edgy. I'm thinking the high center of gravity of the rig might precipitate an el rollo or two, leaving me, my dog and everything I currently own in a shattered heap at the bottom of the ravine.

But I'm picking up a strong whiff of sea air in the freshening afternoon westerlies and figure that beyond that next rise, where this track straightens out and seems to know where it's going, the pale green of the mesquite, chaparral and various cacti of the sweltry rust-red *llano* will give way to cool Pacific blue; and that remote point break those off-road cruiser pilots up at Ensenada raved about should be around here somewhere, wherever here is. Besides, I don't want to be caught driving off-road after dark and I'm burning daylight with the fuel of indecision. So I trot back up the hill, fire up the Ford and press on. Have to find out eventually what this rig can do when the going gets questionable. Might as well be now.

. . .

If the ride down that rambunctious side hill cum vertical-drop arroyo shook up Shiner and me, it did likewise to La Casita Viajera. I've crossed an ocean under sail and lived aboard all manner of seagoing craft, from seven-figure custom yachts to tall ships to flat-bottomed banana boats to commercial cargo carriers—and survived the chaos of a beam-ends knock-down and subsequent foundering in one of the latter. Countless times I've seen the havoc a rolling beam sea with a cross chop can wreak with the accommodations, but still I was astounded by the disorder inside La Casita. In spite of having Velcroed or bungee-corded down everything that could possibly shift or fly, it looked as if a troop of psychotic chimpanzees had thrown a crack-crazed wingding in there.

Parked on a precipitous headland just above the point break I've spent the last three hours searching for, Shiner alerts me to an approaching figure. Someone is following the path up from the little fish camp a half mile or so to the south, the only visible work of man along this wild, distant coast.

His name is Valentine, he says, a swarthy fellow of slight frame and intense eyes that deepen and darken gravely when he speaks. He's the caretaker of the fish camp, and he's brought his two dogs, a quart of Tecate beer and three small lobsters, which he adamantly refuses to take payment for. Examining Valentine closely, I find I can't decide whether he is handsome or homely, such is the chiseled yet uneven angularity of his features. Nor can I tell whether he is 30 years old or 50: is the deeply creased topography of his face a function of advanced years or the shorter-term work of Baja's erosive sun, wind and weather?

On impulse I abruptly ask Valentine if I can photograph him, a query I'd normally make after the development of a degree of familiarity, but the light is good and I'm struck by the mood to record his visage now, before my instincts are skewed by too much knowing. Valentine nods, cheerful and unsurprised by my bold request; he fastidiously primps, straightening the lay of his tattered garb and using his fish-grimy fingers to sweep back his hair.

With half a roll shot, I break out a bottle of tequila and we sit and talk while the three dogs sniff each other and the setting sun busses the fine, clear line of the sea horizon. When Valentine asks me where I live in the States, I tell him nowhere, that I live here right now and I point at the little house that sits on my truck and say, "Es mi casa allí."

He doesn't understand and repeats the question. I realize that *casa* means both house and home so I rephrase, telling him that I used to live in a fishing village in the state of New York but gave that up and now live wherever I am. He nods, looks at my rig and says, "Ahh, eres viajero."

"Sí, sí, sí," I answer enthusiastically because that's how I think of myself now—not so much a "traveler" as a *"viajero,"* the Spanish noun being subtly more Orphic in nuance. He nods, then asks where I'm traveling to. I tell him, *"Al sur,"* to the south, to Central America, in search of an old friend. I also tell him I'm looking for a special place, where the people and the waves are good, and life is sweet and easy. "Busco un pedazo de paraíso," I say, grinning abashedly. "I'm looking for a piece of paradise."

But Valentine does not return my smile. He looks at me for a moment as if he's seeing something in my future, then says that I should please be careful with *"la violencia en el sur,"* the violence in the south. I know a little of what he's talking about, having conversed with people up north who heard that four surfers had been shot up by *bandidos* on the Mexican mainland in the state of Chiapas, two dead and two wounded. And an acquaintance of my expat friend Big Tony had been shot in the spine when he tried to run a *bandido* roadblock and his car was riddled with rifle fire.

I muster a smile and ask if perchance my old friend has passed this way, a fellow surfer running with dogs, two at least, and a sometime commercial fisherman himself. I show Valentine the photo I took of Christopher a few days before he bolted from Montauk back in January of '92.

"Quién es la mujer?" Valentine asks, wanting to know who the woman is sitting by Christopher.

"Mi novia," I say. My girlfriend, then add, "Pero no es mi novia ahora." But she's not my girlfriend now. I don't know how to say "former girlfriend."

Valentine makes a face indicating that the girl is pretty, then studies Christopher's image. I squint over his shoulder at the picture and although I've looked at it a hundred times, I can't help but grin at how it's just so perfectly Christopher: loose-limbed and slouched on a chair in his single-room oceanfront shack, one arm raised with the hand slightly blurred from some crazed gesture, that whacko Christopher grin. My ex, Diana, across from him laughing hysterically but with a startled look in her eye, as if he'd just said something wildly funny yet wholly inappropriate.

Valentine says that no such man has visited here. He shrugs, adding that not so many *nortes* do.

I build a fire and we sit, passing the tequila and beer between us and making small talk. Soon the ribbon of western sky above the dull gunmetal Pacific blue has gone to a pale yellow that exactly matches the color of the fire. As the day itself, our conversation winds down naturally and without artifice.

Soon it's dark and Valentine and his dogs have gone home to the fish camp. I'm drunk and dizzy as I cook and eat the lobsters he gave me, dribbling melted butter onto the stove and down my chin. I nod out after dinner sitting at the settee with the stereo playing Chopin and Shiner snoozing outside by the door.

3.

Nothing like the little adrenaline boost of a first light paddle-out to deconstruct and unaddle your next-morning, tequila-fuzzed faculties. Even in small stuff, like this morning.

A fine, gauzy mist maybe 50 feet thick lays upon the water, and the sun rises as a vague, effulgent white blotch above the massive undulating black silhouette of the Sierras de San Pedro Martir to the east.

The water is noticeably cooler here than just up the coast at San Miguel, probably due to a local upwelling of the California Current—itself a part of the chilly Aleutian Current, down from the far north. At the sea surface, where cold water touches warmer air, mist forms then rises to soon evanesce in the thermal updrafts. The freed water molecules then drift back down to the sea as a sort of ephemeral, microscopic rain.

The waves are just waist-high, and although the sea surface is glassy this windless morning, they are soft and mushy and inelegant. But my joy in being out here alone is of an ineffable intensity. The sea surface swirls over a submerged shelf as I stroke into a little wave that humps up and doubles in size. I rise to my feet as the ocean lifts me up as if in a giant's strong, benign hand, and then gravity's force seems to tilt sideways to effect the controlled fall of my slick, silent horizontal slide. I find a little locus of energy, a sweet spot, on the wave face and cross-step to the nose of my longboard. I'm only up there for a couple seconds before the wave flattens and I have to backpedal, but that familiar noseride sensation—of having no surfboard in front of me, like walking on water or flying or, somehow, something in between—lingers, and I find I'm grinning like a fool as I kick out.

A solo session. The first of many, I'm hoping, now that I've left behind the edgy clutter of crowded stateside lineups. Only one thing better than a solo session, I'm thinking as I stroke back outside, and that's a session with a good friend.

No witness is needed to one's accomplishments out here, nor an adversary with whom to compete in order to make one's efforts meaningful. The activity is sovereign, complete unto itself, and hence it attracts those of a certain independent temperament. But the simple, unspoken act of sharing with a good friend the joys of wave riding adds a precious layer to the experience, like some secret trust between you.

Christopher comes to mind, of course, our many shared go-outs at surf breaks far and wide. The bond of that, and of the common perils, the fearlessness, of young lives lived on the outside, draws me southward down this coast in his faint wake. He is the link, you see, the one clear connection to so much I hold dear, and to so much I regret as well.

I don't know the word I need and I've left my *diccionario español* in La Casita, so I query a young *pescador* named Felix, who is leaning on his *panga* (dory), staring into a fire made from beach wood collected and pooled by the dozen or so crews gathered at the fish camp. "Cuando el aire tiene agua," when the air has water, I say, "Y no puede ver el sol en el cielo." And you can't see the sun in the sky. A fogbank rolled in while I was surfing, supplanting the gossamer brume with a dense shroud of colorless murk.

"Niebla," Felix says. "Niebla impenetrable."

I nod. "Niebla. Cuando la niebla se va, va a pescar?" I'm asking if he's going to sea when the fog lifts.

"Sí. Claro."

Valentine appears, slaps me on the back and tells me he saw me surfing this morning. He is his usual expansive self, his eyes bright but unfocused from the mescal I saw him pour into his coffee earlier by the fire. He drags me off, intent on introducing me around while everyone waits for the weather to clear. As with commercial fishermen everywhere, I feel an underlying connection to these tough, seafaring men, and am unsurprised by their gruff but genuine goodwill. They are a good bunch.

I talk up a fellow in a knee-length olive overcoat. His name is Chicho and he tells me that most of the *panga* crews here dive offshore for sea urchins, which are sold through middlemen to the Japanese market. With his rugged good looks, wild mop of jet-black hair and bushy moustache, Chicho could be cast in an eye blink as an heroic Down South revolutionary of days past, or a wild man *bandido* with a good heart.

I approach a burly fellow named Miguel, who is sitting on his *panga*'s transom and dangling his bare feet over the little fire below it, his right arm draped around the 40-horse Evinrude. Based upon his several layers of threadbare wetsuit, I know that Miguel is one of the divers. Each *panga* crew consists of one urchin diver, plus a helmsman and a crewman who feeds the diver's air hose over the side and looks out for his safety.

I make small talk, using the word *niebla* again in a sentence to further imprint it in my vocabulary, then ask Miguel if he has had any problems with sharks. "The Surf Report," a worldwide surf/travel guide published by *Surfer* magazine, which details the sea conditions and accesses to remote Baja beaches better than any of the publications I've perused, ominously describes several breaks in the area as "sharky."

Miguel's response is curt and vehement. "No no no. Nunca!" Never! He rises abruptly, turns his back on me and spits into the fire. He stares off into the nothingness, toward the ocean we can hear but cannot see. I regard his broad back for a few seconds, wanting to ask if everything is okay but I sense that now is not the right time, so I wander up the hardpan launching ramp to La Casita to make another cup of coffee.

Emerging little more than a moment later, the dazzling clarity of the day makes me blink. The fogbank has moved on, or, rather, disappeared, as if by meteorological magic. I scan the sea horizon, then the inland *llano*. There is no sign of fog anywhere. Poof.

A couple hundred yards to the south where the beach starts a lazy westward curve, a squabbling flurry of snowy-plumed gulls, blue-black ravens and red-headed turkey vultures worry a bloated carcass the size of a cow.

There is no livestock on the local *llano* and I wonder briefly what sort of creature has been cast ashore down there.

With the disappearance of the fogbank, the men on the beach have been galvanized into action. One *panga* has already been launched and is cruising to the northwest, taking small groundswells easily right on the bow, the helmsman's bright orange slicker unbuttoned in front and flapping behind.

I trot down to the beach to find Felix, Miguel and a fellow named Gonzalo turning their *panga* seaward. Valentine and two other men I haven't met grab the gunnels to help and soon the craft is pointed seaward. The other men pause for a breather while Felix and Gonzalo place rollers under the hull. I approach the *panga,* figuring to help in the final push to the sea but Miguel squints at me and seems to frown, meanwhile absently touching the crucifix around his neck. My distinct impression is that he doesn't want me to touch his *panga.*

I back off, more confused than ever.

At a command from Miguel, sea boots and bare feet dig deeply into the beach as the six men commence dragging the boat seaward, chanting "Ya!-ya!-ya!-ya!-ya!" to pump themselves up for the effort.

I tell Chicho what happened when I asked Miguel about sharks. Chicho shrugs uneasily, his gaze wandering south toward the large beached beast. "Es mala suerte hablar de tiburones aquí," he says after a long hesitation, his voice barely above a whisper. It's bad luck to speak of sharks around here.

I ask him why, knowing full well that to answer he'll have to speak of them further. Chicho's words are rushed and sotto voce as he tells me that eight local divers had been killed in recent years by sharks and that a friend of his whose hand-lines caught one of 700 kilos last year near the urchin beds.

"Qué tipo de tiburón?" I know I'm pushing, it but I want to know the species of shark the men fear.

"Bonita," he answers quickly as the scream of a nearby outboard ends the talk of sharks.

I'm thinking that the shark Chicho calls a bonita is maybe a tiger or a hammerhead, but *bonita* means beautiful and the hammerhead is by normal aesthetic standards the ugliest of all sharks. Besides, attacks on humans by hammerheads are rare; so I'm leaning toward tiger. It then occurs to me that maybe he means the great white. Although we're to the south of its typical range, there are kelp beds and seals in the area, which are the great white's favorite prey. And tigers prefer warmer waters than these.

It must be the great white.

Eight men.

I look seaward at Miguel's *panga* as it surges over a small dying line of white water and then follows in the wake of the others, making for the urchin beds to the northwest. Now I'm regretting that I spoke of sharks in front of him, not because I think he will be taken by a shark because of my words, but because of the fear I've created, and I don't believe there is any greater fear than that of being eaten alive.

Come late afternoon I'm relaxing in the hammock with Shiner out cold in my swaying shadow when a pickup and a battered vintage Lincoln Continental with no trunk lid pull up. Both vehicles are packed with *pescadores,* maybe a dozen in all, and I recognize Felix, Gonzalo and Valentine, plus another of the men with whom I'd gotten friendly earlier, Pasqual. Miguel is there, too, back safely from offshore, and to my relief he grins big at me.

Pasqual lifts a heavy box out of the Lincoln's trunk and it's full of quart bottles of Tecate. I produce what's left of my tequila and in short order a party is in progress. Soon thereafter as we sit in a loose circle by the rig, Valentine grabs my arm and tells me I should show the men my photo of Christopher. This is a fine idea, so soon it's being passed from one man to the next, studied intently by each, meanwhile Valentine explaining to the group the story of my search for my old friend. One by one the men shake their heads and say something to the effect that they don't remember the fellow pictured.

The last to look is an older man named Roberto, who speaks passable English from having been a taxi driver in Tijuana. Roberto stares longer than the others and grimaces, as if trying to remember. In the end, he shakes his head, saying maybe up in the city, meaning TJ, maybe not. I tell him that Christopher is not the sort to linger in a place like Tijuana, that he would have gone through there like a cannonball. I then have to explain what I mean by that, which I do in Spanglish with pantomime, and everyone laughs, Roberto even more than the others, saying he understands exactly what I mean. Which is why he moved to *el campo,* the country.

"Tiene tu amigo problemas con la ley en el norte?" Felix asks, wanting to know if Christopher has problems with the law up north.

"No más que yo," I answer. No more than me. This is some subtle macho posturing on my part and was meant for a laugh, which it gets.

Roberto says with a twinkle that Mexico has always been a place for *norte* fugitives and always will be. Then he gets serious and pats me on the knee. "Listen, my friend," he says in his heavily accented English. "There are some bad people around here now."

"Bandidos?"

"Si. Y vienen armados." They come armed. "Pasqual's brother, Chicho, you met him this morning, has a rancho not far to the south. We think you should stay there." From the way Pasqual and several of the other men are nodding, I realize that they have already talked this over.

"No one will bother you at El Rancho de Chicho," Roberto says.

4.

As you approach from the fish camp some three miles to the north, El Rancho seems to rise up from under the desert horizon like an oasis, and indeed Chicho tends it like a garden, trucking in water for the nonnative eucalyptus, Canadian pine and olive trees he's planted on El Rancho's sprawling grounds. A huge oak trunk stands in the northeast corner, imported as a roost for his pigeons.

El Rancho de Chicho is demarcated from the *llano* by a wall of beach stones, a yard or so in height by a yard thick. The stones weigh on average about 40 pounds each and I estimate that each cubic yard of wall is comprised of no less than 30 stones. By pacing it I found that El Rancho's rectangular perimeter is 120 yards by a shade under 80: Using their rattletrap old Toyota pickup, Chicho and his brother Pasqual had hauled nearly a half million pounds of stones up from local beaches, taking two years to complete the task.

Although the wall serves no overtly practical function—an intruder could hop it in a heartbeat—I believe the stones were carried and laid in part as a not-so-subtle warning. Who after all would dare to trespass onto land territorialized by so Herculean an effort? And, indeed, the fishermen of the area, when learning that I was a guest at El Rancho de Chicho, invariably nodded gravely, and their manner toward me waxed more deferential, as if my presence were under special aegis. Although he is not a wealthy man—far from it—Chicho is a man of respect on the *llano*.

. . .

It's now my fourth night at El Rancho de Chicho and Felix's face is barely discernible in the dim twilight. The other *pescadores,* Miguel, Gonzalo and Chicho himself, *el dueño,* have gone for water and batteries for Gonzalo's tape deck and we've been sitting by the rig eating, drinking and talking since before sundown, with Shiner curled snoozing between us by our feet.

Felix more than the others understands the limitations of my Spanish and speaks slowly and distinctly. He smiles patiently and rephrases his thoughts when he uses a colloquialism with which I'm unfamiliar and I request *otras palabras;* or he'll spell the word I need translated while I'm flipping through my *diccionario español.*

There is no electricity on this remote, desolate chunk of Baja coast, so Felix has gone to get a candle. I hear a match strike and flare and through the cracks in the lean-to that serves as an open-air kitchen and communal living area I can see shadowy movement as Felix putters about. I hear the clanking of a pot and the rattle of silverware and catch a whiff of propane in the still night.

Felix returns with coffee; softened by candlelight, the young man's features reflect his Caxaqueno Indian ancestry. When I ask how old he was when he fell in love with *la gringa* in Cancun he'd talked about earlier, he counts back slowly on his fingers, nodding and murmuring to himself, as if remembering specific occurrences in the intervening years as a way of calculating the passage of time. It occurs to me that many desert Indian peoples used painted symbols and hieroglyphics of the most memorable event of each year as a written history. Clearly, if Felix's history were to be depicted in this way, his sixteenth year would have been represented by a bawdy pictograph; or perhaps a sad one, since after their brief affair *la gringa* flew back home to the States and he never saw her again.

Nothing is said for a while, then Felix asks about my job as a writer and whether I've written any books. I tell him, "Yes, one book," but I only nod when he says he'd like to read it. I'm hoping Felix will let the matter drop, but instead he asks me the title. I tell him, "*Bandidos Cósmicos, Cosmic Banditos,*" to which he tilts his head and smiles. I have a copy of the Spanish translation in La Casita but I don't want to show it to him because the story is about a high living, nihilistic marijuana smuggler, and even though that part of my life is long gone and over with I'm embarrassed about it here and now, sitting with a man of his simple tastes, who works so hard for very little.

It's full night now and Felix stretches and yawns and says he's going to bed. He goes off and the darkness and the crisp desert air and the sweet scent of eucalyptus and the hushed resonance of surf breaking a half mile to the west make my thoughts clear and hopeful.

The desert night is not much stirred by its creatures, they of padded foot and muffled wing; and neither do the desert shrubs rustle or shake, with their rigid pointy leaves like broken bones. My mind wanders in the roaring silence and as I connect dots to make mythopoetic pictures in the starry sky, I'm reminded of a conversation I had with Christopher many years ago on a remote beach in North Africa. It was an exotic, far-flung chunk of coast, strikingly reminiscent of Baja. Both are west-facing with predominantly right-handed points (the wave peels right to left from the shoreside view) which break best on northwest groundswells; and both shorelines are flanked by coarse, rugged badlands sparsely inhabited, mostly by seafaring folk.

Christopher and I had been surfing in the wind shadow of a rusted-out hulk of a freighter aground in the shallows just above the mouth of a Moroccan river called the Sebou. We had found the break after a long, mazy, disorienting pilgrimage in our VW van on some desolate back roads, and after our surf session and after smoking a bowl or two of hashish I mentioned something about our not really knowing specifically where we were on the face of the planet. Which set Christopher to extemporizing about the theory of curved space. How the fabric of space is thought to be curved, not straight as logic would seem to dictate, and how this would mean that the universe is finite yet unbounded, of definable size yet with no edges or borders; no beginning, no end, a perfectly enclosed system. And if there is a center to it all, that center is simply wherever you are at the moment. His subtextual point was that one is never truly lost unless and until that condition is admitted to: this is a very Christopher notion, as is the idea that the center of the universe is wherever one happens to be.

Thinking further of Christopher, I wonder if he's found some jungle niche to the south—some other center of the universe—and fashioned for himself a stronghold-by-the-sea like Chicho's. It would be very much like him to do that, with his warrior and honest-criminal past and essential wariness toward all except a few friends and his dogs. If so, our youthful ambition to find a special place may have come to pass, for Christopher at least.

We'd hatched our exploratory plans on that North African adventure a quarter century ago. All giggly yet dead serious in our heady enterprise, we checked off the paradisiacal negatives of our current geographical coordinates: water temp too chilly, groundswell arrivals too seasonal and spotty (flat Atlantic summers), the endemic Arabic culture way too tightly wound, and what with the veiled, reclusive local women the very antithesis of what we sought, a world map was broken out and circles and arrows etched according to the pragmatic dictates of mother ocean and wild and fanciful endless summer assumptions.

By God we were revved and raring. And we had come so close, hadn't we?

And then Christopher came to me in '92, a day or two before his final, solo departure. The bitter January wind blew into my house as he and his dogs arrived, and not that much was said. We had grown apart, I suppose, and I was distracted by yet another conflict with yet another movie studio I was writing a screenplay for, and in the distracting throes of a deteriorating relationship with my girlfriend, Diana.

I might have gotten impatient as Christopher showed me the new surfboard that had just arrived by airfreight from Hawaii, a Dick Brewer rounded pintail. He'd gone on about how he and Dick had conversed by phone about the intricacies and refinements of its shape. I picture myself nodding at his animated discourse, my smiling stare a thousand yarder, while Diana grumpily stalked about the house, neither of us listening or giving a shit. We each had our snide and vital points to make to the other, and were impatient for Christopher to finish up and make himself scarce.

I think he said he'd be in touch as he exited with his dogs and his new Brewer amidst another cold blast. My recollection is vague of that last time I saw Christopher. I clearly only remember that it was very cold that day.

5.

In the late summer of 1944, 22-year-old Megan Riley Conner lived within an easy walk from Islip Long Island Railroad station cafe where she worked as a waitress. William, Megan's husband of less than a year, had been gone to the war in Europe for six months. Megan took extra care to be cheerful and friendly to the servicemen she served in the cafe, for they were mostly very young and frightened about going off to war—and there were so many being sent that summer, replacements for those killed since D-Day.

One of those soldiers was, at nineteen, barely more than a boy, but he seemed to Megan even younger. He was from a small town in the Midwest, on liberty before being shipped overseas. The two got to talking and when Megan was finished with work they went for a walk.

Megan let the young soldier stay with her that night. In the morning she walked with him the short distance from her little apartment to the railroad station, which would carry him to his troop ship. Megan had not hidden the fact of her marriage, nor the love she felt for her husband. She and the young soldier were two lonely people who had sinned, been intimate, and now would never see each other again.

Nine months later, a boy, given the name Christopher Conner, was born of that brief union. With the war still raging in Europe and Megan's husband having been away for more than a year, a scandal ensued. Because of the intense patriotism of the time and the rabid loyalty felt for the men fighting overseas, Megan was legally (and completely unfairly) deemed an unfit mother. Christopher was made a ward of the court.

Soon after Megan lost custody of her son, William Conner returned from the war, found out about Megan's betrayal and divorced her.

Christopher was bounced from various foster homes to an orphanage; and then, at age 12, he was sent to a reform school. Not surprisingly, he had become a troubled child. He was small for his age and physical violence with other troubled, institutionalized kids was common. But Christopher had developed survival smarts; he'd learned how to avoid a fight, or, when that was not possible, how to end it quickly in his favor. He'd also become adept at making himself inconspicuous in situations he sensed might become dangerous. This ability was so striking that his orphanage nickname, "Shadow," followed him into young adulthood.

His mother had been fighting to regain custody and finally succeeded in 1957, when Christopher was 13. But Christopher was unmanageable and over the next few years he was again institutionalized, in reform schools, then in adult jails.

Christopher had only one childhood friend, a neighborhood kid named Danny Quinn. Quinn, who was two years older and looked up to by Christopher, introduced the younger boy to surfing in the spring of 1961. A few months later, Quinn committed suicide by stepping in front of a Long Island Railroad train. Devastated and angered by the tragedy, Christopher was at a crossroads; he was on the verge of going down an antisocial path from which there would be no return.

But instead, Christopher dedicated himself to surfing, which was just becoming popular on the East Coast. It was mainly a handful of high school kids from the towns in Christopher's area, committing themselves to this water-borne, athletic art form. Christopher had entered a whole new world, abandoning a sad, sordid, stifling past for a bright future of fresh sea breezes, white sand beaches and the camaraderie of dawn go-outs with new friends.

As he often said, surfing saved him.

6.

It's early morning of my last day at El Rancho de Chicho and I've paddled out to the rocky point where I had that first solo session. I think about sharks while waiting for my first wave and now that it's me in the water and not Miguel I wonder whether it's bad luck after all, to talk of them.

Time passes and all seems well, though, and with many waves ridden I sometimes let good ones pass me by as my mind wanders. Bobbing in the lineup I can see the fish camp, which is deserted now except for Valentine and his dogs, and the distant bump of El Rancho on the high ground to the south. I think about staying on and making a deal with Chicho to live at El Rancho with Felix, Gonzalo and Miguel. I think of becoming an urchin diver myself and how I could surf this point alone after working the urchin beds or when the waves are too big to launch our *panga*. I'd prop up La Casita on stones I collected on the beach, like Chicho'd done to build his wall, and we'd use my truck to go into town for water and provisions and batteries for Gonzalo's tape deck. We'd listen to Mexican *canciones* at night and talk by candle or fire light.

As a rising sun clears the cliffs to the east, the image of this fresh life *is* sweet and easy, but I know I'll in fact be on the road south when I come ashore, for the life I've chosen for the foreseeable future is one of movement across the land- and seascapes, in my search for new waves to ride, and for my missing old pal.

SOUTH

CURVA PELIGROSA, says the sign on Mexico 1 as you're skirting a bottomless canyon cleft with a roadside crucifix leaning over the abyss (Christ on a stick, oblivious), then (Jesus!) ahead around the funneling switchback caroms the king hell of all trucks, horn blaring, brakes hissing, wheelman grimacing and then FAARRUMPH he's gone, one note basso profundo caterwaul echoing along the escarpment.

Weird. Really spooky. Shiner's shaken up, too, and I don't blame her. I mean what *was* that thing? About half Shiner's size but all teeth and wild eyes and knotted sinews and frizzy gray fur, attacking without notice from behind a privy at the entrance to the remote *pueblo* at the end of another long off-road ramble to the sea. A dog I guess, at least technically. Shiner held her own against its bull-rush onslaught, I'll give her that, but she leaped right back into the rig when I opened the door. Goddamn correct move.

For my part, I got us out of there after little more than a cursory look at the place and I hadn't been attacked by anything. Didn't *see* anything, in terms of life forms, aside from that diminutive hellhound, which circled the rig once slavering and murmuring like some cartoon doggy-demon, then slinked back to its lair behind the outhouse.

What I did see was a vision of an apocalyptic hellhole, made all the more grotesque by its stunning locus on a rugged headland jutting a half mile from the arid desolation of the *llano* into an azure sea. The scenery was a disorienting pastiche of strewn fishing gear and crazed surf graffiti scrawled on twisted kitchen appliances, clatter-board hovels, cockeyed motor homes, junked vehicles and toredo worm-ravaged vintage yachts propped up rotting in their cradles. The *pueblo* was apparently part home base for psychotic local *pescadores,* part *norte*-nazi surf lair and part repository for the detritus of man's mechanical follies.

In the center of the litter-strewn, dusty main drag a directional arrow assembled from the swaybacked spinal column and snarling, elongated skull of some odious, unidentifiable predator pointed toward a sheer drop to the sea. Hang a left here, the skull seemed to be whispering between dagger canines, and you'll end up like me.

I suddenly had a vision of a Mad Max-esque wave rider—surf racks atop his tricked-out, turbocharged steel mount bristling with knife-railed tri-fin thrusters bearing death's head logos—blowing in from the wasteland for a wave-check at the point. "If you wanna surf here, friend," he'd growl, backed up by a band of wild-eyed expats with major localism concerns. "You talk to us."

It was deathly still. Of several dozen decrepit domiciles, not a one showed any signs of life; even the sea breeze felt quiescent. Perhaps what was missing was the tinkling theme to *The Twilight Zone* rising above the silence and completing the impression of an open-air asylum, its patients recently whisked away by aliens, or devoured, bones and all, by the snarling beastie behind the privy. No. Uh-huh. This place was altogether too out of whack, too demented even for my aberrant sensibilities.

As I scatted south out of town along the rollicking coastal track with my dog pressed close, her ears flattened and fur erect from her violent encounter, it occurred to me that in my travels I had crossed some fundamental, unmarked boundary between north and south, between up there and down here, between where I was coming from and where I was going.

SOUTH

Diesel depleted, you roll into the hardpan lot of a sprawling, ramshackle Pemex to find a hand-lettered NO GAS NO DIESEL *cardboard sign lashed to the pumps, but a young fellow with jerry cans at five times the going rate lounges smug and smiling in his Bulls jersey and knockoff Nikes, enterprising keeper of the desert juice. You unleash your own jerries from under La Casita's after works and answer his waning grin with a helpless shrug in mock-empathetic lament at your own foresight, then you top off your tank and are gone up the road in a cloud of that red Baja dust.*

7.

The Pacific's next northwest groundswell having expired to an effete slurp and, further, having suddenly been possessed to see the sun rise over the water rather than set, I find I'm camped on the Sea of Cortez—on North American maps referred to as the Gulf of California—the narrow body of water that separates the Baja peninsula from mainland Mexico to the east. Apart from two local fishermen ensconced at an ad hoc little fish camp a half mile or so down the beach to the south, I have encountered not a soul since my arrival here two days ago.

It's in these more remote places that I tend to picture Christopher, running across him. I'll be rounding the curve of a little point, driving on hard sand or mollusk cultch, or on foot, taking a beach walk with my pooch, and suddenly in my mind's eye there on the beach is his battered old Chevy half-tonner, paint-job lumpy indigo like Big Blue front-lit over the abyss, surfboards and dogs all askew in the shade of a sagging, makeshift tent, with Christopher his-own-self sunburnt black and lolling in a beach chair, one of his droopy straw hats pulled low. Snoring, the very image of mindless euphoria.

Wouldn't it be a kick to stumble upon him thus, in some remote, beachy stopover? Strongly as I suspect that he's long gone further south, that the trail I'm following is stone-cold, it could happen. Just maybe could. As I say, you flat never know with that sonofabitch.

So I talk up the locals, stay alert for sightings. As for my feckless visions, they are of brief, distractive comfort when I'm feeling down or jangled or nonspecifically fearful. And I calm myself through communion with this special place I have come to.

The beauty of central Baja is coarse and unrefined and possesses a jagged and unruly elegance. It's a rough-and-tumble and masculine place, all cuts and edges and quietly fierce, like a bloodied but unbeaten boxer resting in his corner between rounds. Its vistas, while breathtaking, are not comfortable to look at, as are, say, the shorelines of the Hawaiian Islands, which are of such exquisite femininity even when impossibly massive and heroic and immodest. And married with these endemic qualities of the landscape is the pervading presence of the adjoining sea. Although the land and water are profoundly separate, the aesthetic union created is a kind of emotional symbiosis. You cannot look at one without being deeply affected by the other's proximity.

But the sea, I would submit, one-ups its partner in terms of psychical impact, not only through its apparently endless enormity but in the force of its personality. It is a three-dimensional and lively entity, that watery world. It has depth and mobility and with these qualities come the capacity to cover the adjoining land if it is moved to do so; to subsume the earth and make it a part of itself.

At any given time the sea is not only what it is (calm and tranquil, say; a soothing influence), but it is also its capacity to be something else (a medium for wave riding); and then, a moment later, something else altogether (a destroyer and a killer). Imagine gazing at the *Mona Lisa* with the knowledge that her little-girl smile could at any moment transmute to a vicious snarl or a lascivious smirk or a goofball grin. An indication of caprice as to the artist's intent would add an edge to the fascination, no?

It has been claimed that the Eskimo language boasts some ridiculous number of terms for snow, thirty-something, I seem to recall. There is a school of anthropology that postulates that this large number of nouns for "snow" reflects not only a utilitarian need (ease of communication between Eskimos as to what sort of snow fell last night), but an actual difference in perception as well. In other words, goes the theory, when an Eskimo looks at snow, he doesn't merely notice more about the snow; he actually "sees" it in a much more detailed way. The problem with this theory is that one can't just ask the Eskimo if he perceives the snow in a way different from, say, a Trobriand Islander plunked down wide-eyed and shivering in the Arctic. The Eskimo may rattle on about how crusty or grainy or sparkly or deep the snow is (while the Melanesian is stumped in going beyond "white and cold to the touch"), but his words don't tell us anything about his inner life.

The theory can't be proved or disproved, but I'm quite sure it's correct. As a surfer, I don't merely notice more about the sea's condition than a hayseed from Nebraska upon his first viewing; it's an altogether *different world* out there I'm perceiving. As the Eskimo instinctively notes the texture of freshly fallen snow for its capacity to delicately define the track of a wandering wolverine, so the surfer analyzes the sea's finish to gauge how it will hold the edge of his planing surfstick. This perceptual phenomenon is automatic and so deeply ingrained as to be beyond volition. And it can be a distraction. When a movie cuts to a beach shot with waves breaking in the background, it matters not how dramatic the cinematic moment, how drastic and ingenious the plot turn—my mind is immediately absent from the narrative proceedings. I'm off on an imaginary surf check, assessing the size and health of the swell up there on the silver screen, noting the wind direction and state of the tide, maybe muttering for the actors to please step aside for a moment so I can see if that boomer behind them holds its shape through the inside section.

For a surfer, this Sea of Cortez beside which I am camped is an altogether different sort of piece of water from the Pacific Ocean, the illusoriness of the boundary distinction notwithstanding. (Big Blue is a contiguous presence, worldwide.) This is despite the fact that the two may appear identical to an observer standing on the beach—both are wet and stretch to the visible horizon.

There is a corollary to the assertion that the sea is at any given moment capable of being something other than what it is: bodies of water, like human beings, are not created equal, in terms of what they can be. The Sea of Cortez, for example, is largely incapable of producing good surf, due to its limited breadth. This narrowness results in what surfers and oceanographers refer to as a short fetch; "fetch" is the reach of unbroken water across which wind can blow in order to raise a groundswell.

By contrast, the Pacific Ocean has a fetch of many thousands of miles. Looking south from my last west coast campsite, for example, there is nothing of any significance to impede the production of a groundswell until we come upon the pack ice of Antarctica, some 8,000 miles distant. So even when the sea is flat, you may still find yourself gazing horizonward with an alertness in your surfing soul, for—however many miles out there, however many days' journey away—there likely is a slew of waves in transit in your direction at that very moment.

In July of 1996, world champ bodyboard-surfer Mike Stewart experienced in a very personal way the implications of the Pacific's vast fetch. Stewart was on a surf trip in Tahiti when he learned that a huge groundswell was battering the islands to the south—some of the smaller, low-lying atolls had disappeared underwater. The next day the head-high vanguard of the northbound swell arrived in Tahiti. Within 24 hours, the island's south-facing reefs were under full, thunderous assault. Through satellite imagery and modern communications technology (and with the expertise of wave guru Sean Collins), Stewart realized that the size, location, wind vortices and projected track of the southern ocean tempest that had spawned the big swell were exactly right for him to try to accomplish something that had never been done before, never even been tried. It was the chance of a lifetime.

Stewart spent two days in Tahiti searching for a break that wasn't mutated out-of-control. He finally surfed the peaking swell in near-survival conditions, then packed up and flew to Hawaii. Arriving simultaneously with the likewise north-traveling groundswell, he surfed a legendary speed break on Maui called Maalaea, which he was told hadn't gone off that big and fast since the '70s. Wild-eyed with hair still damp, he mad-dashed to the airport to catch a flight to the mainland.

And so it went. Stewart followed the swell's northward progress, next surfing the classic Newport Beach, California, break known as The Wedge. Although the storm that had parented the great swell was blowing itself out thousands of miles to the south, the vigor of its wave-progeny had dimished but little during the journey north: The Wedge was maxing in the 25–30-foot range.

Speeding up the coast by automobile, Stewart surfed central California at two secret spots reachable only by boat. Here, after five days of crazed travel and extreme conditions in the water, he began to feel a synchronicity with the groundswell's rhythms, and to sense its idiosyncrasies; to develop what he terms "an anthropomorphic" relationship with the waves he was riding. The swell "had taken on a personality," he later wrote. "Like a friend . . . (or) a primitive life form."

Three days later, as Stewart stood on a remote point on the Gulf of Alaska, watching head-high waves march up from the blue expanse to the south, a feeling of almost psychedelic unreality swept over him. He felt he understood, in a visceral and soulful and inexpressible way, the machinations of the sea, and, by subtle inference, the universe at large. Although he had not been present at the tumult of the groundswell's birth, he had experienced it throughout its existence in space—and in a sense, time as well. Through his travels he had conjured a sort of time machine, which enabled him to remain in "the present" of a phenomenon that over a period of some ten days had spanned nearly half our planet's circumference. Moreover, the waves he rode had, in a very real way, affected virtually the whole of the Pacific basin, as the ripples from a pebble dropped in a bucket spread across the surface of the water within.

Stewart's was a conceptual and logistical achievement of no small merit. And being a wave rider of great talent, his quest resonated on a creative level as well. In his wave-pursuit across the vastest of oceans, Mike Stewart had enabled himself to personally, holistically, experience the process of the continual transfer of energy through matter on a grand scale. And he knew that the elemental progenitor of that energy was the sun itself. In its giving up of heat to the sea and the land and the air, our local star is the creator of all the earth's winds. It is wind that creates waves.

Finally, as the physicists now tell us—and as Eastern philosophers have long implied—the "stuff" of matter is waves, if on the tiniest and most ephemeral of levels. The universe vibrates in many ways, and on many planes, producing many different realities: from vibrations of nothingness (of space itself) spring galaxies and stars and planets and human beings; similarly, from the sea's vibrations arise groundswells that traverse the limited physical realm of our world. And perhaps consciousness itself—the universe turned inward to reflect on its own vibrations—manifests itself as yet another plane of vibration. Another sort of wave.

SOUTH

The narrow two-lane strip of winding and climbing and dipping and vertical drop-skirting pockmarked tarmac has straightened to a gradual descent to a parched and lifeless llano, *the distant saw-tooth ridge a sleeping Jurassic beast, armored plates serrating a hazy blue late-afternoon sky and descending to a hulking, horny head with jaws agape, granite tongue lolling onto sere grit as if Godzilla had had a bad night. You blink at the hallucination, squint at the white line to shake it off, gulp lukewarm mocha to stay alert as gusty dust and wavering heat and the lowering sun obscure a far distant blot on the blacktop where here in the middle of nowhere no blot should be. What the hell is this? After another blink, squint, shake of your head it's still there, distance closing, deimmaterializing now as a car—no, a truck, a vintage Dodge immobile in the left lane with two men waving in the right—hapless travelers in need or brazen* bandidos *out for mischief? Remembering The Three Rules of Survival of Mexico 1: Eyes ALWAYS On the Road, Never Drive at Night, and, Never Stop for Anyone, you blink your lights in warning and barrel on through—oh shit, farm tools, hay bales, bleary exhausted wife sitting on the truck bed a blurred image in passing. You cackle, harebrained from this wearisome heat, this lunatic road. Fuck 'em, you're thinking, but you ease off the gas, coast to a quarter mile stop, turn around and go back to give your fellow travelers a hand.*

8.

As dawn broke clear and windless, I stepped to the steep, rocky drop to the sea where I'd terminated another southward run on Mex 1 with a harrowing late dusk 4WD low-range westward rumble. The tiny off-road fishing village I'd come upon was all abustle, or as abustle as a village can be when its permanent population is in single digits. One *panga* had already been launched and was planing out the channel in the nook south of the point, while a second crew turned its craft seaward on a stone beach just above the high-water mark. A woman and her young son watched the action from the doorway of the largest domicile, a raw, ramshackle cinder-block rectangle with a tin roof.

My immediate interest lay to seaward, where the substantial swell I'd sensed in the deep dusk was wrapping around the point from the northwest, generating perfectly walled-up shoulders of feathering blue pursued by cylindrical hooks of whitewater. I estimated the surf at a bit more than head high with what looked to be a bigger set stacked and looming outside. Based on a quick toe test of the water temp I opted for a full wetsuit and booties.

It's no coincidence that fishermen and surfers are attracted to the same pieces of coastal geography. Here, for instance, a sharp bend in the coast created a deep-water channel where both small craft and surfboards could be safely launched even when a groundswell was running, while the point of land served as a focal point upon which the swell could expend its energy, in the form of breaking surf. This point/channel configuration was also ideal for surfing from the standpoint of wave shape: the deep water of the channel would cause a wave to break across the shore as it followed the sea bottom contour, instead of dumping all across in one heave, hence affording a long, fast glide down the line. An ancillary benefit of this arrangement was that surfers, like small fishing craft, could use the channel to reach deeper water outside without the nuisance of having to blast through breaking waves on the inside. Indeed, there will generally be an out-flowing channel current to ride to the lineup off a point. Point breaks are especially convenient when the surf is big. In my younger days at Sunset Beach, Hawaii, for example, I'd often paddle out to 15-foot waves without getting my hair wet.

I was about to commence my paddle that morning when a high pitched "Yeee-aaahhh!" pierced the still morning air, followed by a wavering series of yips and yodels. Ankle deep in the wash, I froze. The strangest pair of surfboard-toting dudes I'd seen in 30-some years of globe-trotting go-outs was hoofing it across the inland sandy scrub, angling in my direction. One looked to be tall, 6 feet 5 inches at least, and absurdly thin, 120 pounds maximum including his wetsuit. His cohort was a full foot shorter, squat and well muscled. Both were high-stepping in unbridled mania to reach the water.

"Alemán!" the tall one cried (Spanish for "German"), thumping the hollow bodily indentation where his chest should have been. "Surfingk!" the short one added, redundantly holding up his surfboard. Early twenties, shaved heads, pasty complexions, cigarettes dangling. The short one sported a silver chain linking his right earlobe to a nose ring.

With an inward flick of his tongue and an audible gulp, the short one swallowed his lit cigarette, his witless grin widening. Then, resuming the yodeling that had announced their arrival, the two hit the water and stroked for the outside. But instead of walking the few yards down the shore to the channel, they launched themselves directly toward the point, meaning they would have to paddle over the rock reef itself, through what surfers call the boneyard, or impact zone.

"I think I'll use the channel," I said in Spanish to the crew of the second *panga*. As I waded past, my exaggerated smirk indicated that, notwithstanding our shared passion for wave riding, I was of a different sort, no, a different species, from those two nincompoops.

The Germans never made it to the lineup. Maybe a half-hour after I'd effortlessly ridden the channel current to the point and had several waves to my credit, they'd been swept a quarter mile to the south down the bleak, uninhabited coast. Two forlorn dots on the seascape, still in waist-deep water no more than 40 yards from shore, gamely flailing into line after line of white water. It was the last I saw of them.

Later that afternoon, after an onshore wind had blown out the surf, I lay in my hammock and thought about these unlikely fellows, for whom, now that they were sight unseen, I'd come to feel some surf-brotherly affection. I tried to picture how they'd come to be so far from home on this wild foreign coast. I saw them in some subterranean Berlin nightclub, brainpans sizzling with drugs, slam-dancing to the foul blaring of a rabble of Teutonic misfits. Videos were being offered, I fancied, jagged images of violence and death and desecration. Upon one screen, however, jeeringly offered as ironic counterpoint to the blessed, anarchic chaos, was featured a surf flick—maybe the archetypal images of *Endless Summer* itself. A chord having been struck, these former neo-nazi miscreants were summarily off to see the surf wizard, the shenanigans of their former lives abandoned.

Their story—I would lay odds that my version differs from reality only in the details—is essentially mine as well, and Christopher's, and that of thousands of others. Listen: when someone tells me he or she wants to learn the athleticism, the art, of surfing, my first reaction is invariably, "Careful, it can change everything."

Surfing can not only change everything, it can change everything about everything, as it were: the very roots and principles of causation become subject to a sort of domino effect. You might not only find yourself in some strange and exotic place searching for waves to ride, but because of your unique view of the world, situations may suddenly arise to dramatically test your mettle and expand your horizons in unexpected ways. Although it's easy to make light of the German fellows for their flaky facades and waterly incompetence, I have no doubt they had their worlds shaken to the bedrock by some of their experiences.

Such was the case with Christopher and me in 1970, not long after we came to the remote North African shore where we began planning our worldwide search for surf paradise. Making our winding way to the far side of the Sebou river mouth just to the south of the stranded ship, we camped in the lee of a jetty, with a fine right-hander in clear view outside our tent flap. We found the living cheap and easy and decided to stay for a while. Although, as we would discover, other surfers would occasionally pass through the area, for several weeks Christopher and I surfed in solitude.

About a half mile up the river was a village of Arabic-speaking fisherfolk. Their craft, the largest of which was maybe 25 feet, found safe haven from Atlantic storms inside the same sandbar that formed the waves Christopher and I rode almost every day.

At first the fishermen would walk down from the village and sit on the jetty to watch us surf. But soon the novelty wore off and the spectating dwindled to one fellow, Omar, a young man about our age in a tattered *jalaba*. He'd always sit on one particular rock, and although he'd busy himself fishing with a little bamboo pole, we could see that he was in fact watching our wave riding very closely. He wouldn't speak to us or approach us directly, but occasionally, after one of us would get a particularly good ride, he'd grin from his perch. Aside from Omar's smiles while he watched us surf, because of language and cultural barriers, about the only contact we had with the people of the village was an occasional nod in passing and some minor sneak thievery from our camp.

One day, a month or so into our stay, the surf came up very big and very quickly. By late afternoon the river mouth was closed out, with churning white water flooding the river almost as far as the village. With a rising tide and the swell still on the increase, our camp, normally a good fifty yards above the high water mark, was in imminent danger of inundation. While moving it, we spotted Omar sprinting along the jetty from the inland end. Following behind was a throng of turbaned men and veiled women from the village. They would alternately run, then stop and look seaward. There was obviously something wrong.

When he came abreast of Christopher and me, Omar gestured toward the river mouth and yelled something in Arabic. We watched as one of the smaller fishing boats briefly appeared at the top of a peaking groundswell. Two men were aboard, one in the stern by the outboard, the other clinging to the gunwale amidships. Based on the scale of the boat, the wave had to be in the 15- to 18-foot range. Behind, the rest of the set was stacked and looming.

That first wave closed out the river mouth with an explosive roar; the vibration shook the jetty under our feet. "They're gonna get caught inside," Christopher said. This was going to be close.

Another half dozen waves rose and dumped, each noticeably bigger and steeper than the one before. But the boat miraculously managed them without pitchpoling end over end and made it to outside of the impact zone. The little boat's escape, however, was only momentary. We knew that the two men were in dire circumstances.

Christopher and I having joined the gathering on the jetty, an argument broke out among the men. From the finger-pointing and fiery looks cast in our direction, Christopher and I soon realized that the argument had something to do with us. Finally, the fellow who was apparently the leader came to a decision; he and Omar approached us. As it was, Omar spoke the barest bits of English and Spanish, which in combination with grand gestures enabled him to communicate with us.

Omar had persuaded the other villagers that Christopher and I, having displayed through our surfing a measure of mastery over inshore breaking waves, were best qualified to guide the men to safety. Although there was no question that we would do as asked, Christopher and I shared a long, fearful look, knowing two lives had been put in our hands. Scrambling to a high narrow promontory on the jetty, with sweeping gestures we first directed the craft to wait outside the deepest area over the sandbar, where the waves broke with a little less ferocity. Then we analyzed the rhythm of the swells marching in from the northwest.

The big sets were coming at intervals of about five minutes and were comprised of six to eight waves, with the last two being the biggest. The first two or three tended to be of relatively moderate size. This seemed to us to be key. If the men's shoreward dash was timed just right, they might be able to outrun the first few waves of a set. If not, and if they kept their boat perpendicular to the line of the wave, there was a chance they could surf a smaller wave over the sandbar to the relatively safe waters of the river itself.

As we debated strategy, the fisherfolk milled about uneasily, with many an impatient glance cast in our direction. Omar was off to one side, staring out at the distant figures in the craft. Based on his anguished countenance, the possibility occurred to me that the men in the boat were relatives of his. As it turned out, one was his cousin.

The swell and tide were still on the rise and the possibility that a rogue wave would sweep us all off the jetty and into the swirling river was increasing by the minute. And the period between sets appeared to be diminishing—the fishermen's already narrow window of potential escape was on the verge of slamming shut.

Finally, there seemed to be a lull. Sensing that it was now or never, Christopher and I waved our arms for the men to power it for the river mouth. The crowd of fisherfolk joined in vociferously—yelling, jumping up and down and gesticulating wildly.

Although we couldn't see the fishing craft behind the intervening walls of white water from the previous set, the distant high whine of the outboard told us that the men had gotten the message. But then as if by some malevolent magic, a mountainous array of shifting peaks materialized to the northwest, clearly angling for the river mouth. It was the biggest, meanest set we'd seen all day, and I had the sickening feeling that Omar's faith in us had been sorely misplaced.

The emotion of such a moment, along with the passage of intervening time, can play havoc with the details of memory. The next thing I can recall is seeing the men in the fishing boat waving at us as they surfed up the river on the crest of a small, dying line of white water. I remember the sound of cheering, the impact of hard slaps on the back, and hearing what I took to be utterances of gratitude.

Friendships were forged that day; a wide cultural gap was not only bridged but closed and sealed tight, in a way no amount of formal socializing or superficial interpersonal dealings could effect. And under Christopher's and my tutelage, Omar would become, so far as I know, the first of his countrymen to take up surfing. And he would learn English through its unique lingo.

Many years after leaving the little village, I heard from a traveler who had just returned from the area that a local had drowned while surfing a big day off the river mouth. A local named Omar. I suspect that it was my old friend.

9.

Following the goofball Germans' brief appearance, I spent the next week getting to know the fisherfolk of the little Baja fishing village. Although fishermen from neighboring inland *pueblos* would come to use the launching beach in the nook of the point, the village was actually comprised of just one family: a young couple, their five-year-old son, the grandfather and two fellows in their thirties, brothers of the husband or wife; I never found out which. I got along particularly well with the grandfather, Anuncio, who lived alone in a small cinder-block cottage closest to the point. We'd often play checkers and drink beer and discuss the matters of the day as the sun set in front of his cottage.

Anuncio didn't fish much anymore, but he loved the ocean and the life he lived far from cities and towns, where, he told me, men became confused and lost sight of God's plan and artistry. Although Anuncio never used the word in talking about his home on the point overlooking the Pacific, I suppose he had found his piece of paradise.

Anuncio liked surfers and enjoyed watching them in the water when they visited the little village, although he said he didn't understand the ultimate purpose of their calling, since nothing of value resulted from it. To this I could only reply by asking what he thought was the ultimate purpose of performing music, or drawing, or writing.

Those things are different, Anuncio replied, since a man could be paid for them and feed his family with the money. He said that many of the surfers he'd met did not seem to be concerned with anything other than surfing, which earned them no money. He thought that this was a bad thing, although he hastened to add that it harmed no one. To this I countered with another question: What does the pursuit of money have to do with God's plan, or with His artistry? That, too, was different, Anuncio replied impatiently, as if his logic were self-evident and the discussion not worth pursuing.

Okay, I said, then what about the case of a person who has no family to feed, only himself? Doesn't that free him up to do what he wants?

"Por qué no tienes una esposa?" was Anuncio's narrow-eyed reply, asking why I didn't have a wife. My thought was that he was merely ducking my question, and I told him so. Anuncio got impatient and cheeky again, issuing an equine snort.

"Ha tenido una?" Now he wanted to know if I had ever had one.

"No."

"Por qué?"

"Es un cuento muy largo." It's a long story.

"Ya dímelo." So tell me.

"Es muy complicado," I said, flapping the fingers of one hand in a gesture indicating copious speech.

"Emplee tu diccionario," Anuncio said, indicating the Spanish-English dictionary I always carried. He wasn't going to let me off the hook.

"El cuento es sobre una ola y una mujer," I said as preamble. "The story is about a wave and a woman." "Una ola muy especial." A very special wave. "Y una mujer muy especial." And a very special woman. "La noche que se encontraron cambió toda de mi vida." The night they came together changed everything about my life.

The story as I would liked to have told it was beyond my capabilities with Anuncio's language, so I didn't even try. Minus grammatical errors and with a bit of fluffing, the simplified version—sans intimate details and historical setups—went something like this:

Many years ago when I was a young man I lived on a faraway tropical island, set like a jewel in a stunning azure sea. (Okay, more than a bit of fluffing.) One day a beautiful woman came to stay with me. Although the woman was wonderful in many ways, she did not love the sea and the waves that broke upon the island like I did, and was jealous of my love for them. She told me I would have to choose between her and the sea.

I adored the woman so much that I thought I might give up the sea so that I could marry her. But one night the sea sent a very special wave to come and show me both the power of its wrath and its ultimate beauty. And I would never again be tempted to stop loving the sea because of the love for a woman.

My tale had the trite, preposterous ring of a parable; even as such, it was mediocre at best. But it nevertheless had the desired effect, which was to shut Anuncio up on the matter of why at my age I am not, and never have been, married.

10.

The woman I had told Anuncio about was named Candice. We'd had a tumultuous, on-again, off-again affair since meeting in 1967 at a rock concert in Miami, where I had been attending college. The following year I switched to the University of Hawaii, securing an oceanfront house on Oahu's North Shore—a stretch of beach that is to surfers what the Himalayan range is to mountain climbers—just north of the legendary big wave break called Waimea Bay. Christopher, who had recently returned from Vietnam, joined me a few months later. His plan was to stay for a couple weeks of surfing, then return home. In fact, he stayed for nearly a year. And as it would turn out, in a sense, he never left the North Shore. Neither of us would.

As the late '60s were a time of radical social and ideological change, so were those years also a time of revolution in the arena of wave riding. The traditional blunt-nosed, 10-foot-long, 2-foot-wide, 40-pound surfboard that functioned as an unwieldy platform upon which you glided in a relatively straight line across a wave had been suddenly transformed into an elegant 7-foot, 8-pound, needle-nosed pocket rocket ("pocket" here refers to the curl—the tube or barrel; the breaking part of the wave) that could literally carve rings around the old equipment.

Like early jet aviation pioneers, the North Shore surf crew was expanding the limits of physical capabilities on radically advanced, previously unproven equipment, at a venue which provided the ultimate testing ground, and a patently perilous one. Breakthroughs in speed and control parameters quickly mounted, resulting in a progressive perception of what humans were capable of achieving in the water. We—especially a certain few of Christopher's and my particularly gifted, ballsy brethren—were truly going where no man had gone before.

An elitism amongst those surfers involved was a natural outgrowth of the stunning accomplishments during the last two years of the decade (elitism being another trait held in common with rocket jocks), an elitism over and above that which existed in the late 1960s hippie subculture, from which we'd largely come. We had, in our own snobbish worldview, gone beyond even the most extreme of that element in distancing ourselves from the bourgeois masses and their mundane priorities and mores. We were in essence an outlaw subculture within an outlaw subculture, as far removed from the *Gidget/Beach Blanket Bingo* image that still lingered in the zeitgeist as Abbie Hoffman was from Ozzie Nelson.

Our waterborne elitism created a de facto sexism in our sociological hierarchy, a throwback to the 1950s mentality that in all other ways we had left far behind. A sexism based upon the reality that, in those days—with a tiny handful of exceptions—women did not surf.

Upon coming to live with me in this wild and paradisiacal surfers' enclave in the fall of 1969, Candice found herself sequestered in a physically and socially isolated, male-dominated society in which the female's chief duty, apart from providing postsurf-session sex on demand, was keeping the brown rice steamy and the joints rolled.

Candice would have none of it, barely tolerating the North Shore's misogynistic, locker-room view of women; her sarcastic asides and refusal to toe the sexist line were a constant source of embarrassment for me. Thing was, however, Candice was both witty and beautiful—wide blue eyes, thick mane of flaming red hair, a more than passing resemblance to the Faye Dunaway of that period (*Bonnie and Clyde* had recently hit the theaters)—so she got away with it. The boys more than put up with her.

Despite some peculiar intellectual leanings, not the least of which was her claim of proficiency in the art of witchcraft—which she referred to as her "arcane proclivities" (I had to look up both words)—Candice was and remains to this day one of the smartest, most literate people I've ever encountered, and she was just twenty then. She and Christopher, who was likewise given to esoteric discourse, would often leave me in the conversational dust, shaking my head in befuddlement or disgust.

Candice's wry yet inscrutably feminine mind-set presented a very direct drawback, however, in terms of our relationship. She simply didn't *get* surfing. She didn't comprehend the physical aesthetics of it, nor its ultimate, not to say cosmic, significance.

I remember coming in from a session at Pipeline on a sizable day and approaching Candice, sitting there on the beach with an open book on her lap, Proust maybe. The wave at The Pipe breaks very close to shore. With its big and thick booming and spitting barrels being ridden by the most progressive surfers the world had ever seen, Pipeline, in my admittedly parochial view, was simply the greatest show on earth.

I stared at Candice for a long moment: I was jacked up and tingling on adrenaline with a testosterone chaser, waiting impatiently for some indication that she was impressed by the spectacle she had just witnessed. And although I wasn't among the best of the best, just my having been out there should have put her heartstrings into an all-aflutter mode.

Candice gazed back at me deadpan. Then—not nastily but with a listless sigh—this is what she said: "Big fucking deal."

My ego, my world at large, effected a quick and disheartening droop. I hoped Christopher, sprawled on the sand nearby, would offer some support or sympathy, but his face was contorted in suppressed hilarity.

If I'd known then what I know now, I would have summarily cut and run at that juncture, as I have done in similar situations since, but I loved Candice and indeed had visions of spending the rest of my life with her. My fantasy was that we'd somehow work it out. On the morning of December 4th, however, Candice and I had what would turn out to be our final tiff. It was over surfing, of course. How my dedication to it prevented our having any semblance of a social life, my conception of which rarely transcended pot-addled surf jive with those she termed my "mindless, waterheaded frat brothers." Even our erstwhile stupendous sex life had suffered, due to my up-before-dawn, asleep-at-dusk routine.

Sometime around midmorning Candice packed up her belongings and bolted for a girlfriend's up on the hill. She left me with a parting shot that I laughed off, but which would come back to haunt me in about twelve hours' time. "You're gonna regret this," she said, with the bright-eyed, knowing grin she affected when talking about her arcane proclivities. With that, she turned and huffed up the road.

Christopher was standing on the porch, shaking his head and frowning. "Well, buddy," he said. "That's either the best thing that's ever happened to you or the worst."

"You mean Candice or Candice leaving?"

"Take your pick."

That morning Christopher and I paddled out at Sunset Beach, took one wave each, then came in, our tails tucked up between our legs. It was just too damn big out there, for us at least, and for most of our cronies as well. And it was definitely getting bigger.

By late afternoon we had a first-class boomer on our hands. Only a handful of the lunatic fringe of big-wave junkies was still in the water at Waimea Bay; all the other breaks had closed out and were unridable. By sundown, even The Bay was out of control and devoid of humans. It was breaking far outside of its second reef, a phenomenon no one had ever seen before.

And yet the swell was rising.

Around 10 P.M. the fire department came knocking at the door, telling Christopher and me that the North Shore beachfront neighborhoods were being evacuated due to the high surf. Several homes in the Waimea area had been flooded and the full moon tide was still on the rise. High water would be around midnight.

We watched our neighbors pack their valuables and retreat to higher ground. We, however, decided, to smoke a bowl of hash then go up onto the roof to catch the show.

This would turn out to be an error in judgment.

As was often the case in those days, one bowl led to another, and to another, and so forth. As the booming of the groundswell shook the house and everything in it, we amused ourselves by watching in cross-eyed fascination as an ashtray vibrated across the table between us, then fell to the floor, while the din of rattling dishes and falling pots in the kitchen simultaneously increased in intensity. The house was rattling and groaning as if it were loaded on a careening freight car.

Around midnight we were ready to make the move to the roof. Christopher opened the door, which faced side-shore, then stepped onto the porch and looked seaward. Like a bad actor in a low-budget horror flick, he immediately sprang back inside, slammed the door and spread his arms against it, as if attempting to bar the entrance of an approaching monster.

There are moments in one's life that become frozen in time, images hung in the gallery of the psyche. That tiny fraction of time, that image of Christopher leaning backward against the door of our house on the North Shore of Oahu on the night of December 4, 1969, his mouth hanging open in dunderheaded disbelief, is surely a masterpiece of my collection.

What Christopher had seen was a two-story wall of white water charging across our backyard, the remnants of a groundswell wave that, when it originally broke outside, was possibly the biggest wave ever to peak off the Hawaiian Islands, or even on the planet earth (discounting tsunamis, or tidal waves, which are of different origins than groundswell waves). The implication of the moment, of the look on Christopher's face, was that we, Christopher and I, were about to ride that wave, with our house as the wave-riding vehicle.

The claim that that wave was perhaps the all-time, ultimate one is not as unlikely as it may seem. The swell that night was the aggregate result of two massive low-pressure systems that had converged in the far North Pacific, creating a tempest that would make the Atlantic "perfect storm" of 1991 look like a summer squall. Suffice to say that another groundswell of those proportions has never hit the Islands in historical times.

The Hawaiian Islands themselves—and the North Shore beaches in particular—are geographically, and by virtue of the deep water off the coast, one of the very few locations on earth where waves can reach such monumental size. Moreover, due to the physics of wave formation, there comes a point where a wave approaching shore cannot rise in height any further before gravity causes it to break. In effect, it will self-destruct. It's likely that the wave in question had reached that point, meaning no greater size would be physically possible.

So it was in some sense an historic moment.

At the instant of impact, the house disintegrated. It was not flooded or knocked down—it flat out *disintegrated.* The floor opened up and I found myself underwater, trapped beneath wreckage as the whole neighborhood swept inland. I surfaced into a haze of vibrating purple sparks; indeed, I was very nearly electrocuted. Our house had run down the roadside power line, blacking out the entire North Shore in the process.

In the parlance of surfing, our takeoff was a bit late and lacking in style points.

Probably no more than a minute after the inundation, I came across Christopher standing in waist-deep water, with cars, uprooted trees and pieces of ours and our neighbors' houses swirling around him, and looking even less sentient than he had been when our eyes last met in what was then our living room. Whatever pleasantries we exchanged at that point have been lost over time; they were probably of no more note than our usual surf-jive, i.e., "Far out, man," or "Hey dude, gnarly wipeout, what?"

Apart from superficial abrasions, we were both uninjured. This was singular enough that a picture of the two of us standing by the pile of splinters that was our former abode made the front page of the *Honolulu Advertiser* of December 6th, under a headline proclaiming "LUCKY TO BE ALIVE!"

Christopher and I waded across the rural two-laner called Kamehameha Highway, then trudged mindlessly uphill, a couple of surfy Laurel and Hardys after dropping the piano. Candice was lying in wait in her friend's yard, which overlooked the whole of the North Shore. Her wild red hair was spread over the sunburnt fracas of freckles on the elegant curve of her shoulders, her dewy blue eyes wide in mock surprise. A little smile played on her lips, verging on demented hysteria at the sight of the dripping-wet, disheveled nincompoops before her.

I turned and looked seaward. Stacked to the far distant horizon, and appearing to rise up from below the rim of the world like migrating cordilleras, were impeccably spaced, towering processions of falling white water. In their gargantuan proportions and great distance from my vantage point, the aqueous mountains appeared to advance shoreward not at all, although they were moving at a speed greater than the fastest human can sprint. Likewise, the time taken for a breaking crest to cascade to its trough far below was distended beyond all reason. The seascape seemed suspended before me like a surrealist's painted image. To paraphrase a lyric from the song of the moment: logic and proportion had fallen softly dead.

Imagine a mountaineer gazing up at a peak that pierces the vault of the heavens. Or an astrophysicist allowed to peer into the divine engine that burns inside a star. For a surfer, this surfer, what I saw that night was akin to a glimpse into Creation itself.

Meanwhile, Candice's smile had widened slightly and her eyes were dilated in glee. Pointing at the offshore furor, she said, *"That* is what happens when you screw around with me, Allan."

Looking back, I believe that what followed was a defining moment in my life. For I truly loved Candice and I knew that had I put my arms around her and told her as much, and vowed to change my ways, she would have accepted me. I'm quite certain she loved me, too. The tumult she'd claimed to have raised was, after all, a function of her passion.

But there was something else going on. My slate had been wiped clean, you see, not only by the events of that day and of that night, but by the preceding year or so, and by the very times in which I was living. The Vietnam war was at its height in 1969. My best childhood friend and inseparable buddy throughout high school had, a few months before, been killed there. And Christopher had returned wounded, with psychological scars that would surface in the years to come. These two casualties had the effect of distancing me from both the establishment that had sent my friends to that conflict (and that yearned to do likewise to me) and from my past.

My commitment to surfing, not only the activity itself but the mindset, the life of it, had been honed through advances I'd made in my own abilities during my tenure in Hawaii, and from living among those who were at the apex of the art form. To an extent, all else was fading in the face of that commitment. The maxim that had been going around the North Shore that winter surf season, inspired by the astounding feats of its denizens, seemed to refer to me personally: Surfers Can Do Anything.

And apart from the tattered surf trunks I was wearing and the hash pipe somehow still clutched in my fist, I had been stripped of my physical possessions. Was not the sensation of rebirth inevitable?

In front of me stood the woman I loved, and all she implied; at my back, the ocean, another She, and also a focus of my sensuality and deepest desires. Two profound, implacable forces of nature vying for the nod of total commitment, mutually exclusive in their coveting of my attentions.

The decision I ultimately made was not an instantaneous one. For a short period I resumed my life of uneasy cohabitation with the two Shes. But in the end, the less contentious (though no less demanding) She won out. Two months later, in February of 1970, Candice gone, slate immaculate, I dropped out of school and Christopher and I left the North Shore to go on the international wave hunt.

In making that commitment to the sea and shucking all the rest of it off, a new life had begun. And after that night, after that wave, after Candice, I never again harbored a thought of marriage, or looked at any relationship as a potentially lifelong union.

Of course, many factors other than the intersection of my lifeline with the demise of that ultimate wave could be the basis of my enduring bachelorhood; and, in the longer view of causation, of my presently far-flung geographical coordinates, my seemingly desperate personal straits; all that. But I prefer the transcendent explanation to a mundane one; some failure of character, say, or ambition.

11.

The morning of my sixth day at Anuncio's little village, I was about to commence my paddle out to the point when I noticed a four-foot-long sickle-shaped fin flowing seaward in the backwash by my feet. I recognized it at once as the disembodied tail fin of a fair-sized thresher shark, no doubt caught by one of the *panga* crews, the tail discarded after the butchering of the animal at water's edge. I looked around for someone to ask about the prevalence of inshore sharks in the area, but both dories had already gone to sea and Anuncio was nowhere to be seen. He'd probably gone off on one of his extended beachcombing forays.

Just as well, I was thinking, probably better not to know. Besides, if there were a real problem around here, someone would have said something. Right? Definitely . . . unless . . . come to think of it, the boys up north by El Rancho de Chicho didn't mention anything until I did . . . *Es mala suerte hablar de tiburones aquí.* It's bad luck to speak of sharks around here.

The paddle out at an unfamiliar break, especially a remote one with no one else in the water—and for who knew, ten, twenty miles in either direction along a wild coast?—is a subtly unnerving endeavor, for several reasons: unseen, possibly dangerous bottom conditions like sharp rocks or metallic debris in the impact zone; urchin-covered shoals to fall onto after an ill-timed maneuver; the knowledge that there is no one to come to your aid should you find yourself in trouble; a long ride to a Third World hospital in case of serious injury, if there's anyone to carry you there. All that, plus a generalized apprehension of the unknown below—a primal fear. But your overriding concern stroking out alone at a remote break is sharks. Or,

57

rather, *a* shark. One big, voracious brute that maybe has had a lean time of it offshore and is jacked up and pissed off and very hungry and is now on the hunt for easier inshore pickings, and possibly drawn from the deep by the pelagic blood trail of the sea-dumped offal of his late thresher cousin.

Shark. The word itself has an almost onomatopoetic ring to it, the sharp, lean sonance being closely akin to the animal itself. Say it aloud: SHARK. A mean, jagged sound, cruel and malevolent and severe in utterance. And the word "attack" follows so easily in its wake.

Surfers have sundry nicknames for sharks: The Man in the Gray Suit, Mack (as in "Mack the Knife"), Old Toothy. These terms function, with uneasy humor and subtextual intimacy, as euphemisms, a way to avoid voicing the common, scarier moniker. But the most apt, implying as it does ultimate dominion and power and the violent abuse thereof, is my personal favorite: The Landlord. The Landlord is out there where you're blithely headed, somewhere, count on it. And the rent due him, my hapless friend, just might be you.

I know: Statistically, it's more likely you'll be struck by a lightning bolt than taken by a prowling *tiburón*. But what statistician's tally includes the eight men known to Chicho, offed by sharks just up the coast? By what means are the attack/fatality numbers gathered for Baja, or any remote coastline where men go to sea daily? By no means, I'd venture. Poor Chicho is running low on leathery, callused fingers in the count of friends lost; he'll soon need his toes to keep up. And speaking of the lightning bolt theory of fate, isn't a paddle-out just down the beach from where those eight men had been slaughtered the doom-tempting equivalent of climbing a lone oak tree and waving a three-iron at an ion-bloated, crackling thunderhead rolling across a flat-prairie golf course? Would you do that?

If it is indeed bad luck to name that sea-dwelling devil, as Chicho, Miguel, et al. believe, how much more dangerous must it be to pooh-pooh his menace? No, speak not of how safe you are out there on the edge of the abyss, with limbs like live bait dangling.

And what of Chicho's whispered sobriquet for Big Blue's netherworld beast—bonita? Beautiful? Irony is not the vogue among these forthright men, I would submit. No. The assumption here is that not only is the creature sentient, but omniscient, and capable of mercy toward those who venture into his lair. It's truly best not to speak of him, but if you do, placate the sea demon with sweet talk, my friend. Call him beautiful.

I wax hyperbolic here, admittedly, but my fearful ramblings reflect no untruths; and anyway, who would negate the incessant badgering of the mind? In reality, the lurking shark is almost certainly illusory—almost—an irrational yet potentially debilitating fear, an accompaniment of all the rest. So you do your best to put the fear aside, and successful or not, you paddle on out there and get on with things.

SOUTH

Around a big lazy curve skirting a flathead mesa you pass a made-in-America pickup, make eye contact with the lone charro *in back—bushy mustache, chaps flapping, boot on saddle; he looks away,* muy macho.

12.

Not exactly feeling 100 percent these days.

Symptomatic of what Melville would call my hypos: when the girl with melonic breasts doing back-arching yoga on the beach in front of her tent asked how old I was in reply to my inviting her to my birthday party tonight, I shaved a year off the truth.

Today is in fact my forty-ninth, the first day of the last year of a half century of a bumbling stumble of a search for something to do on planet earth. More specifically, midmorning on a day in which my temperament and concerns have waxed gloomy if not morose, harassed if not paranoid. I am, in short, in a foul, self-pitying mood. Aside from the age thing—and from my general predisposition to melancholia—a part of it is the female problem, as in, I haven't been with one in a while. Not since Denise came for a visit to the town at which I used to live. Last summer. It's now winter. My forty-ninth birthday.

I'd meant to spend no more than a week camped on this half-mile-long series of rock reef points and sandbars south of Punta Lobo (Wolf Point), down near the bottom of Baja, but it's now going on eight weeks since my arrival. I rationalize my tarriance with matters practical. During the time spent bouncing back and forth from remote Pacific to Sea of Cortez campsites I've been essentially incommunicado with the dwindling vestiges of my old life. Now the message center in nearby Todos Santos has allowed me to catch up: To complete the negotiation of an option agreement for one of my old screenplays; wrap up the sale of *Cosmic Banditos* to an Italian publisher (my seventh foreign sale; the French are quite taken with the thing

I'm told); harass magazines delinquent in monies owed; try to find out why a new surfboard, paid for months ago, was never shipped (I've broken two so far in the rambunctious Baja surf); make calls to Denise, far to the north, who does love me, *sans* promises, *sans* future.

As is my habit, I've been talking up the surfier expats and itinerants here, flashing my photo of Christopher and my ex. A longboarder of about my age, Theo, who lives in a ramshackle tent/shack affair with his dog over by the arroyo, claimed he'd run into Christopher here at Punta Lobo four or five years ago, then again last year around this time. Said they'd spent last Christmas Eve together. Problem was, parts of Theo's story didn't jibe. The guy who was supposed to be Christopher was traveling in a pickup with two dogs, but then Theo got vague as to the make and color of truck and the breed of the dogs. Also, he hadn't come up with the truck/dogs aspect on his own. He agreed when I brought them up in my initial description, saying, "Yeah, dude, he was in a pickup with two dogs." The other problem with Theo is this: he's noticeably out of his mind.

So who knows? Christopher was here, maybe. Maybe even twice. Or maybe not. Once, twice or not at all. Take your pick. Phantomlike, the specter of Captain Zero, Shadow, Popeye (another of his nicknames), Christopher, whatever the tag, has materialized in the lee of Punta Lobo.

I've also been inquiring around as to the situation to the south, the status of the civil wars, anti-Americanism and general strife in Central America. I in fact do not know much in this regard. I hadn't looked into it before I left. I mean I was going in any case, so what would have been the point? But no one I've quizzed has ventured south of mainland Mexico, at least not by the overland route.

I've heard more horror stories about southern Mexico, however, more of what Valentine at El Rancho de Chicho referred to as *"la violencia en el sur."* A few days ago, a surfer named Cormac told me a friend of his from Santa Cruz had been found in his van dead from gunshot wounds on a stretch of road in the state of Michoacán known as Bandido Alley. He'd been traveling alone, except for his dog, which had been murdered, too.

Like most of my life's designs, my plan to somehow find Christopher by the New Year, now some three weeks past, has gone by the boards. Which, come to consider it, frets me but little. What, after all these years, is the hurry? The road south beckons, though; I have reservations on the La Paz to Mazatlán ferry tomorrow afternoon.

13.

I've taken to riding a longboard nearly exclusively these days, a personal evolution that on the surface might be interpreted as retro, given that I had been a ground-zero participant (if a very minor one) in the revolution in thought and design that resulted in the abandonment of the longboard for the shorter, lighter, highly maneuverable equipment that today dominates the lineup worldwide.

Looking back, the total rejection of the longboard was a mistake, if an understandable one. Truth is, 90 percent of all surfing is done in the less-than-ideal conditions of size, speed and power that best suit most shortboard surfing. The shortboard revolution, in its wild-eyed enthusiasm, failed to take this into account.

If it seems assbackwards that smaller boards work best in bigger surf, consider the basic hydrodynamics of a planing surfboard. In bigger, faster surf, less lift is required to achieve maximum speed, hence less planing area is needed. In fact, the greater wetted surface area of the longboard creates added friction at high speeds, which actually slows the board down. While it's true that in really big surf, surfers return to bigger boards, the reason is related to problems in catching big waves on a smaller board, not riding them. (When this problem was recently solved through high-speed jet-ski "tow-in" takeoffs, big-wave riders immediately returned to the faster, more maneuverable smaller board, albeit with some interesting design modifications.)

Until the mid- to late 1980s, when the dinosaur gradually began its rise from extinction, it was virtually impossible to find a longboard in the quiver of even the most freethinking waterhead. My own eureka experience came one day in the summer of 1987 at Montauk. I was out with a mob of other shortboarders when a buddy of mine, Tony Caramanico, a gifted short-boarder himself, suddenly appeared in the lineup on a 9-foot longboard he'd had built.

Well, there was a lot of smirking and snide commenting, the wittier of the latter relating Tony's age (mine minus two) with that of the antiquated equipment he was riding. He had some problems that day in maneuver-ing and regularly caught a rail or had his nose pearl (submerge, stopping the board and sending Tony flying) and so forth, which only increased the ridicule. But he stuck with it and within a week or so he had that big plank pretty wired. His turns became deeper and smoother, and his movements to the nose were done in a cross-step rather than a shuffle. Not only did he look good, but, with the ease of paddling of a longboard, he was catch-ing way more waves than anyone else, and riding them right through to shore, while the shortboards were stalling out and losing the wave wher-ever it flattened a bit. Having myself learned to surf on a board similar to the one Tony had had built, I found myself stirred by a deep nostalgia.

So I got myself a modern longboard, much lighter and more elegantly designed (and hence more maneuverable) than its 1960s-era predecessors. And what gradually has happened since is I've found myself sticking with my longboard even when surf conditions are big and speedy enough to allow full-performance shortboarding. Why this is so is in part a function of per-sonal aesthetics; and, to be honest, I find the switching back and forth dif-ficult, the approach and mentality of the two styles being so different. (Few enough surfers regularly ride both that it may be said that a longboard/short-board schism exists, with longboarders currently greatly outnumbered; maybe ten-to-one. The division is deep enough that the two major surf pub-lications, *Surfer* and *Surfing,* virtually never mention or feature photos of longboarders.)

As far as the aesthetics of the two approaches go, there are conflicting factors at work. One result of the move to the shortboard was to put the surfer in more intimate touch with the wave by melding the surfer with his equipment, the overall ideal being to make the surfboard "disappear." For the highly evolved surfer, the shortboard goes where he projects it with no thought of the board itself; and the rider's feet, once planted, rarely shift more than a few inches during various turning and trimming maneuvers. In contrast, the longboard is turned from the back and trimmed for speed from up front, making movement upon the board sine qua non to that approach. The end result is that the wave-riding vehicle becomes much more of an active psychological factor in the surfer/wave equation. In other words, the longboard surfer is much more aware of his equipment.

On the face of it, the Zen factor would seem to give an edge to the shortboard approach, with its theoretically "purer" relationship with the wave. In practice, however, and in the view of some, shortboarding has developed stylistic drawbacks. These style factors have had inevitable repercussions in the nature of the shortboarder's deeper relationship with the wave.

For one thing, most shortboards—again, due to their sparse planing surface—will not effectively trim (reach and maintain maximum planing speed), except in those relatively rare moments when they are in the most critical (steepest and fastest) part of a near perfect, sizable wave. The result is that the shortboard, in order to keep momentum up, must be constantly worked, i.e., turned, in order to achieve a state of constant acceleration. Otherwise, it will go dead in the water, with the result that the surfer will either be overrun by the approaching curl or lose the wave altogether.

All well and good, one might respond, a state of constant acceleration based on high-speed turning sounds exciting, an interesting state to inhabit out there. Consider skiing. How boring would a downhill run be without the edge control challenge and high G-force rush of a deep slalom turn?

But the other side to this implied value judgment lies in the medium itself, and in that aspect of surfing that makes it unique. Unlike skiing or any other earthly endeavor, wave riding is a creative interface with an active, in some sense living force of nature. Given this, is not an aesthetically valid relationship with the medium the obvious goal of the act of riding a wave? In other words, the wave's the thing. The surfer must follow its lead, respect its diversiform flow.

Yet one only need watch the shortboard shenanigans at virtually any break worldwide to suspect that many surfers have lost sight of this simple, obvious objective. What began as an attempt to mate surfer and wave has deteriorated to a fierce puff-and-grunt struggle to not only keep yourself moving but to do so in ways that take little regard of the will and pleasure of the wave. Where is the ideal of merging with the medium when every muscle and fiber in the body is tensed and the mind consciously fixated in a rabid need to do something, anything, radical—"catch air," say, a maneuver that 90 percent of the time results in a fall or loss of connection to the wave? But even as the downed surfer tumbles head over heels in white water, the beach erupts in applause at his splendid derring-do. I'm meanwhile thinking, *he fell fucking down,* wasting the rest of a now-expiring-and-never-to-exist-on-this-planet-again miracle that he showed such little respect for in his jumpy gymnastics—in his desire to "shred the wave," to "tear it apart."

Coming off decades of longboarding—an approach wherein style was everything, maybe to a fault—the innovators of the early days of shortboarding retained their individualism while transitioning to total commitment to following the wave's lead. A glimpse of one of those surfers, or even a skilled-but-not-great buddy, up and riding, would identify him by name: his body posture in turning, the carriage of arms and legs during weight shifts, the arch of the back or cant of the head in tube riding—plus a myriad of subtle flow factors, the sum of which equaled each surfer's distinctive line drawn upon the wave—were as unique as his personality or the tiny whorls at the ends of his fingers. (Guys like Barry Kanaiapuni, Billy Hamilton, Jeff Hakman, Joey Cabell, Terry Fitzgerald, Jock Sutherland and Gerry Lopez come to mind from my North Shore days, with their characteristic power-to-elegance variations in approach.) Now, the tension-wrought need to blast the deepest hole in the trough with a bottom turn or raise the biggest rooster tail with a cutback blurs diversities in style, the dubious aesthetics of domination eclipsing the poetry of the wave/surfer ensemble.

For true style to surface, a surfer must inhabit that seemingly contradictory mental state of relaxation/total concentration that is the essence of the creative act; a state that necessitates the dissolution of the ego of "I." Although I see no lack of concentration in what I suppose can be termed this postmodern era of surfing, I see very little evidence of relaxation out there—and a whole lot of ego.

The deterioration of individualism in the water is an annoyance of sorts, a blot on the aesthetics of the seascape, but in reality a minor one. More disturbing is the blatant commercialization of what once amounted to a secret society—the lifestyle's grinding assimilation into a ravenous pop culture image machine. In becoming economically and culturally significant, surfing's specific importance has somehow diminished. It's become a *sport,* complete with all the coarse, irrelevant trappings that concept implies.

The dissolution of style, along with commercialism's inexorably rising tide, appear to be themselves reflections of this media-addled era and the nonexistent attention spans and discordant predilections of its denizens; the lack of rhythm and class in everything current—music, visual imagery, fractured, simplistic storytelling.

One need only examine the history and current state of what used to be known as the "surf movie" (now the "surf video") to understand the interconnection between style in the water and in landward creative efforts, and to assess their simultaneous descent. The definitive masterpiece, *Endless Summer,* aside, compare both the filmmaking panache and the wave riding grace of 1972's *Five Summer Stories* to those of most of its postmodern counterparts—the aptly titled *Water Slaughter,* say. But wait. Isn't all a matter of individual taste? Sure, and so is the difference between Coltrane and Kiss, or Mozart and Hell Rot.

But lest I be rightfully accused of the brand of old-fartism I myself ridiculed in my younger years, there are moments on quick green water when today's truly gifted young shortboarder, through sheer and enlightened athleticism, achieves such soulful union with the medium that I find myself thunderstruck in witnessing his accomplishments. With these special individuals extreme athleticism has *become* style, art.

Amidst the rabble of any era, genius will surface and have its say.

. . .

Although the late 1960s Surfers Can Do Anything maxim may have an absurd ring to those whose image of surfing was forged by the mass media of that (or any) era, the character trait it reflected was a straightforward one, and applicable to landward endeavors as well: the ability to exhibit grace under pressure. *The unruffled retention of personal style in truly hair-raising, even impossible situations.*

Grace under pressure is Gerry Lopez at Pipeline that all-time winter of '69 (still the biggest, most consistent North Shore season ever: as if the surf gods had given us a year to refine the advances of the revolution, then said, "Okay, boys, let's see what you can do"), streaking across a massive, top-to-bottom breaking boomer that is clearly and viciously intent on overrunning him and the last thing you see before he is consumed, buried, pummeled and thoroughly traumatized by untold tons of churning white water driving him down toward that shallow, jagged reef is his silhouette against an upwardly rushing emerald wall, stance indifferently narrow, knees slightly bent in blasé deference to the need for balance; arms hanging loosely down with hands limp by his sides and fingers lightly curled as they would be in pleasantly dreamy sleep; shoulders limp and perhaps indicative of an easy expiration of breath, a meditative sigh; head canted forward and cocked to afford a casual gaze up at the concave metaphor for fate or what-have-you towering over him; overall not an ounce of tension in his slight, upright frame.

And then the world beneath your feet rocks as the curtain of ocean comes crashing down on the water-play and Gerry is . . . gone. . . . No, wait, no no no, that's not possible! There the son-of-a-bitch still is, that cracking green monster spit him back out, his casually upright posture unchanged since his disappearance into the belly of the beast. And now his board is decelerating to a slow plane on the shoulder, the fellow absently touching his nose as if to shoo a fly that had landed there. Or perhaps it was an admonitory wave to quell the standing ovation from the beach. This is not theater after all; it's bigger than that. It's a personal thing.

Grace under pressure is Jock Sutherland at Waimea Bay a week or so after that ultimate wave came ashore and truly rattled my cage. Jocko riding big surf deep into the night in a solo full-moon session, his staggering accomplishments visible from shore only through the luminescence of his deeply snaking board wakes, Jock himself invisible in the lunar shadow under the freight-training wave crest, 25, 30 feet above him. If big waves are measured in increments of fear, the equation for Jock broke down that surreal night; he had entered another realm.

Then some time around midnight, a section of his board washed ashore, a forlorn shard chewed up and spit out, Jock having committed some minor faux pas, like being out there to begin with.

Those of us on shore squinted uneasily into the hazy glow of stacked-up hillocks of whitewater, imagining the dark speck of a head, then Jock dragging himself to land, wild-eyed and disoriented. But no one, nothing, not even the rest of Jock's exploded board emerged from the shore break. Then the fire trucks and ambulances were there, their crackling radios and rotating lights adding an unnatural rhythm to the night. The rescue chopper's efforts—the beam of a gargantuan spotlight futilely searching the churning inside froth—were a joke in those appalling conditions.

An hour or so later, a crowd having gathered, hoarse whispers inquired the inevitable: "What's going on?" "Jock?" "He was what?" "But it's the middle of the night!" And the thought, left unspoken by Jock's surf-brethren, was finally voiced by a man in a firefighter's hat and boots after examining the remains of Jock's board: "He's drowned, that's for sure. No one could survive out there."

But then, still later, as the crowd commenced its disheartened dispersal, a figure was spotted walking down the coast road from the north. Lean frame, sandy-blond hair, yellow surf trunks dry from land ambling, it was Jock all right.

A stunned silence. Then: "Where'd you come in, Jock?"

"Umm, down around Pipeline."

Pipeline? That's over a mile. How did he . . .

"Anyone seen my board?"

"Broken, Jock."

A pause, Jock squinting out at the roaring offshore tumult, then at the high moon and you could see it in his eyes: *he wants to go back out there.*

A few words were exchanged with the authorities, then, having no surf-board to ride, Jock hoofed it on home. He was so relaxed, still so deep within himself, that no one thought to offer him a ride. No big deal, fellas, just another go-out.

One more thing about Jock's little moonlight romp. It was undertaken with a headful of Orange Sunshine LSD, the most potent psychedelic around back then. Jock's feat was perhaps the ultimate Up Yours to the powers-that-be that demonized the freelance chemical exploration of the mind so in vogue amongst the youthful counterculture, through invoking an image of acid-whacked flower children jumping out of windows in a hallucinated belief that they could fly. Listen to me here, because I was there. It was as if Jock had taken that leap, and lo and behold, *he did fly.*

Jock's moonlight session was, of course, a very personal thing.

Yes, my pining eulogy for what-once-was suggests displeasure with the current state of things in my country of origin, the United States of America. And yes, this dissatisfaction to some extent accounts for my having abandoned my old life and bolted south. But I'm not such a zealot that I would have taken this drastic action solely based on the state of wave riding up north. A part of surfing's essential allure is in the solitary nature of it; the way the act itself exists apart from one's fellows—their style, or lack thereof; all that—and from the techno/socio/economic conditions surrounding it.

Admittedly, my grumpiness belies my weakness. It should be just the wave and me out there and let the zeitgeistian rest of it be damned, right? Yes, but . . . but . . . but . . . but if my rant sounds clichéd ("Hey, fella, you mean to say your precious surfing's gone the way of everything else and become crass and commercialized here at the end of the millenium? Duhhh . . ."), maybe that's precisely the point.

Which, in theory, makes me the predictable sour expat, unable to hack it Up North and therefore having fled south into the literal and metaphorical realms of the unridden, or less ridden. On top of that, with my quest to find my old chum—and with what some may view as my subconscious attempt to return to my youth with this reversion to longboarding—what we're also dealing with here is an example of a midlife crisis run amok.

The truth is, I don't *believe* it's as simple as that. In the here-and-now of my last birthday before the benchmark five-oh, I can only say *maybe* so. I do wrestle with what's behind this thing I'm doing, this life I'm living.

14.

I paddled out late this afternoon into some inconsistent waist-high waves and worked my longboard into three shortboarders in the lineup at the point, guys I know casually from in the water and on the beach; guys in their mid-twenties from up on the West Coast of the United States somewhere. Casual nods exchanged, I edged my way outside of them and pretty quickly a little three-wave set came through. I took my pick of the biggest of the little, which also happened to have the best taper to its shoulder.

Now, what waves there were were pretty few and far between and these guys were there first. Theoretically, I'd pulled a rude move by placing myself at the front of the lineup and immediately availing myself of the best wave. Seeing who was out there, I had immediately made a subconscious pecking order assessment, and finding myself at the top, did what I had to in order to get things done. This is how it works in the water, although there is definitely a line between taking what's rightfully yours due to your history/ability and blatant infringement of another's rights. From the stink eye I was getting it was obvious that one of these young fellows thought I'd crossed that line. And you know what? He was probably right.

But it was my fucking birthday and if I'm not getting any sex I'm at least gonna take my pick of waves, and besides, I was riding Pipeline when this kid was in diapers. No, wait, he wasn't even born yet. So I returned eye contact, the old primate stare-down that's been around for about 10 million years: Who's the silverback around here?

Me, that's who, young fella.

This distracting business went on for a bit, then a Mexican surfer I know,

Julio, hit the water and after he paddled over and high-fived me and wished me *feliz cumpleaños*, the whole idea of a pecking-order conflict became irrelevant since the cranky young shortboarder was gone. He'd paddled down to the next point, wanting to have nothing to do with Julio in the water. Or, suddenly, Julio's buddy, me.

My history with Julio goes back to mid-December, a week or so after my arrival at the Punta Lobo camping grounds. Being new, I'd been gradually working my way up in the scheme of things, mostly through surfing well and giving the already-entrenched expats and itinerants some room. I didn't push it out there, didn't get in anyone's face. No matter how skilled you are, if you push it, you're in for trouble, either in the water or on the beach or through some sabotage of your shoreside belongings or wheels; or even a nocturnal ambush/gang shit-kicking to throw a more serious dose of humility into your act.

Then Julio effected his entrance from his normal stomping grounds up north in the Ensenada area and a knowledgeable expat immediately informed me that he's a full-blown nightmare in the water, given to fast and furious fisticuffs in asserting what he regards as his absolute right of eminent domain. And I already knew a bit about him: he had been the instigator of the Ensenada cantina brawl back in November, single-handedly taking on a cadre of SoCalers that had offended him, probably through their mere presence in his country.

A few days after Julio's arrival, the surf came up and I found myself deeply involved in an inspired session in perfect head-high point surf in front of my campsite. This particular day I was inhabiting that quasi-mystical state known in certain physical endeavors as The Zone, and which longboarders sometimes refer to as The Glide.

Having ridden one particularly fine piece of watery work to the beach, I glanced up to see Julio standing in his surf trunks on a rise just above the wrack line, his surfboard stuck in the sand and leaning against his shoulder like a spear. He was no more than 20 yards away and the eye contact we sustained was not reassuring. Although Julio is not a particularly big guy, he's very solidly built, with near-zero body fat; and with his swarthy complexion sunburnt to a fervid red-black, unkempt shoulder-length hair and feral gleam, he veritably exudes insolence and intimidation. As I stroked back out, it occurred to me that my inspired session was about to deteriorate into some sort of surfy showdown at the O.K. Corral.

I should also mention that Julio also rides a longboard exclusively, the only Mexican I've come across to have made that commitment. And he rides it very, very well. Unlike many new-era longboarders (Julio is somewhere in his late 20s) who manhandle their equipment as if it were merely a larger version of a shortboard—wide, squatty stance, a lot of arm waving and grimacing—Julio rides with the classic upright and relaxed posture of the golden era of longboarding. Although his surfing is notable in many areas, his walk to the nose is particularly distinctive: a functional yet showy sashay falling somewhere between a matador approaching the bull and a butch version of a Vegas showgirl strutting her stuff.

Julio is also very adept at finding The Glide, which, aside from a state of mind, is also a physical place on the wave. While the shortboarder is looking to rip the wave apart, the longboarder is searching for the perfect position of trim that affords him a moment of utter relaxation—a state of grace, you might say—because any further movement or weight shift on his perfectly planing surfboard would only serve to disturb the elegant equilibrium of his place in the world.

This delicate condition, The Glide, for reasons relating to both style and complex physics, is generally best arrived at from a position right up on the front of the surfboard, and in the steepest, fastest part of the wave. The nose position—and, less directly, any maneuver that leads to it—is the name of the game in longboarding in all but the biggest, hollowest surf. It is the ideal posture of speed and implied aplomb; a precarious perch is that position on the tip, difficult to maintain over time and distance. The noseride is in fact such an unlikely physical circumstance that the best longboarder in the world—a young phenom named Joel Tudor—has said that he doesn't really understand how it's possible at all.

Julio paddled straight on by me and then sat his board no more than five yards to seaward, his back turned; the same rude move I had pulled today with the young shortboarder. A lull ensued; the only sounds were the gentle slap slap of wavelets against my surfboard and the background roll and hiss of white water inside.

Then the horizon stirred with an incoming wave-set and everyone commenced jockeying around and edging his way further outside. Everyone but Julio. Julio just sat there. Now, this would have been the time to stroke past him and reclaim my outside position. In fact, Julio had in effect dared me to do so by not edging further outside himself. He was waiting to see what I would do.

Well, I pretty much froze up. I sat there like a craven fool, immobilized by Julio's daunting presence. Though not a word had been spoken nor even eye contact made, it was as if Julio had called me out at high noon and I'd remained cowering in the saloon. Somewhere in the primitive recesses of my brain—my conscious mind had shut down in denial—I knew that wherever I thought I had been numerically ranked in the pecking order in the point surf that day below Punta Lobo, I could now subtract one.

But then came the unexpected. As the set loomed, Julio swiveled around on his board and looked right at me. Although his eyes remained hard as ever, he vouchsafed me a short nod along with a slight hoisting of his brow, indicating that I should take whichever wave I wanted.

There was only a matter of a few seconds between this startling development and my launch into the second best wave of the set, but, nevertheless, the beat of confusion in the lineup was palpable. Until Julio's precipitant appearance, I'd been getting nearly all the best waves through what must've appeared to be blind luck (it wasn't, trust me: it was The Glide). Then, not having done the necessary strategic jockeying to maintain a preferred position, I ended up in limbo in the midst of the pack and no more entitled to take my pick of waves than anyone else. But then this maniacal local with whom no one wanted to tangle or even make eye contact had given up his top-ape spot to me, a *norte* newcomer. To further mix and stretch metaphors: I had prostrated myself at Julio's feet, but rather than cleaving me in twain, his highness had anointed me.

What the hell was going on here?

He who hesitates, as it's said, is lost. The beat of confusion was all I needed to grab the wave and disappear shoreward from the socio-confrontational disorder in the lineup. Having ridden to the beach, I pulled out and looked seaward. As I knew he would be, Julio was on the wave behind mine—the best of the set—and, having easily located The Glide, was relaxing on an extended noseride, throwing in a little soul-arch in the middle to further indicate his capacity for nonchalance in a critical place.

The two of us naturally fell in together for the paddle back out, and our casual Spanglish surf jive sowed the seeds of an actual friendship. For the rest of that session and in those we shared in the days and weeks to come, the confrontational vibe between us dissolved completely. In fact, as is often the case in the beginning stages of a surfbuddyship, we wound up bending so far over backward in an attempt to give the other guy his pick that we would occasionally both miss out—"you take it;" "but I'd rather you take it;" "no, it's your turn;" "now that other guy got it," kind-of-a-thing.

Thinking about it, several factors were at work in Julio's choice of me as a *norte* ally. Certainly our being the only two longboarders in a sea of short-boarders helped, as did the fact that I was surfing at, or near, Julio's level that day—surfing buddyships tend to be between those of similar ability. And the little water drama had played itself out the only way possible, if we were to become friends and if the proper balance of things was to be simultaneously preserved. Julio couldn't have just paddled over and said *Hola.* He had to assert his dominion first, which he did with his original rude move, then his disdainful refusal to partake in the standard jockeying procedure. My submission was also a necessary element in the scenario, as was my subsequent selection of the second best wave of the set, thus leaving Julio the best as a sign of gratitude and further respect. Our age difference may have played a role also, my avuncular distance mitigating any perceived territorial threat. Had I been ten years younger, some real foolishness might have transpired out there.

What I'd like to believe is that maybe Julio sensed I had some surfy tales to tell around the Punta Lobo campfire. Maybe some wisdom to pass on.

But perhaps it was this simple: It is good to be king, to be the top ape, the most feared gun, but it's also lonely. Maybe Julio just needed a friend.

15.

Deep dusk now and as the beach fire and revelry in front of my campsite attracts the assorted wave-obsessed misfits, bohemian athletes, stoned idiots and former and current outlaws who have settled at or are passing through lower Baja, my birthday party is starting to have the feel of a tribal gathering.

Sitting on La Casita's driftwood stoop clutching a well-dented bottle of 100 percent agave cactus juice, I observe the peculiar interplay among my guests as the proceedings bloom. To my left, by my pile of beachcombing spoils, Chip and Ralph—two of five Alaskan smoke jumpers who have wintered here since discovering that the adrenaline rush of wave riding is the perfect complement to their summer vocation of hurtling from flying machines into wilderness conflagrations—are trying to decipher the singsong surf-jive of the unlikely Norwegian waterhead from two campsites down.

To my right by Shiner's little tent, J. Boy Crispin—a flamboyantly tattooed artist whose roots go back to the late 1950s Malibu heyday of the surfing life—rends the deepening dusk with the booming, gravelly, tequila-laced laugh that I'd first heard at the Hotel California bar in Todos the night before a big New Year's swell swept in from the northwest and the wave riding around here turned outright serious. "Shady" Lane, an aging surf gypsy, is J. Boy's cohort tonight. The two lean in for a conspiratorial aside, J. Boy cocking his head and prodding the fire with an ironwood walking stick he sheathed with the skin of a rattlesnake that bit him before he killed it, and which he refers to as Silent Bob.

Big Tony, former real estate developer, now keeper of the point break from up north at Ensenada, wanders over from the adjacent campsite with his soul mate, Barbara, a Swiss beauty he'd encountered on a surf trip in Bali. Barbara has just returned from Zurich, where she performs open-heart surgery to help finance their wandering life Down South. They come bearing birthday gifts, a pitcher of margaritas, and a bowl of peppery pasta. Tony gives the stink eye to whatsisname who's just stumbled in, a punked-out moron from an enclave of NorCals and Oregonians at the Punta Lobo end of the beach, and with whom Tony's had constant problems in the water. Tony looks at me questioningly, and I shrug. *I* didn't invite the guy. Hey, word spreads when festivities loom.

Frank Henley, former NFL running back, self-proclaimed big wave specialist and proprietor of Shut Up Frank's, a Todos Santos cantina that is a gathering point for local exiles and itinerants, blows in with his motley entourage, precipitating a chorus of "Shut Up, Frank!"s from the crowd, although Frank hasn't yet launched into one of his wild-eyed tirades.

Scott and Vanessa appear with a blazing cake as Tony and Barb fire up the crowd with the birthday song, accompanied by a pair of knapsack-toting sisters on guitars and the sibilance of a dying groundswell, rolling in weakly from the northwest.

I look to the north, up the beach toward Punta Lobo. Campfires are strung along the shore in an uneven line like little suns, with shadowy, planetoidal figures hovering and circling. More waterheads drift over to the party, bearing beach wood to add to our fire, as is the custom here when paying nocturnal social calls.

Julio won't be making it. He said he had to make a Cabo run tonight, some sort of business. He was coy; who knows what he's up to. Like many of the wandering wave riders down here, Julio's means of support is not wholly obvious.

There are a lot of surfers here at Punta Lobo, too many. With all the empty breaks between Ensenada and Cabo San Lucas, just to the south, why so many have amassed on this stretch of beach is a question I've pondered. Aside from my feeble rationalization that Christopher might have been here twice and therefore might show up again, given the sometimes crowded lineup and the distraction of pecking order games, why have I lingered?

The vast, sprawling encampment has the feel of an outpost, a frontier settlement; more than that, the edgy vibe of a sort of point-of-no-return. As if in their migration south, these various travelers have pulled up in hesitation here at the bottom of the peninsula. A place to re-evaluate the level of commitment. Some will press on to the mainland, then further south. Most won't.

As the birthday song ends and the ensuing catcalls and drunken guffaws wind down, I raise my bottle in a toast to the friends I've made at this faraway place, and then power down the remaining cactus juice.

16.

Ferry to Mazatlán now, although I missed my reservation for the day after my birthday, due to the magnitude of the resulting hangover. Did a leisurely three-day convalescence, lurking with some *pescadores* at a secluded fish camp on the Sea of Cortez a couple hours north of La Paz. Then I moved my camp about a hundred yards and stuck around for a couple or three days more. This would make the date the 27th or 28th of January.

Today is Sunday, which I figured out from the church bells ringing this morning and how quiet the streets of La Paz were. This would make it the last Sunday in January. Which in turn would make it Superbowl Sunday, I'm pretty sure. I have no idea who's playing.

The ferry crossing is some eighteen hours and I won't have access to the rig, so I've sprung for a *cabina,* which has a bunk and a writing table. Tonight will be the first night in four months I won't have slept in La Casita Viajera, which I feel weird about; I've truly come to see my little house that travels as home. Dogs are not allowed on deck, so Shiner will be stuck in the cargo hold for the duration. I feel weird about this too, since she'll probably think she's being punished for something.

I've always found sea voyages conducive to reflection, and often in my life they have also augured some sort of significant change. No matter the size or type of vessel, the body of water traveled upon or the nature of the deed being done in doing so, there is a deep-rooted psychological commonality among sea voyages. Perhaps it's simply the state of being afloat. It seems such a miraculous condition, given the insubstantiality of the fluid medium. Stick your hand in the stuff and see what I mean: it just keeps going, water apparently being hardly more supportive than air. But then again, possibly my view on the naturalness of sinking is skewed, a disproportionate number of my voyages over the years having terminated in catastrophic submersion.

In any event, lying on my ferry bunk with the familiar rumble of a big diesel engine below and Big Blue's vast and inspiriting presence conveyed by the ship's easy pitch and roll, I can so easily summon images of those past voyages.

She had no name, this 80-foot Down Island former banana hauler of questionable provenance (and no legal registry) that since 1977 has rested in 40 fathoms and within sight of my beloved Montauk Light. At first we simply called her *The Boat;* and then, having been subjected to her chronic foibles and nuisances, coupled with her acute and more flagrant failings, we called her *The Fucking Boat.*

In the late summer of that year, Christopher and I, along with a crew of two (one of whom was—or rather claimed he was—on the run from a history of multifarious felonies) ran the vessel up to northern waters from La Peninsula de la Guajira, the wild west epicenter of the mammoth Colombian pot trade of the mid- to late 1970s. Our 20,000-pound load of chaffless gold buds was the most ambitious we'd as yet transported between international borders. The venture represented a turning point for us, not only in terms of the immediate money it represented, but also with regard to our credibility with the Down South connection we'd been cultivating.

The voyage north had been an eventful one, mechanically, with Murphy's Law combining with the entropic principle (the inexorable slippage of order into chaos) in ways I'd never before experienced, and I hope am unlikely ever to experience again. Within a week of embarkation only three pieces of the ship's equipment remained functional: the twin turbocharged Detroit 1271 diesels, the microwave oven, and the massive sound system Christopher had insisted upon installing for crew morale. The autopilot didn't work, nor the loran nor the radar nor the sonar depth finder nor the

RDF (radio direction finder) nor the log (a seagoing odometer for measuring distance run) nor the marine frequency radios nor the bilge pumps (I found that in a pinch a frightened man with a bucket suffices) and so forth and so on. Even the compass had suddenly and without warning given up the ghost. The direction it pointed seemed a semi-random function of the RPMs of the engines.

I could have dealt with the resulting navigational dilemma through celestial means—I'd long ago mastered the use of sextant and chronometer for position finding—and our course could have been steered using the sun's azimuth in daytime and by putting the North Star, Polaris, over our bow at night. The latter lay in exactly the direction we wanted to go, true north. The problem was that heavy overcast skies predominated for most of the voyage—the heavenly bodies were not visible.

So we barreled blindly ahead, employing largely what Christopher termed stone-age navigation—sporadic and very skeptical use of the compass, along with the prevailing winds (the northeast trades in the Caribbean and the westerlies in the North Atlantic; each has a different feel and look upon the water than the less "natural" antipodal flows) and what we could discern through the cloud cover of the sun's direction. A bit of flotsam thrown overboard at the bow then timed in its apparent movement aft over the 80-foot length of the craft in effect gave us our speed through the water; simple extrapolation gave us distance run. (This is whence the term "log" springs; in the age of sail a piece of wood was used.)

Just before midnight of our eleventh day out, I climbed to *The Fucking Boat*'s wheelhouse roof in hope of spotting Montauk Light. If my gut instincts were correct, it would hove into view somewhere ahead sometime soon. But having run well over 2,000 nautical miles with no reliable position fix, I was harboring no illusions about pinpoint accuracy. It would not have surprised me if I'd been off by as much as 300 miles, which was more than a full 24 hours' run.

Well, by the sea gods, I was up there squinting into the darkness for no more than ten minutes when that familiar 5-second-period beacon appeared, dead ahead. I found that the flashing light would disappear under the horizon when I was squatting and reappear when I was tippy-toeing (this is called "dipping the light"), with eye level about 18 feet above sea level. Plugging 18 feet—plus the height of the light above sea level as given on the chart—into the Distance of the Horizon table in Bowditch (which is based on the exact degree of curvature of the earth), I defined our nautical mileage from the peeping beacon. (I had also proved that the earth is round.) With Polaris directly above the light, I didn't need a compass to know that we were due south of it. That knowledge, coupled with our distance from the light, gave me an exact position fix: the latitude and longitude I'd worked up based on stone age navigation had been off by no more than two miles, a margin of error of less than one tenth of one percent.

Even Christopher was impressed. As I sensed from his dour, tight-lipped nodding and starchy stalking of the deck, he was also inexplicably somewhat vexed. I would find out what was on his mind soon enough.

We were not, however, out of the oceanic woods yet. The initial ensuing bad news came when my engineer—a truly twisted reprobate from south Florida with a more than passing interest in satanism—informed me that a broom handle plumbing of our 12,000-gallon main fuel tank (the gauge was inoperable, of course) came up bone dry. He had underestimated our rate of fuel consumption by some 15 percent. *The Fucking Boat* was now running on whatever residue that remained in the lower reaches of the big tank, and within the filters and fuel lines between the tank and the engines. Further, when I dug out my northeast coastal charts, I found that the ones I'd ordered that covered Long Island Sound, the sight of our planned offload, had been omitted by the stoner who'd done our initial provisioning and outfitting.

But most seriously, as we rounded Montauk Light an hour or so after raising it offshore, we ran headlong into the densest fogbank I've ever seen or heard about, a seemingly preternatural barrier. The sensation of entering it was as if somehow the atoms that comprised *The Fucking Boat*, through some statistical quantum glitch, found the void between those of an otherwise solid wall—the fog's edge was *that* sharply defined—allowing a miraculous passage into substantial matter.

The first thing I did was shut down *The Fucking Boat*'s engines, both to conserve fuel and to give myself some quiet in which to think. I also wanted to discuss our predicament with the others, mainly Christopher, who was my equal partner in the venture. The other two were hired hands; neither were surfers. I would have anchored up, but we'd lost our ground tackle during the onload Down South when it hung inextricably on a coral head and we'd had to sever the line. (Admittedly, we should have had at least one spare aboard—an anchorless vessel is potentially in great peril in inshore waters.)

The four of us gathered in the cramped quarters of *The Fucking Boat*'s wheelhouse, with Christopher rolling a joint from one of the bales lashed between bunks. The fugitive deckhand, call him "Chet," was the first to speak.

"We got to get off this fucking boat," he said, eyes wide and fearful in the dim amber of the chart light. The guy had been getting edgier since the onload; since before that, actually. I'd more or less seen this coming.

I glanced at Christopher who, for some reason, grinned big, barely holding back an outright laugh. I definitely needed to speak to him in private.

"This fucking trip is cursed, man, doomed." Chet gestured at the satanic icons and posters, screaming death's-heads and upside down crucifixes that our engineer, "Luke," had hung on the bulkheads and over his bunk. "I mean, look at this bullshit, man. What kinna karma we dealing with here?"

Luke shot Chet some cartoonish daggers with his Charlie Manson eyes and jabbed the Sign of the Beast with extended forefinger and pinkie. Chet retaliated by crossing himself.

Great, I thought, on top of all my other problems, now I have the forces of Christian Good and Evil battling it out in the wheelhouse.

"You ever see stuff break down on a boat like this? How could a compass act this way?" Chet had lowered his voice in a forlorn attempt at reasonableness.

It *was* weird the way one by one, things had just quit working for reasons that could not be fathomed through normal causal logic. "It's a wiring problem causing some sort of variable magnetic field," I improvised, but privately I had to admit that having a device as unsophisticated as a compass malfunction was unnerving. Standing at the helm for hours on end watching it whirl randomly as if under the control of an invisible hand, it was easy to imagine we were being toyed with by some malevolent force.

I frowned at Luke, who shrugged. My problem with the guy was simply that he hadn't been able to fix anything. I was also aggravated about the fuel issue. I'd pointedly asked him during the outfitting if we needed extra diesel, which could have been secured on deck in drums or a bladder tank, and he'd said no, the 20,000 gallons in our main tank and two auxiliaries were plenty. The fact that we could now run dry at any moment was preying on me as much as anything else.

Chet had worked himself into a genuine panic. "Aside from everything else, we got no radio to tell the offloaders to meet us! Just find the shore and we'll jump ship and run," he pleaded. "This is hopeless, man!"

"I sure am glad Fredi can't see you now," I remarked in disgust. Fredi— the Colombian pot lord—had fronted us the cargo, agreeing to wait for his end until the successful completion of the voyage; a major indication of trust on his part. Normally, a minimum of $20 a pound would be paid up front by the smugglers just to cover the expenses in growing the product, plus various forms of necessary protection, including both the Colombian army and Fredi's private troops. Fredi was in effect lending us $400,000.

Chet, when I'd introduced him to Fredi, had attempted to wow the latter and his *bandido* cronies with tales of his criminal exploits—all bullshit, I now suspected. Chet was right, however, in regard to the hopelessness of our situation. But hopeless or not, abandoning the load was not an option. I grabbed a flashlight and motioned Christopher to follow me out on deck.

The fog-enshrouded night was beyond dark, the air so dank with moisture that breathing labored heavy, as if underwater. The sense of gloom was so viscerally overpowering that it seemed to suck into oblivion the spectral red and green of our running lights. From somewhere across the Sound a foghorn moaned disconsolately, as if it were itself lost and crying out for the way home.

Wanting to center myself, to in some way reconnect with planet earth,

I leaned over the rail amidships and shone my flashlight down, toward where the ocean should have been, but the light's beam was brought up short and rejected by the reflective density of the night. The super-hydrated air glowed so brightly that I had to blink and look away. But by cocking my head just so, out of the corner of my eye I could make out tight swirls etching the oily slick blackness of the sea's surface down there, evidence of a strong current.

"Tide's on the flood, sucking us west'rd," I said. Barely five miles downtide lay the narrow, rocky shoal-skirted neck known as The Race, which led into the inner sound—a hair-raising night passage even under the best of conditions, and in a sound, well-appointed vessel. And here we were, deaf, dumb, blind and without a cane, drifting down on it at a good two knots.

I looked over at where Christopher was standing, no more than a couple yards away, but all I could make out was a Cheshire cat incandescent smile. "We're gonna be just fine," Christopher said.

I stared back at the teeth-in-the-mist, trying to figure their owner. Christopher and I had successfully weathered some tense times together since those early North African hashish smuggling days and the subsequent loose bale running in the Caribbean, and we'd regularly relied upon each other during numerous hair-raising go-outs in sizable surf. But, given our present dire circumstances, this enigmatic grin he was subjecting me to was starting to rankle.

"With no radio and if by some miracle we make it to our offload coordinates," I reasoned, "there's no way the boys are gonna know we've arrived." The offloaders were ensconced in a motel near the mouth of the Housatonic River in Connecticut, waiting to hear from us via radio, their souped-up flotilla of speedboats tied up at nearby marinas. "I mean, what are we gonna do with the fucking load?"

A match flared and for a moment I could see Christopher clearly as he fired up the cigar-sized joint he'd been holding. "The more ridiculous the situation gets, the more convinced I am that in the end we're gonna be fine," he said, and that goddamn grin widened further.

Okay. This explained his disappointment at my navigational coup. He'd been hoping our situation would completely deteriorate, in his mind thereby ensuring ultimate success. I couldn't help but grin myself. This was quintessential Christopher.

Then, suddenly, I heard something. "Listen, Christopher."

Yes. There it was, the deep, rhythmic grumbling of what had to be a distantly approaching diesel-powered vessel. The sound of another ship in dense fog is normally daunting, for fear of sudden, headlong collision, but given our dire circumstances, my response was one of guarded hope. In that unseen ship's functioning navigational gear, I suspected, lay our possible salvation. But where was she, and which way was she steering, east or west? In our state of utter disorientation, it was impossible to tell.

I called Luke and Chet out of the wheelhouse, placed them in the stern and amidships, respectively, and put Christopher up on the bow, instructing the three to call out the direction from which they sensed the other vessel's engine sound was emanating. I meanwhile stood in the wheelhouse door, ready to fire up our engines and make chase. My plan was to run right up under the other vessel's transom and follow her until the fog lifted, which I hoped would be no later than dawn.

The tricks that fog plays on distant sounds was immediately and comically apparent. The three all adamantly shouted different directions—"Off the port quarter!" "Starboard amidships!" "Dead ahead!"—and I was quite sure that they were all wrong. The other vessel was most certainly off the port side, amidships.

Tracking the phantom stranger down under those conditions was a painstaking, exasperating and hazardous task. Once there was a majority opinion on the general direction of the distant engine sound, I'd fire up *The Fucking Boat* and run that way at full bore for 15, 20 seconds, then shut us down so we could listen again. The very real danger, of course, was that we'd smash headlong into our target in the near-zero visibility. Yet my forward bursts had to be at full speed, since we would lose ground each time we stopped to listen. And the rocks at The Race were somewhere out there, the graveyard of untold ships manned by better men than us.

And deep down I knew that if we somehow weathered the night, the possible increased visibility of the coming dawn would be of little consolation. We'd be able to see where we were, but so would everyone else, including the Coast Guard. A quick glimpse at our ramshackle 80 feet of turbo-charged patchwork timbers and they'd also be able to clearly see *what* we were: a bunch of fruitcake desperados running ten tons of pot into the yachting mecca of the East Coast.

But finally, and to my great relief, Christopher called out from the bow that through a crease in the fog he had spotted the other ship's stern light. We fell in behind, as distant as possible while still maintaining visual contact.

With the ghostly gloaming of first light, the fogbank behind us shone a nacreous pale as we emerged into startlingly clear air. The ship ahead—an oceangoing tug, as it turned out—bore off at a good clip, with a cadre of crewmen staring stonily after us from the bridge wing. With *The Fucking Boat* stalking them on their radar screen, we'd undoubtedly been a harrowing aspect of the past few fogbound hours. I blithely waved at the boys, then attempted a blast on our air horn as a token of our appreciation, but the pressure within had fizzled. My attempted paean came out an effete, atonal squeak.

I throttled down to idle and scanned the shoreline for clues to our whereabouts, but came up as dull-eyed and ignorant as ever. Although I knew the waters off eastern Long Island quite well, we were many miles to the west here. Nothing looked even vaguely familiar.

There was no lack of aids to navigation: whistle and bell buoys, cans, nuns, black, red, striped—they peppered the inshore waters all around, all duly numbered, but without a chart to define their position they were perversely useless, like signs in the wilderness saying YOU ARE HERE but nothing more.

For a moment I felt a kinship with the explorers who had opened up the northeast half a millennium past. Names like Adriane Block, Sebastian Cabot, Henry Hudson; and, perhaps most fittingly, the inimitable William Kidd, hanged for his seagoing felonies around the turn of the eighteenth century. Having raised land after a harrowing ocean crossing, these voyagers had sailed this same inshore course and, likewise clueless as to exactly where they'd fetched up, faced the possibility of hostile action from irate locals on shore.

Christopher, blasé as ever, was still up for'ard, firing up another hand-rolled bomber; maybe his plan was to smoke the whole of our cargo as means of avoiding the forthcoming bust. Chet was out of sight, off cowering somewhere no doubt, practicing the denial theory of arrest avoidance: if you can't see the cops, maybe they can't see you. I'd sent Luke down to the engine room with a drill and hacksaw to open up the cavernous main fuel tank for a plumbing to its real bottom (the inspection port bolts were frozen solid by corrosion). We'd burned around 400 gallons of diesel since discovering the tank to be "empty" and I knew we had to be very close to being actually empty.

But the immediate order of business was to find out where we were. In spite of the risks inherent in an up-close disclosure of our appearance, we needed to find someone to ask directions of. A few craft were out and about that morning, mostly sport boats and day cruisers. Scanning our environs with binoculars, I spotted a small boat adrift about a half mile inshore on the Connecticut side. I gradually eased the throttles forward and headed its way.

A few minutes later we pulled alongside two fat guys wearing dumb hats, bottom fishing in a 16-foot Boston Whaler. As the two squinted up at me, wide-eyed, I tried to imagine what *The Fucking Boat* looked like from their point of view.

Over the years of being bought and sold (cash on the capstan, with minimal, if any, paperwork), then used for one-shot pot runs, each new owner of *The Fucking Boat* had slopped onto her topsides a new and different color in a comical attempt to change her identity, the result being that the multiple layers peeling off in ragged sheets had given her the look of a seagoing Jackson Pollock. The thickest, bumpiest layers of paint were on the transom, evidence of multiple name changes. We hadn't bothered with such nonsense when we took possession of her down islands, figuring that to try to look like anything but what we were would have been akin to slipping sunglasses on an elephant and expecting it to walk around incognito.

The two appeared for a moment to be speechless, staring wide-eyed at the 80-foot monstrosity towering above. Affecting as casual a tone as I could, I wished these two fellows a pleasant good morning. And, by the way, how was the fishing? They had recently caught a flounder, said the one further aft. I nodded, noting that the forlorn little fish lying on deck was a fluke, not a flounder. I then felt someone's presence beside me, and hoped it wasn't Luke. He really did bear a startling resemblance to Charlie Manson (in Luke's demented worldview, a source of pride) and I figured with one glance at him these two would immediately sense that we were up to no good, if they hadn't already.

But it was Christopher, grinning that fucking grin of his. He pointed with his nose at the Whaler's bow and raised an eyebrow significantly. I sneaked a look. An orange stripe had been painted on up there, running diagonally from the waterline to the gunwale—the insignia of the Coast Guard Auxiliary. Oh, fuck. Of all the boats I could've picked to ask directions of.

Christopher cleared his throat then glanced through the wheelhouse door, which I had left open. Clearly in view just inside was a stack of marijuana bales. The top bale was all torn up and dribbling product; it was one of those that everybody rolled joints from. Jesus. I eyed the Whaler's VHF ship-to-shore radio and the whip antenna with the little stars and stripes flying from its tip, along with a miniature Coast Guard flag. The radio was turned on and set to channel 16, the Coast Guard's hailing frequency. I casually swung the wheelhouse door shut with my foot.

The Coast Guard Auxiliary is a civilian organization largely comprised of wannabe watermen, dipshit law-and-order types who join up for the paramilitary vibes, the testosterone-rich conviviality of meetings with other faux watermen, and the patches and hats they get to wear. True idiots, the vast majority has never been out of sight of land. These two perfectly fit that profile. And had no doubt attended one of the Coast Guard seminars meant to alert the boating public to be on the lookout for crazed smugglers like us. I couldn't help but picture some junior C.G. officer unfurling a poster-sized image of *The Fucking Boat* as the archetypical smuggling vessel, along with giant mug shots of the four of us as your basic dope runners.

I sensed that Christopher beside me was trying to keep from laughing; he had probably summoned up a similar image. For my part, being giddy from lack of sleep to begin with, I couldn't help myself—I laughed outright. This set Christopher off in a fit of hysteria. In the end, it may have been our happy-go-lucky mien that saved us—evil dope smugglers weren't supposed to act like this. The two representatives of the Coast Guard Auxiliary relaxed and grinned back at us, as if they were in on the joke.

It was also in our favor that we were just so flat in their faces. Returning to the elephant analogy, it was as if they had been shown a picture of one and told to keep an eye out for it in their neighborhood, then had run headlong into it and found they couldn't recognize the beast with their noses pressed up against its hide.

"What kind of boat is that?" one of them inquired.

"She's an old PT Boat," Christopher said, still giggling like a fool. If there was one thing *The Fucking Boat* didn't resemble, it was a PT Boat. But the two Coast Guard Auxiliary guys nodded, as if they'd known that all along and were merely testing us.

"She looks like she needs some work," the fellow aft observed.

"We're gonna fix her up for exhibition at the Smithsonian," I said. "She has a valiant history."

More nodding. "Where are you coming from?"

"Just up the coast," I said, gesturing vaguely. "She was in mothballs up there. We're looking for the Housatonic River. We sorta got turned around in the fog down east'rd."

The two guys suddenly got all serious. We had now become fellow seamen in need of assistance.

"It's right there," the guy sitting aft said, pointing west with his fishing rod. "That buoy's right off the mouth."

"Terrific," I said, and meant it. We'd finally had a turn of luck. Then I suddenly had a great idea. "Are you guys going in soon?"

"We were just about to when you came over," the guy up forward said. "We've been out here since before dawn."

"Would you mind taking one of my friends ashore?" I inquired casually. "He's in the wheelhouse. Never been out on a boat before. He's really seasick and . . . all rattled. You guys obviously know your way around the water and, well, maybe you can calm him down."

"Sure. No problem. Pass him over." A rescue at sea! they were probably thinking. I was figuring that with Chet aboard their boat as a distraction, the two would be less likely to commence a discussion between themselves that might lead to an "Aha!" experience about what we were so obviously up to.

"Just a second." I rushed into the wheelhouse and found Chet in a paranoid funk on his bunk. "You're getting your wish," I said. "You're getting off *The Fucking Boat.*"

Chet nodded in vehement agreement as I told him about his ride ashore. I gave him a wad of currency and piece of paper. "Get to a phone," I said. "Call this number and ask for Harry. He's the guy running the offload. Tell him to meet us two miles south of the river mouth buoy at sundown. Tell him to bring some diesel and local navigational charts. Can you do that?"

"No problem, man," Chet replied, suddenly recovering his lost machismo. "A piece of cake."

"If these guys ask you any questions, just pretend you're seasick and scared," I told Chet as we went back out on deck. Christopher and I helped him over the rail and down into the Whaler. Chet huddled in his seat, moaning softly.

As the Whaler sped off in the direction of the Connecticut shore, it suddenly occurred to me that Christopher had been right. With the Coast Guard Auxiliary having come to our rescue, we'd finally reached the height of ridiculousness, and as a result it appeared everything might actually be all right in the end.

17.

Stretched out on my bunk on the La Paz to Mazatlán ferry 20 years later, with someone else burdened by the concerns of nautical command, the recollection of my youthful fearlessness produces in me a state of giddy, borderline euphoric optimism.

But what an era it was, those 1970s, for guys like Christopher and me, born a couple centuries too late. It was the twentieth century's return to the Great Age of Piracy, minus the moral indelicacies of rape, pillage and slaughter. So many fortunes made and lost at sea; so many hair-raising chases, escapes, near misses. And some of us were caught, some did jail time. And some, along with their cargos of the new treasure known as Guajiran Gold, were simply never heard from again, victims of the inherent hazards of sea passage or of real pirates, the murderous rovers who stalked the waters off the north coast of Colombia, once known as the Spanish Main. But *c'est la guerre,* no? As with a go-out in big surf, the asspucker factor was a given. In a very fundamental way, it was why we were there.

And lest we forget: Surfers Can Do Anything!

Indeed, it was as if the job description of the international pot mover had been composed by a well-buzzed wave rider in a postsurf session hammock drowse on some reef-ringed tropical strand: "Vagabond waterheads wanted to travel to exotic coastlines! Make friends with colorful indigenous people! Learn how to barrel-roll a Learjet without spilling the bubbly in back onto your suitcase full of cash! A capacity to exhibit grace under pressure and a cavalier attitude toward international law the only prerequisites!"

And insofar as the cultural sentiment of the time was concerned, our antics were nothing if not encouraged. By the late '70s, the incarnation of your basic dope-addled hippie of the 1960s had evolved into a mainstream force, largely due to economic factors—he had become a legitimate, big-time consumer. And he had brought his predilection for the mellow pot high along with him into the ensuing decade.

The government's bumbling, disingenuous attempts to portray this benign smokable as "the weed with its roots in hell" backfired. With well-documented evidence of the CIA's heavy involvement in cocaine and heroin trafficking worldwide beginning to surface, the "war on drugs" was perceived as yet another hypocrisy perpetrated by the lying slugs who had so recently given us Vietnam and Watergate. (None other than archconservative William F. Buckley, Jr. has now come out in favor of legalization, calling his vilification of the substance "the only mistake I ever made in my political career.") These factors served to increase an otherwise largely law-abiding citizenry's identification with those involved in the pot trade.

And in an era when rock groups—surely the embodiment of the 1970s youth-culture sentiment—through their three-piece-suited, Madison Avenue PR men, painstakingly cultivated outlaw images, the trend toward canonization of the real thing was to be expected. America's love affair with outlaw types, even down-and-dirtily violent ones, was of course nothing new, but the perceived victimlessness of the smuggler's criminality facilitated this new infatuation.

The 1970s era *contrabandista*-as-folk-hero phenomenon was best exemplified by the troubadourical odes of Jimmy Buffett, who, through his own rambling waterhead lifestyle, knew whereof he sang. Ballads like "Son of a Son of a Sailor" ("Son-of-a-gun, load the last ton, one step away from the jailer") struck a deep chord in those involved in the trade, while reinforcing their heroic image amongst the vast segment of the populace already predisposed in that direction. In part, Buffett's rise from cult minstrel to superstar was based on his understanding of the youthful masses' natural affinity toward the seafaring antihero. It was a sentiment he not only stroked, but helped create.

But like the fortunes of the intrepid scoundrel in Buffett's sea-dreamy

"A Pirate Looks at Forty" (he did his share of smugglin', ran his share of grass; he made enough money to buy Miami but he pissed it away so fast), looking at not only the Big Four-Oh but at all the years and all the mad times that preceded it, the era was "never meant to last . . . never meant to last."

18.

The offloaders never showed, nor did Chet put in an appearance to explain why, which was especially aggravating. I'd given him enough cash to buy a boat, let alone rent one, to come back out to inform us of any new and catastrophic developments. No doubt he was afraid I'd drag him back aboard and his panic attacks would resume.

Although the odds were still excellent that someone would notice us and call the Coast Guard, with the inevitable result that we'd all be behind bars by sundown, we spent an uneventful, even pleasant day drifting south of the mouth of the Housatonic. I even managed to get some much needed sleep.

Luke had refused to perform the exploratory surgery on the fuel tank that I'd ordered, and we had a few words, Luke claiming it was better *not* to know how much diesel we were carrying—one helluva questionable attitude for a ship's engineer, I pointed out. I stopped him short of saying anything about trusting in some Dark Power to see us through (I'd sensed it coming), not out of the fear of bad karma Chet had voiced, but because I just flat wasn't in the mood to hear it.

But fuel or no fuel, come the night, we had to make a move. Our hide-in-plain-sight luck could not be relied upon for another day. One way or another the load had to be put ashore. The problem was, of course, that ten tons of loosely packed contraband are somewhat unwieldy to move around and difficult to conceal.

My plan was to make an exploratory foray up the reach of the Housatonic River, the feeble hope being that some miraculous opportunity would present itself. It was around 9 P.M. when we commenced our creep past the industrial area at the river mouth. Passing under a busy highway bridge (I-95, I think), we eventually found an industrialized shoreline turning to middle class suburbia.

"Buzz on over there for a look-see," Christopher said, pointing to a home on the western bank.

The grounds were enclosed by high hedgerows, isolating the house from its neighbors. Set back from the water, the residence faced inland, toward where the road must have been. A well-manicured lawn sloped right down to the water and was peppered with willows and stately hardwoods, heightening the sense of seclusion. Whoever owned this place, he liked his privacy.

"Looks like deep water right up to the lawn," Christopher remarked. He was no longer goofing around; he had finally made the transition to his serious, get-it-done mode.

I eased us up to land for a test of the water's depth and found we didn't touch bottom even with our stem kissing the bank. The house, which was maybe 30 yards distant and partially hidden by trees, was dark, except for a porch light and a single lamp in a downstairs corner room.

"I don't think anybody's home." Luke had come back from his position on the bow.

"You can't see the riverbank from the driveway, right?" Christopher asked him.

"We'd see car lights if they came home but they wouldn't be able to see us. Not right away."

"That's it, then," I said, backing us down toward mid-river. I did a long, slow turn until we were a couple hundred yards from the residence and pointed dead at it. We were all quiet for a moment—the asspucker factor was kicking in as we contemplated what we were about to do—then I gave *The Fucking Boat* full throttle. The big Detroits shattered the night with their dull roar.

"The tide'll be on the make for the next couple hours!" I called out to Christopher as we barreled across the Housatonic.

Christopher nodded. "And with the ship lightened up, we'll float back off, no problem!"

We were doing a good 10 knots when we struck the riverbank. Our bow plowed a deep furrow into the lawn as we came to a sudden stop, stuck fast, with the front dozen feet of *The Fucking Boat* sitting on terra firma in the good old U.S. of A.

I shut down the engines and went out on deck. Christopher and Luke were up on the bow watching the house for any signs of activity. I went aft and looked at the home directly across the river. Although its residents had probably heard our crazed sprint, the river was wide, the night moonless. It was unlikely that they had seen anything. And with many of the local yachts powered by big diesel engines, we sounded no different than some investment banker out for a cruise.

What we now desperately needed was manpower and at least one truck, so Christopher was delegated to find a pay phone and make some calls. Our best hope was a wholesaler we knew who lived about a half hour away. He was an associate of Harry, the offload guy, and was one of the people waiting to distribute our cargo. He most likely had a direct line to Harry, wherever Harry was.

Luke shimmied up a porch column and cut the phone line, while I crept around the outside of the house, peering into windows to make absolutely sure no one was home. Doing my Peeping Tom bit, I spotted something that gave me contemplative pause: hanging in the kitchen was a framed Grateful Dead poster, one of those black light deals from the '60s. The thought occurred to me that if the situation arose, maybe whoever lived there could be reasoned with.

Then again, maybe not.

About an hour later Christopher returned with two trucks, a van and Harry and his crew of a dozen guys. As we'd figured, our wholesaler cohort had been sitting by the phone waiting for news of our arrival from Harry. After Christopher's call, the wholesaler connected Harry and his crew with Christopher and now here they all were, the cavalry coming to the rescue.

A quick grilling of Harry explained Chet's failure to contact him. Suspecting that it was tapped, Harry had recently disconnected the phone number he'd given me. Chet, who was from Florida, knew no one in the area. He could be anywhere. Partying with the Coast Guard Auxiliary guys, maybe.

Christopher had wisely been coy about the specifics of our arrival onto dry land, not wanting to spook our only hope for a successful completion of the operation. But I now felt it would be a breach of etiquette to not inform the crew that the off-load was being conducted under somewhat less than secure circumstances.

"You're kidding, right?" was Harry's initial reaction to the bad news that we didn't know the home owners from Adam, nor if and when they'd be returning home. "This is no time for lame jokes, man."

When I assured him that it was no joke, Harry turned the color of mother-of-pearl. He looked at *The Fucking Boat* with a start, as if he'd just noticed its looming presence. "Everything'll be all right, Harry," I said, and meant it. "We'll just deal with things as they come up."

I've never seen anyone work as fast as that bunch, in transferring our cargo from *The Fucking Boat* onto the lawn and then into the trucks. Within an hour we had half the load stacked inside one truck and a small mountain of marijuana piled up next to the other. And still the bales flew off *The Fucking Boat*. She seemed bottomless.

It was at about this point that we had visitors. I was taking a breather by one of the trucks when Harry said, "Oh, fuck," then pointed toward the river. A little sailing dinghy with its canvas furled was furtively edging its way along *The Fucking Boat*'s topsides, the two occupants peering in our direction. Not knowing what else to do, I stepped to the riverbank and bid them hello.

"We have guns," one of them said in a shaky voice that sounded barely post-pubescent.

"That's nice," I said. "So do we." This was only technically true. We had an old double-barreled shotgun somewhere on *The Fucking Boat*, but that was about it as far as armaments went. The AK-47 we'd started the voyage with was solely for self-defense against pirates in the waters off Colombia (we had in fact been shadowed the first night out, then lost our pursuers in the dark); we'd tossed it overboard upon approaching U.S. jurisdiction.

Harry was likewise a nonviolent type and I knew he didn't allow his crew to carry arms on an offload. In the event of a bust, you either surrendered or ran like hell, preferably the latter. Shootouts with the law were virtually unheard of amongst pot runners. It just wasn't done.

There was an uneasy silence, with Harry and the boys frozen immobile wherever they were standing. Then, voicing what was actually on my mind, I said to the new arrivals, "So what do we do now?"

"I don't know," came that squeaky voice.

"Tell you what," I said in as offhanded a tone as I could come up with. "Why don't you guys give us a hand?"

Silence.

"We'll make it worth your while. Say, a bale apiece."

They were a couple of high school-aged kids from the neighborhood who had seen us go by down river, suspected what we were doing and decided to investigate. Nice kids, as it turned out (as I'd figured, they didn't have any guns), and could manhandle a fifty-pound marijuana bale with the best of Harry's crew.

About a half hour later, *The Fucking Boat's* cargo hold was empty. All that remained was to load the couple or so thousand pounds piled on the lawn into the second truck. Unfortunately, right about this time the people who lived there came home. As car headlights swept the shrubbery at the bottom of the driveway, everyone instinctively ducked down as if to hide, which was ridiculous, given the magnitude of the scene on the riverbank. But as we already knew, the curve of the driveway was such that the house blocked from view the part of the yard we were occupying. Still, the tension mounted as we listened to two car doors slamming, then, a moment later, the front door of the house opening and closing. Lights started going on downstairs.

The question was: *What now?*

It was theoretically possible that if we were very quiet we could wait until the couple (I assumed a husband and wife) went to sleep, then finish loading the second truck. We'd then barrel-ass out of there and be long gone before they could do us much harm. With their phone line cut, they'd have to run to a neighbor's house to call the cops. By the time an APB could be put out on the trucks, they'd be cruising down I-95 with thousands of others.

But we'd have to leave *The Fucking Boat* where it was, which made me nervous. There were too many ways we could be connected to it by a highly motivated and resourceful government agency like the DEA. There'd be fingerprints, stuff we'd no doubt left aboard, not to mention that those two Coast Guard Auxiliarymen could certainly provide descriptions of Christopher, Chet and myself. (They'd have fun describing how they'd helped out by giving one of us a ride ashore.) I thought of the month we'd spent outfitting on the little island of Bonaire. If *The Fucking Boat* were traced there, which would not be difficult, and given the spectacle we'd made of ourselves every night in the hotel casino and bar (we'd somehow managed to abuse an unlimited expense account), the likelihood was that *The Fucking Boat* would come back to haunt us big time.

But wait. No matter what, we weren't going to get out of there without alerting these folks. Just starting the trucks would do that, never mind the poorly mufflered, turbo-charged beasts that powered *The Fucking Boat*. We were perched on the horns of a serious dilemma, no question.

I looked up at the second story of the house, wondering where the master bedroom was. Probably the room on the near corner, which directly overlooked the river and our little circus on its bank.

Okay then. I tried to put myself in the home owner's place. I come home from dinner and a movie, I'm about to turn in with the little woman. I glance out the bedroom window to see a banana boat on my back lawn, along with two trucks, a van, a small mob of sinister figures and a bunch of square objects scattered about.

What do I do?

Christopher must have been wondering the same thing. He, too, was looking up at the second story—and that grin was back. I was about to ask him what he thought of all this when the grin widened and he said, "Bingo!"

I looked up at the second floor again. The light had just come on in the room I'd suspected was the master bedroom. A male figure appeared in the window, looking right at us.

In a sense, all hell broke lose, although the only things that actually happened were that the figure disappeared from the window, the light went off, and one of the dinghy kids said something that sounded like "Oh, boy." The rest of us just stood there. But, as I say, it seemed like all hell had broken loose.

Then a pang of guilt shot through me as I suddenly realized how rudely we were conducting ourselves. "Okay," I said, quickly recovering from the guilt attack. "He's just picked up the phone in the bedroom and found that it's dead." I imagined the scene. "Now what does he do?"

"Not a fucking thing," Christopher said, and I sensed that he was right. "Locks the bedroom door and cowers with his wife."

"Still," I said, "we better put lookouts on the other side of the house in case they decide to bolt."

"This is not the way I'm used to doing things," Harry hissed as he sent two of his guys off.

I asked the dinghy kids if they knew the guy who lived there but they didn't. Under the circumstances, I told them, they could collect their bales and go; but they shook their heads, saying that they'd stick it out with the rest of us. Looking back, I completely understand where they were coming from. Truth is, when you're young and out of your mind, there's no rush like the one produced by an iffy offload, maybe apart from a go-out in big surf. Certainly way more fun than a night at the mall.

"Okay, let's finish up," Harry said, glaring at me, and the rest of his crew set to completing the work. His turn from fear to anger was fine with me. Whatever kept the adrenaline pumping, the bales flying.

But I was still concerned about *The Fucking Boat.*

I thought about that Grateful Dead poster.

"I have an idea," I said to Christopher. "Why don't you go over to the house and see if you can strike up a conversation with our friend." Christopher had a natural charm that made him the perfect choice for the mission I had in mind. "Tell him we're sorry about all this and that we'll be finished in a half hour or so. Tell him we're leaving something on his front porch to offset any inconvenience we've caused."

Christopher nodded. "It's the least we can do."

"Grab one and come with me," I said to one of the dinghy kids. We each shouldered a bale and set off for the front porch. Meanwhile, Christopher walked over to the house. I could hear him calling out "Excuse me, sir . . ." in his politest, lowest key voice.

When the kid and I returned from the front porch, Christopher was still under the window, which was now part way open, although, from my angle at least, there didn't appear to be anyone there. I could hear the placating murmur of Christopher's voice.

"Let's put two more bales on the porch," I said to the kid.

Less than an hour later the trucks were packed to the gills and ready to roll. Two bales remained on the lawn. There was just flat no more room in either truck, no matter how hard we tried to pack them in, and it was verboten to use the personnel van for bale transportation. The kids had already put the two bales that were their end in the dinghy. "Well, boys," I said. "You might as well take those babies, too."

As I watched the kids set sail for home, their little craft nearly swamped by the weight of ill-gotten gains, I made a rough calculation. If they took their time and offed by the pound, they'd made better than $100,000 (in 1977 dollars, remember) between them for a couple hours' work. I hoped they'd use it wisely; for college, say.

Harry came over, sweating and out of breath from exertion and the tension of what he perceived as an out-of-whack offload. "We gotta hit the road, man," he said. "Are you coming with us or what?"

"Just give me a second to think," I said. I looked up at *The Fucking Boat*, towering over us. Beached in suburbia and massively silhouetted against the starry sky, it looked like some awful apparition, an abominable reincarnation of the *Titanic*, maybe.

"Those bales you put on the porch are gone," Harry said, derailing whatever train of thought I had going. "He must've taken them inside."

I looked over at the house. Christopher was back under the master bedroom. The home owner was clearly visible in the window, looking down at Christopher and saying something. According to Christopher, the fellow hadn't said much during their previous chat, apart from an assurance that he and his wife would stay inside.

But he had apparently scarfed the four bales from the porch, which was an interesting development.

"Come on, man," Harry said, nervously hopping up and down on one foot. "We gotta get out of here. I mean like now." I heard the van start up, followed by both trucks.

Christopher sauntered over, his expression deadpan.

"What did he say?" I inquired, referring to the home owner.

"He said we can come back any time we want. He said he'd build us a dock."

With the home owners as de facto cohorts in our criminal enterprise, we were now pretty much free to do with *The Fucking Boat* as we pleased. After a quick conference with Christopher, the following decision was made: given that *The Fucking Boat* was in such abominable condition and was no doubt near the top of the shit lists of a myriad of federal law enforcement agencies, the proper course of action was to retire her from service. In other words, take her offshore and pull the plug.

The plan was to have Christopher leave with the trucks and then fly out to Montauk, where he'd enlist one of our commercial fisherman/surfbuddies to come out in his boat to meet Luke and myself in *The Fucking Boat* the following night. The scuttling done, he'd bring us back to shore.

As we'd suspected, backing *The Fucking Boat* off the lawn was easy. Since the onload Down South we'd burned off more than 150,000 pounds of fuel, plus of late had unburdened her of the 20,000-pound cargo. Added to that, the tide had come up some since we'd run ashore. Her ass end was bobbing around like a cork, as if the poor old girl were impatient to get back to sea. She was evidently unaware of our plans for her future.

Luke and I spent the remainder of the night drifting leisurely downriver, meanwhile sweeping the decks and cargo hold clean of incriminating debris. We must have shoveled a hundred pounds of seeds, stems and loose buds into the river.

Harry had brought the charts I needed to the offload but only 50 gallons of diesel, which was a joke. The big Detroits sucked that much up in twenty minutes. So we had to refuel. This was accomplished just after dawn the next morning at a marina near the mouth of the Housatonic. There was an amusing aspect to this. We pulled up at the fuel dock next to a splendiferous sportfisherman with spit-polished bright work, uniformed crew, etc., just as the dock guy, a kid in his late teens, was about to refuel her. Seeing us, he immediately abandoned the yacht and came over, dragging the diesel hose with him. With the sportie's skipper glaring from the fly bridge, the kid commenced pumping the requested six hundred gallons into *The Fucking Boat,* meanwhile grinning like a fool from under his mirrored shades and shaking his head as if he were on the verge of voicing some profound witticism.

Notwithstanding the sunglasses, even a casual once-over told me the kid was stoned out of his gourd. As the refueling dragged on, the grinning and head shaking continued. Finally, he could no longer contain himself. "You guys are sooooooo fucking cooooool," he said, as I paid him.

I nodded in acknowledgment, reflecting that the dinghy kids had apparently wasted little time in distributing their merchandise, and spreading word of their adventure amongst their peers.

With the improbable success of the offload, I must admit I *was* feeling pretty cool, and more than a little cocky. The sense of invincibility I'd been living under since Hawaii and North Africa was in full effect and then some. (On the other hand, if I'd had an ounce of self-reflection in me in those days—what a double-edged sucker *that* is, I can tell you—I might have pondered the fine line between grace under pressure and outright lunacy.)

Despite our efforts at cleanup, *The Fucking Boat* was far from devoid of cannabis debris—a pot-sniffing dog would probably have keeled over in delirium. Plus we were in violation of about every international and domestic maritime regulation one could think of, including conspiracy to import a controlled substance, which carried the same jail time as the deed itself. Our cruise east to Montauk should therefore have been a low-key affair, fraught with some degree of tension.

Predictably, such was not the case. We faroomed *The Fucking Boat* up Long Island Sound as if she were a hot rod on a Saturday night, veering this way and that on flighty little sightseeing excursions, and buzzing by the various pleasure craft we came upon. Lightened up and with the turbo-charged V-12s at full throttle, our souped-up 80-foot banana boat was up on a semi-plane and doing something like twenty knots. (In her original incarnation, she was probably powered by a single, meek, low RPM eight-banger and had a top speed of under 10 knots.)

Christopher and a surfbuddy of ours met us in the buddy's little lobster boat off Montauk Light just after dark. We cruised together a few miles further offshore then shut down our engines. It was a beautiful night, clear, calm and windless and very dark; ideal conditions for the job we had to do.

The Fucking Boat, however, was not so easy to put down. In fact, we almost failed altogether. A long past previous owner had equipped her with huge seacocks for ease of scuttling (a common add-on feature in a smuggling vessel), but they were frozen solid by corrosion and could not be turned on. We opened the engines' seawater intake valves but by that means it would take forever to pour sufficient water into the bilge.

We had a fire ax and the old double-barreled shotgun aboard and in the end this was how we did it. We stood in the cargo hold and chopped her and shot her full of holes until we ran out of ammunition and out of energy. Then we sat waiting on our friend's boat while she settled in the quiet water until her decks were awash. She would sink no further, however. We had forgotten about the fuel tank, a huge bubble of air that offset the dead weight of the engines, which, because of the vessel's all-wood construction, was the only reason she would sink. So we went back aboard and tore into her again, into that big fuel tank, taking turns with the ax until our calloused hands were raw and blistered.

And then she finally sank, just before first light. It had taken a good eight hours, but like Rasputin she finally went down. Weighted by the engines aft, she pointed her bows straight up at the heavens and then, after one final faint, illuminative sweep of the distant lighthouse beacon, she was gone.

And I'll tell you what: though I'd cursed that ship and ultimately came to hate her for all her maddening defects, seeing her vanish like that made me shiver. The sinking of a ship you've lived and voyaged aboard is no small thing, even when done by your own hand. Maybe more so then.

We sat there for a while, absently watching the sun come up and glancing at the place in the ocean where the vessel had sunk. We were all very tired and not much was said. Then our friend tried to start his little lobster boat but the battery had gone flat. So he radioed the Coast Guard and they sent out a cutter that obligingly towed us in, and then with that little irony the fun and games were over.

19.

The La Paz to Mazatlán ferry plies on eastward through the Sea of Cortez. Out the little porthole adjacent to my bunk, the crimson smear of the dying sunset over the Baja peninsula fades in our wake.

I took a turn on deck a while ago, circling the ship once around. Out of guilt and concern, I tried to go down to the ferry's off-limits cargo deck to visit Shiner, but a crewman caught me sneaking along the line of vehicles and my offer of a 20-peso *mordida* for a quick five minutes with her only seemed to aggravate him further. Like it was some sort of insult; like this country doesn't hum-fucking-along to the bribery tune. I got a bit melancholy at this, worrying about my current partner in things, hoping she's all right. If it isn't one thing it's another, these days, with these damn moods.

I also stopped to have a beer at a little cantina overlooking the fantail. There was quite a party going on there, an assortment of mostly Mexican tourists and travelers drinking and dancing to a quartet of *mariachi* players. I've become very fond of the Mexican style of music, *mariachi* in particular, which I can only liken to country music in the states; the way they both skirt the fine line between the sublime and the ridiculous in their portrayal of the doings of humans. These fellows were quite good, able to take the revelers along with them as they changed moods. The place quieted right down during a tragic love ballad and I became quite sad myself, in a nonspecific way, although I did briefly think of Denise, wondering where she was and what she was doing at that moment. An older couple danced to the song and it was obvious that they were very much in love. The crowd formed a circle and watched the two move elegantly about, holding each other tight, and even the drunken fools were openly moved. This easy emotionality is one of the things I like most about the people down here.

As the *mariachis* returned to an up-tempo, yodeling *canción* and the crowd waxed once again boisterous, I noticed a pair of fellows who must have arrived during the love song, now sitting in deep conversation at a table near the companionway to the lower deck. One was a swarthy *latino*, a Mexican no doubt, and through his facial features and the way he quietly exuded a kind of power and potential for action—menace, even—he recalled to me my Colombian partner in crime, Fredi. His companion was a North American, I felt sure. He was fair-skinned and from the hesitancy in his speech I sensed he was not fluent in Spanish. The other thing I suspected, and quite strongly, was that the two were involved in some illegal activity; they were up to no good.

The last time I saw Fredi, I recalled, was at his fortified compound in a little town called Rodadero on Colombia's north coast, in the summer of 1981. I'd come down to tell him that I was getting out of the pot business, that I was going to Hollywood to write movies. Fredi didn't ask me why I'd made this decision, but merely wished me well and asked that I let him know when I had a movie out so he could go and see it. There was an awkward moment then, because I'd just lost 9,000 pounds of pot Fredi had fronted me, and due to the informality of our business dealings it was unclear whether I owed him any money.

I'd brought a newspaper clipping from Puerto Rico that told the story of how the U.S. Coast Guard had interdicted Christopher and me on our motor sailer near the Mona Passage. I'd done this as proof of the loss, which was the custom when things went sour, but Fredi refused to even glance at the article. This was his way of saying he trusted me completely. I then broached the subject of money I possibly owed him, which could have amounted to several hundred thousand dollars that I no longer had, but Fredi waved me off, that it was a small thing between us.

When I left later that day, Fredi waved good-bye from his compound's gate, wearing the red silk robe I'd given him on a previous visit, a 9mm pistol tucked in the sash. He was gone less than a year later, killed in a gun-fight in the streets of Rodadero. A rival pot lord ambushed him coming out of church with his family, I heard.

I still think of Fredi often, and fondly.

I've found that reliving the past has had a double-edged effect, like looking through an old photo album. Lots of smiles of recognition but also some sadness, some longing for the way it used to be. And some regrets, for the way it used to be.

20.

There was another aspect to the pot run I've described, which surfaced the night after the scuttling. To explain, I have to go further back in time, to 1970 in North Africa. When Christopher and I first decided to dabble in the arena of international crime, it was merely in order to finance a few more months of surf exploration abroad. We were too young and too focused on our passion to see beyond this modest yet crucial goal.

But with our immediate and highly remunerative successes in the movement of hashish to the waiting masses in the United States (a pound bought for $40 from the Berbers in the Rif Mountains went for $1,000 stateside), we expanded our ambition, now visualizing an open-ended world surf tour; perhaps under sail, a trade wind-friendly schooner of classic design. One more run, we kept telling ourselves, then off we'd go to put some personal Xs on what was in those days a largely blank world surf map. One thing led to another, however, and to another, and, flushed with success, our ambitions grew. After one really big score, we now told ourselves, we'd not only find our paradise but buy a piece of it. We'd do *Endless Summer* one better. Unlike the vagabonds who lived that seminal fable, we would never return.

Then, in the late summer of 1977, the big score we'd envisioned had transpired, in spades. The money was there—or would be in a few days— suitcases of it, more than enough to secure our personal, far-flung little surf kingdom. But celebrating in a Montauk bar that night, the subject of wave riding, let alone of our planned withdrawal to surf paradise, never came up.

"Now that we're rich," the conversation essentially went, and it matters not who said what. "What should we do next?"

"Get reeeeeeaaaally rich!" was the reply and laughter followed and glasses clinked and our fates were sealed with that betrayal of the faith.

PART 2

Deeper, Mainland Mexico and on to Central America

Who hath desired for the Sea—the sight of salt water
    unbounded—
The heave and the halt and the hurl and the crash of
    the comber wind-hounded?
The sleek-barreled swell before storm, grey, foamless,
    enormous, and growing—
Stark calm on the lap of the Line or the crazy-eyed
    hurricane blowing.

RUDYARD KIPLING, from
"The Sea and the Hills"

To become the energy of the wave, that's the main idea.
You take when the water gives, and you give when the
water takes. It's a constant interplay of bold confrontations
and mellow respect.

BILLY HAMILTON, surfer

1.

How different women are from the rest of us. Like the miracle of design of their hips, the way it can effect a lower unit bump and glide simultaneously, and on soft, sloping sand at that. And like . . .

Denise notices I'm staring and smiles shyly. That lavish, much-photographed model's hardbody and she's still self-conscious; how do you figure? In a fit of abashment she mad dashes for the water, long legs churning spent white water, goofing it up as she flops, then waving and calling out for Shiner and me to come on in, but at this very moment I'd rather just sit and watch and try not to think too much. Shiner looks at me and I tell her to go ahead so she does and then I'm alone on the towel while the two females swim for the outside.

More than three weeks now since the ferry deposited me and my whole worldly act on the Mexican mainland, and six days since Denise flew down from snowbound Toronto to a quaint little *pueblo* fronting a reef break I found outside Puerto Vallarta, a move of pure impulsivity after I'd called her from the Mazatlán bullfights and blurted how much I missed her. I caught her going out the door and pictured her in her apartment all bundled up and impatient, but then I could hear the whisper of her coat coming off as she sat down and said she was just thinking about me.

Thing was, when I called her, I was already rattled on some other level, by the bullfight. Although I had experienced one before, I hadn't at that time seen the connection between it and wave riding, not so much for the grace under pressure aspect—many endeavors involve that—but for how *la corrida* is likewise a creative interface with an active force of nature. I had been wrong in thinking that surfing was unique in this way. It occurred to me that the essential difference between wave riding and bullfighting lies in the spectacle of the latter. The matador needs the crowd; unlike surfing, the bullfighter's art is not a strictly personal thing.

These realizations set me to a bout of self-reflection, which so often leads to trouble, as it did here, upon the killing of the first bull. When the matador drove his sword down between the bull's shoulder blades, through his spinal cord and then into his heart and the animal collapsed in a heap, the focus of my identification switched from man to bull, and I was overcome by a mix of emotions I had felt once before, at sea. And just for a heartbeat as I found myself doubled over in my seat with my eyes shut tight while the rest of the crowd rose and cheered, I also remembered the lust for the kill I myself had felt those years ago.

It was the fall of 1987. I'd gone to sea on a commercial fishing trip out of Montauk with a surfbuddy named Michael Potts and his mate, Dennis Gaviola. We were after big bluefin tuna; individuals are referred to as giants when they weigh in at over 310 pounds. The meat of the giant bluefin is much revered in Japan and is sold as sashimi in restaurants for around $50 an ounce; the succulent, buttery belly meat brings even more.

Giant bluefin tuna are bought off the dock by Japanese exporters who overnight the animals to Tokyo so they can be consumed the next day. The price the local fisherman gets depends on the quality of the meat (the more marbled with fat the better) and the vicissitudes of supply and demand. In the early 1980s, during a time of bluefin scarcity, one big, fine, fatty fish sold "on the hoof" for $80,000. Although this is an extreme example, really big bluefin, known colloquially as "dinosaurs," routinely bring in five-figure sums.

With this kind of money at stake, the endeavor is very serious business; in lean times a fisherman's season can be saved with the catching of a single fish. But the giant bluefin is a wily, intelligent animal and the quest for one has more the feel of a big game hunt than "going fishing." It is not unusual for a boat to go for years without a hook up, let alone a landing. Mike Potts, however, is an extraordinary sea hunter, blessed with an inborn instinct for finding and hooking bluefin that even he can't explain. He's known as the best rod-and-reel tuna man in the harbor.

We hooked the fish in question midmorning some 10 miles south of Montauk Light at an exact spot in the ocean that would become known as The Weisbecker Numbers, after its loran coordinates, and since I fought the fish. The fact that Mike had put me in the fighting chair was not a tribute to my experience or ability as a fisherman; quite the contrary. I had in fact never fished for giant bluefin tuna before. The catching of a giant is a complex feat requiring instant and intimate coordination between the skipper on the bridge and the mate on the fish deck. The angler is mostly there for the muscle and is the least important presence in the struggle.

An hour or so into the fight we had coaxed the fish to within a few yards of the boat and I caught my first glimpse of him, a massive spectral flash of silver and blue off the stern. He seemed tired, his pull flaccid and spent. I felt that we had him, that the fight was over. And I was surely glad of that; I was about as physically exhausted as I'd ever been.

But then the rod tip moved subtly sideways as the animal turned his head and saw the boat—saw the human animals on its deck, who were intent on killing him—and then instantaneously I was jerked nearly out of the chair and the rod bent double as he ran for the horizon.

It was another hour before the fish's runs weakened and we got him close to the boat again; Dennis hopped up onto the transom and raised a harpoon to his shoulder. Then the fish surfaced and I got a good look at him. I was struck not only by his size—he'd go well over a quarter ton—but by the color of his flank, which appeared to pulsate with every hue of blue I'd ever seen—and some I hadn't, because they were unique to the animal and the situation. They were a reflection, a manifestation, of his will to live, and of the sea itself.

For my part, I had hit a wall of mental and physical exhaustion, and in my lust for the kill my mind was operating on a level of utter here-and-now purity. In a very deep and fundamental way, I wanted that fish to be dead.

But then Dennis's arm and upper body shot forward and down as he planted the harpoon and at the instant the razor-tipped lance penetrated the fish's shimmering flank, a jolt ran through my body like a high voltage arc. I also experienced the phenomenon aurally, in the form of a sharp, hallucinated electric crack. And then, as at the bullfight, I found myself bent over, hammered by grief and remorse for the terrible thing being done.

The commotion on deck and the raised voices of my companions and the scream of the reel and the sharp bending of the rod told me something else was wrong. The fish was gone again on a run for the horizon, his fastest and strongest yet. I turned and looked to my left and through the haze of grief and remorse and awe, I watched as Dennis secured a flotation barrel to the quarter-inch nylon harpoon line, which was uncoiling in a blur from the deck. Then the barrel shot off the transom and was gone overboard as if shot from a cannon.

We watched in silence as the barrel plowed horizonward, submerging briefly then reappearing as the fish fought its buoyancy. How could this be? I wanted to know. How could this fish could be doing that after two hours of desperate effort fighting the pull of the rod, and now with a harpoon through his back? Dennis turned and looked up at Mike and I knew from their expressions that with all their years of killing big fish they had never seen anything like this before.

We chased the harpooned fish for about another hour; then the barrel ceased its movement through the water and we backed the boat up to it. Dennis reached over the transom and tried to haul in the harpoon line, which was leading straight down now, but he could not do it. He looked up at Mike and shook his head and said that the fish was still green, meaning not ready to be landed. He was just resting, Dennis added.

"No, he's dead," I said, and even with all Dennis's experience, I knew I was right. I had felt the fish's death rattle, a tiny vibration that had passed up through the monofilament into the rod and then into me.

The heart down there under the water had stopped beating.

With great effort, Mike and Dennis hauled the fish from the depths, then affixed a tail rope, and with block and tackle hoisted the animal over the rail and onto the deck. His electric colors were fading; even as I watched, the beautiful blues of him were gone to a sickly pale. Like the bull in Mexico, he was no longer a force of nature but just a pile of dead meat skewered by a steely lance.

Around sundown, as a Japanese man oversaw the loading of the carcass into a crate with a Tokyo address on the side, I was given a sliver cut from the fish's massive heart, which I consumed, as is the custom.

"What were you thinking?" Denise is asking me. After her swim we raced through the lime trees and hydrangeas and down the path to our condo and now we're all entwined and slithery and I'm feeling pretty good. Pleasantly dazed from the state of concentrated relaxation I've just experienced and which subtly lingers still. The heightened awareness of nothing at all. The time off from being me.

What was I thinking? There's a question. "When?"

"When I was walking along the beach and you were staring at me with this very serious expression."

Trying to remember. "Things. This and that." Lame. Stalling. Back to being me now.

"Like whaa-at?" Stretching the word into sweetly cajoling multi-syllables and cuddling closer.

"I was thinking how beautiful you are."

She presses herself against me tighter and wiggles for a better fit. "And what else?"

"Doing what we just did."

Tighter still and her breathing quickens. I did good. Told the truth and made her happy. Only left out this and that.

"And what were you thinking about just now?"

Off guard: "Wondering what's down the road."

"For us?"

Confused and maybe a little annoyed by all the questions: "Literally. What I'm going to run into south of here."

Silence as her grip stiffens and her breathing becomes shallow and hushed. She sighs and hugs me harder for a moment then rises and goes to the bathroom and turns on the shower. She won't in any way make an issue of what has just happened. So many women would have just risen abruptly and left me to ponder my gaffe, my whole miserable, selfish act. Maybe issue a sharp parting shot to instill some added fear and guilt. But that's just not her way. I have the feeling she's crying in there, though. Hiding the sound with the running water. Which is more dispiriting than anything she might've said.

In the two years since we began our long-distance affair, Denise has never uttered the phrase "We have to talk," and neither has she ever juxtaposed the words "evolving" or "growing" with the word "relationship." Words and phrases that are the equivalent to the *Jaws* theme in my doings with women.

But then sometimes she goes off and cries.

We met in November of 1994 on a beach on the island of Tobago in the lower Caribbean. She'd come down with her sister for a week's stay in one of the few resort hotels on the pristine southwest coast, near the classic point break known as Mount Irvine. To a sophisticated (but unpretentious and so sweetly so) urban woman like Denise, I cut the romantic figure of an adventurer, she would later tell me, someone out of an outlaw song or swashbuckling movie, my grizzled good looks (her words) and dubious personal history only increasing the initial attraction. But she came to love me, she said, for my forthrightness, my sardonic sense of myself and the world as I saw it, and for a kindness and sensitivity that belied my rougher aspects. Things I was glad she saw in me but that I wondered about. Maybe she just needed me to fit a certain vision and bent her perceptions thus.

Four days into Denise's stay, I joined forces with a couple of other traveling surfers and chartered a local fishing boat to make a run down the coast to surf a break that was inaccessible by road. Denise came along to do some beachcombing on what we'd heard was a pristine, seashell-rich shore. Upon midmorning arrival, however, we found the tide too low and the inshore wash too rocky to make a landing to put her ashore. And although the groundswell was only moderate, the boulder-strewn shore break looked too dicey for a safe swim in.

So Denise was stuck on the shadeless, foul-smelling, fish crud-encrusted little vessel while the rest of us surfed. Twenty minutes into the session I paddled back to the boat to be with her. I felt terrible about the situation, and guilty that I hadn't thought to inquire about possible problems in landing.

"No, go ride your waves," she said when she realized why I'd cut my session short. She turned her sweet, easy smile from me to the horizon. "I love just being out here." Flies buzzed, her sweat ran in rivulets in the gathering swelter. "And I love watching you surf."

It's Denise's last night, so we're splurging, dining at an upscale eatery in the nearby village of Sayulita. Second-floor sea view veranda, tuxed waiters who greet you in English and are surprised and grin when you respond in Spanish; menu prices in dollars first, pesos parenthetically, as if an embarrassing afterthought. I'm formally dressed for the occasion, dug out a shirt with an actual collar and my sole surviving nondenim long pants. I've even unscavenged my belt from its function as an awning tie-down. Denise has trimmed my hair and moustache as a final touch. She herself is quite the slinky center of attention in a tight-fitting dress we picked up in Vallarta.

The atmosphere is hushed, the soft Muzak barely this cultural side of Herb Alpert, but raucous laughter and boom-box mariachi emanating from the string of local beach joints we normally frequent just up the beach to the north remind us where we really are.

I look around. The place is filling up; I recognize the *norte* expat and his Mexican wife who run the real estate agency I used in securing our rental. There's a bizarre story behind these two—on a certain level the most bizarre of any I've come across since embarking on this journey—which I'm dying to relate to Denise, but we're in deep conversation at the moment, so I'll wait for a lull to bring it up.

Denise has been asking me about Christopher, whom she has never met, since he had bolted south two years before she came down for her first visit to Montauk. Although, over the time we've spent together, Christopher has often been mentioned in my backstory tales, it was always more or less in the abstract; he was merely this guy with whom I'd shared some experiences. Her queries tonight have been seemingly offhanded, but laden with a subtext that has made me wary of where she's going with the conversation.

"What does he look like?" she wants to know, after I've told her about Christopher's strange, Dickensian childhood and a bit about his Vietnam experience. How, due to his slight frame, he had been the one in his platoon sent crawling down enemy tunnels with a pistol and a knife, to kill anyone lurking within; how, one time when he was wounded and sure death was imminent, he'd written a letter to his mother on his arm.

"Christopher's not good-looking in the usual way," I'm telling her, realizing I've not shown her the photograph of Christopher I carry, perhaps because my last ex, Diana, is also pictured. And Diana and I have had sex, once, since I met Denise. "Although women like him. Pretty much everyone likes him. He's got this grin." A pause, then, rambling a bit: "He's fearless and he loves kids and dogs."

I go on: "He's very strong for his size. One of his nicknames is Popeye, for his love of the sea and for his outsized hands and forearms." A life largely spent paddling through lines of white water, hauling ropes and nets and manhandling marijuana bales on rolling decks has hardened and corded Christopher's physique, pared his flesh to an efficient minimalism, except for his meaty paws and forearms. An outward minimalism that reflects his personality, he being frugal with language, except on the occasions when he launches himself into a flighty philosophical jag or ridiculous rambling discourse and those hands and arms go all a-blur in emphatic gesture.

"You two were very close," Denise says, maybe too levelly. It's as if she's holding something back.

"Yes, we are." My use of the present tense is not lost on her.

"A guy thing."

A shallow, almost cruel summation. I'm getting the drift now, seeing where she's headed. And I sense the tension. This is not like Denise.

A guy thing. But how to explain a bond borne of the shared perils of 30 years of big-water go-outs and slapdash lawbreaking and all-around ridiculousness, and of the certain knowledge that each will do the right thing with respect to the other and be there, even when it's all going sour? Do the right thing and be there at crunch time, yet without the *quid pro quo* inherent in a love relationship. The purity of the bond of our friendship, perhaps paradoxically, lies in its very passionlessness, and hence in its unselfishness. In its sacrifice without motive. Passion—love—is the quintessence of self-interest, in its all-consuming graspy greed—the ego rules, the I of it, the What's in it for me? of it. Love is so fervently, so needily, sought, because it's after all a hunger, a volitionless imperative. While friendship is all volition; the sacrifices, the bond itself. Perceived this way, deep, true friendship is harder to account for than love, and therefore rarer.

I'm tempted to say these things, but I know the words would merely strike her deep, with no gain of insight. So I don't say anything. Which of course is in itself a very guy thing, and hurtful.

"Why do you think he stopped communicating with you?" Denise asks.

How to explain that that doesn't matter? That Christopher's apparent abandonment of me is not a betrayal of any sort, as it would be between a man and a woman, or perhaps even two women friends. Yes, again, *a guy thing.*

"Maybe he's dead. You ever think of that?" As if this would also be a betrayal.

"I doubt it," is all I say. Even given the inherent risks of the life he's living—whatever the specifics—it would be very unlike Christopher to be dead.

"What are you going to do if you find him?"

"When I find him, I'll ask him how he's been and then odds are we'll go out for a surf." My words have an oblique, unintentional ring of sarcasm. But they are merely the truth.

"Allan . . ." I'm holding her eyes in spite of my discomfort with all this. "Are you planning on ever coming back?"

Although her line of questioning has in no way been a grilling—plenty of contemplative pauses and wine sipping and little asides about this and that—I just now realize she's rehearsed her part in the scene we're playing out.

I lean forward and subtly indicate the *norte* expat and his Mexican wife across the room at a table for two. I lower my voice. "See that couple over there?"

Denise glances, nods. The two are concentrating on their food. The silence between them seems easy.

I met the wife first, I tell Denise, at their real estate agency. The lady spoke no English so we talked about local rentals exclusively in Spanish. She told me that she had exactly what I wanted, but that her husband had the key and wouldn't be back until tomorrow.

The next day, the husband was at the office alone. I dealt with him in English. Just as we were about to go have a look at the condo, the phone rang. He picked it up, said "Hello," listened for a couple seconds, then, in the worst *norte* accent I've ever heard, said, "Yo no hablo español." Butchering the grammar and omitting a necessary preposition, he added, *"Dice mi esposa mañana,"* and hung up. Speak to my wife tomorrow, was what he meant. "Speaks my wife tomorrow," is what he said.

"Turns out he's been living in Mexico for fifteen years, been married to his wife for twelve years, and speaks no Spanish," I tell Denise. "I'm talking functionally zero. And *she* speaks no English."

Denise's eyes flicker then wander the room.

"I mean, think about that."

Denise nods but doesn't say anything.

"They have kids . . ." Something occurs to me. "Maybe the kids are bilingual . . . Of course, they'd have to be. They could translate if anything vital had to be communicated between them."

My camera is on the table and on impulse I tilt it upward toward her and press the shutter. The flash pops. Denise blinks, then fusses with her purse; she's used to my unannounced, shoot-from-the-hip candids.

She excuses herself and heads for the ladies' room.

I'd meant to catch a nap in the airport parking lot after Denise walked through the security gate at Vallarta International for her dawn flight. She stopped and turned, then, holding back tears, asked if she'll ever see me again. But I hit the road south instead, hunched over the wheel, feeling tense and hollow and vertiginous, yet somehow exhilarated, like some fugitive with a newly clean slate, passing some indefinable point of no return.

SOUTH

Late morning and your third coffee isn't working as the copra plantations and dusty little roadside pueblos *blur by, nut husks piled high like skulls, long, hard panning stares from bush-knife wielding campesinos at the unfamiliar sight of a small white house atop a big black pickup rolling through their jungly baili-wick.*

2.

I've lost track of where I am, not to say I'm lost. Stopped on a dirt turnout between two potholed hairpins with a view of nothing but dense bush and high, jagged gorge rising all around into a midday scorcher, I feel like I've fallen into a pit. I wipe my brow with a sweat-sogged bandana and squint at the map. The thick red line labeled "Mex 200" indicates a straight coastal shot south where I thought I was, or should be, not this switchback-laced, up then down, ear-popping, mean mountain twister.

Where the hell am I?

Here comes somebody, from the sound of it a truck laboring up the steep grade behind me, the first traffic in a half hour at least on this bleak, umbrageous excuse for a . . . Well, here we go again, kids, *federales,* a full platoon in a troop carrier, and damned if it isn't pulling up, *los soldados* piling out and headed my way in the rearview, looking very serious in clanking full battle dress.

There's a more businesslike vibe than in my many past encounters with Mexico's finest. As the grunts surround the rig, a captain or colonel—he's well braided and medaled—trots over to my window and peers inside: a quick sweep of large brown eyes and a barked command I don't quite catch over Shiner's snarling uproar. "Todo esta bien?" he asks me, with a direct, concerned look. He's not asking me for my passport, or for money or a souvenir from the United States or a *Playboy* magazine. Just wants to know if I'm okay.

"Sí, por supuesto," I assure him. He nods, glad of that, then issues another order. The troops double-time it back to the carrier and are summarily gone up the road around the next hairpin. Well, that had to be the quick-est, least aggravating encounter with *federales* in the annals of . . .

It suddenly hits home where I am. I'm on the stretch of road where Cor-mac's friend from Santa Cruz was found in his van, he and his dog dead from gunshot wounds. I'm in the state of Michoacán on the stretch of road known as Bandido Alley. Which was why the locked and loaded troops fanned out facing *away* from the rig, scanning the deep roadside bush and the jagged overhangs of the escarpment above, instead of covering me. Those boys were ready to rumble; they saw my stopped vehicle on the side of the road as a *potential combat situation.*

"The Surf Report" is succinct in its general view of the hazards of this area: "Avoid traveling alone," it cautions; and, if waylaid, "you and your life may not be held in high esteem."

A couple weeks ago at Mazatlán, I talked up an RV wagon master named Tom Walker of Caravan Adventure Tours—20-motor-home convoys trav-eling from RV park to RV park, the safety-in-numbers-circle-the-wagons-at-night theory of Mexican tourism. Tom and his wife had been leading such tours south of the border for many years but this year had shortened the itinerary to exclude points south of even Mazatlán, due to the recent rise in road bandit depredations.

"They pick off the stragglers," Tom had said. "Haul a fallen tree or a spike-driven plank onto the road in front of you, then one behind you." He'd strongly suggested I find another vehicle to travel in tandem with.

Most recently, I ran into a Mexican surfer at Playa Bruja near Mazatlán who shook his head and started in with more tales of woe when I told him of my southern travel plans. "Por favor, amigo," I'd interjected. "No quiero oirlo." I don't want to hear it.

I'd heard too much, the reverse-cumulative effect being that I erased from my mind the possibility of coming to grief. But now, the behavior of those *soldados,* the look of concern on the officer's face as he peered intently into my rig, has shaken me up.

I fire up the Ford and floor it. A couple miles up the road I fall in be-hind the troop carrier, right on its ass.

Avoid traveling alone . . .

Find another vehicle to travel in tandem with . . .

As together we tool on down *la carretera* known as Bandido Alley, with points of no return piling up in my wake, it occurs to me that my direction of movement warrants a new description.

DEEPER

Late afternoon now and you're viajando solo *again, the troops having turned off inland into the hills. God bless 'em. But you've got to find a safe place to camp before dark. Safe? What's that word mean down here, you wonder, as you negotiate deep curves and cavernous potholes that keep your speed down and hence your vulnerability up, squinting at high crags above that seem designed as brigand lookout points; and on the inland side dimly glimpsed lairlike hutches in deep emerald bush; and now to the west, the beaches, seemingly pristine and deserted until you spot a shadowy figure lurking on the edge of a banana or coconut grove—the long curved blade of his bush knife a dark scar against the white of the sand—craning to watch you go by, your little house that travels no doubt looking like a bank vault on wheels rolling on down the road in the direction of deeper.*

3.

I almost missed the turn off. Cruised right on by the sign, big as all get-out on the right, "Playa Nexpa." A wandering mind I guess. I was probably thinking about Denise, or *bandidos,* or this growing sensation that I'm a fugitive, although I don't believe I'm currently wanted for anything anywhere. Turned around when the bridge sign RIO NEXPA hove into view and went back and on down the dirt road.

"The Surf Report" extols Nexpa with the words "Seems safe," high praise in comparison to its assessment of the area's alternatives: "Not safe to stay overnight" and "Not a safe place to camp and don't bring your girlfriend if you do."

Not the first thing but the second thing I liked about Playa Nexpa was how easily defensible it is: surrounded on three sides by water, one way in. Someone has it in his head to fuck with you, he has to come down the dirt road, the end of which is guarded day and night by campground dogs. The first thing I liked was that long left point break that is the enclave's focal point. It's been shoulder-to-head-high or better since my arrival last week—I have no plans of leaving in the immediate future. Never drive away from good surf.

Shiner's fitted right in with the dogs here. She's a full fledged member of the pack, guarding the end of the dirt road alongside Shorty and Oso and the rest of the rowdy mongrel crew. "The Surf Report," regarding the dirt road: "Don't drive down the road at night if it can be helped. Stories of holdups are many." Indeed, Tonia, the local woman who runs the campground, was ambushed a few years ago on the road and shot when she hesitated in forking over her jewelry.

The geographical setup, along with the mutual concerns of the people ensconced here, gives Nexpa the feel of a stronghold. A surfers' stronghold.

Places like Nexpa rouse the sensation that I'm closing in on Christopher. Every so often I'll catch a glimpse of someone from behind in the surf lineup or at an angle just so on an otherwise deserted beach, or late night at a raucous, surfy cantina like Nexpa's overlooking the break, and for a skipping heartbeat I'll think my search is over.

Predictably, down here in the heart of *bandido* country, still more horror stories of the "*la violencia en el sur*" theme surface, some verging on the apocryphal. The latest: last season a young *norte* surfer was walking the beach from the nearby town of Caleta with some groceries when he was accosted by a young Mexican with a gun, a .22 caliber sidearm. The situation went sour and the surfer was shot point-blank in the head.

That much of the story, and that the surfer survived, I know is true—I spoke to someone who was here at the time. The rest of the incident, which I could not confirm but I believe to be true, goes as follows: the surfer did not have travel or emergency evacuation insurance and did not want to go to a Mexican hospital, so he flew commercially from Zihuatanejo to Mexico City. In Mexico City he waited overnight at the airport for the next available flight to the States, where he took a taxi to the nearest hospital and had the bullet removed from his head.

I tend to believe this not only because on a certain level the story is so archetypically Mexican, but also because as a group the surfers entrenched here at Nexpa are hard core and I can picture one of their kind doing this.*

But it's not all crazed surfers and fear and loathing at Nexpa. One of the travelers here is a middle-aged lady named Jody, living in the open-air palapa next to mine on the bank of Rio Nexpa. Jody has made thirteen trips this deep into Mexico, or deeper, and almost always travels alone, except for her dogs. Jody doesn't fear *bandidos,* or anything else.

---

*Months later I confirmed the story via a surfer who had seen it on *Surfer* magazine's Web site; the guy had indeed flown home with a bullet in his head, after waiting overnight in the airport in Mexico City.

Camped two palapas down from Jody is a perky young blonde named Peggy, who surfs, and on whom I at first had designs, but then we became friends and I let it slide. Peggy lives alone in her van and will soon be on the road, solo.

Karen is from British Columbia and lives out at the point in a clatter-board lean-to. She is here because she had a dream about Aztec ruins and hence believed it was her destiny to come to Mexico. Karen hitchhiked to Nexpa, right through the heart of Bandido Alley. (She was sexually assaulted "only once," she blithely told me.)

There *are* hazards to life deep down on the Mexican mainland. Aside from the threat of violence from humans, there are earthquakes (Nexpa was recently rocked by a 6.8) and tsunamis (the campground at Boca de los Iguanas, just to the north of Nexpa, was inundated last year). The threat of sharks and poisonous sea snakes in the lineup is real and there are alligators and big boas in the rivers; the deadly fer-de-lance viper, along with a plethora of venom-squirting creepy crawlies, may be encountered virtually anywhere. There are bowel-dissolving, potentially fatal tropical diseases that may be contracted despite elaborate preventive measures. And possibly worst of all, there are the Mexican motorists, who are as a whole among the most unbalanced I've encountered anywhere in the world.

Despite all this, throughout my journey I have found Mexico to be a fine and beautiful place, populated mostly by kind and gentle folk. I've come to like it very much. And I've come to feel safe here.

4.

Although with surfing's emergence as a mainstream sport the times have changed stateside, south of the border the lifestyles of wave riding and out-lawism are still closely linked. In other ways, too, my southward travel amounts to a trip back through the decades of the sociological evolution of surfing. The crowded lineups thin, the individuals I encounter wax leaner and scruffier and of harder core and wilder eye. New Age sporties, week-enders, the uncommitted masses, have largely been left in *La Casita*'s dust. No beemers in the parking lots down here. Or would be none, if there were parking lots—beach access being somewhat primitive.

Surprisingly, considering my own irregular background, it had not oc-curred to me that my habit of asking around about Christopher—and in the process flashing my water-stained, increasingly-rumpled-from-being-sat-upon, barely al dente photograph of him and my ex, Diana—might have the repercussion it did: Within 24 hours of my arrival at a certain small coastal *pueblo,* word spread amongst its expat residents to be on the look-out for a deep cover DEA agent traveling in a pickup/camper with a dog and a quiver of surfsticks, and inquiring after someone's whereabouts.

The world of the Down South expat, no matter his or her legal status, is a small one; in the case of remote surf break strongholds it waxes down-right minuscule. The point being that this fellow I'll call Bart was, by virtue of his longtime residency in the area, particularly well connected to the grapevine and he at first avoided my proximity. Bart, you see, was still very active in the smuggling trade.

A couple days into my stay a southwesterly groundswell arrived and the reef break adjacent to my campsite commenced going off in grand style. Although there were other waves to ride in the immediate area, this one was Bart's favorite for the size and swell direction. The morning of the third day his stoke got the better of his discretion and he joined me and a handful of others in the outside lineup.

With wave faces well overhead and of top-to-bottom breaking configuration, the conditions were at best borderline for optimal longboarding, noseriding in particular. In bigger, hollower surf, when the wall of water upon which you are noseriding waxes super-steep preparatory to its forward pitch, a longboard's fin will tend to lose its grip on the wave and break free. As with a rudderless ship, a sideways broach is then inevitable, with catastrophic control loss. So I largely eschewed the tip position and contented myself with a mid-board crouch and fast slide toward the light at the ends of the watery tunnels evolving ahead. In other words, tube—or barrel—riding.

It's here, in more sizable, critical conditions that the shortboard's design advantages come into play. With less wetted surface (hence less friction), the shortboard is faster than its lengthier counterpart, and simply fits better in the tight confines of the curl. And with its shorter turning radius, the shortboard can also be projected into the desired tube riding position with greater dispatch.

A handful of young hotshots on their pointy little thrusters were taking full advantage of these factors, tucking themselves deeply into wave after wave, occasionally disappearing altogether as surface tension shattered and Big Blue's integument folded in upon itself, creating a hurtling, water-shrouded niche, a sort of *locus classicus*. For all my talk of The Glide and its psychotropic effects, it is time spent within the confines of the sea's emerald recess (the term "green room" was coined elsewhere and long ago; it still says it all) that represents surfing's real nirvana-state; its place of secrets. Not that the tube ride and the longboard Glide are mutually exclusive, quite the contrary. The condition of mindless bliss engendered by perfect speed-trim is theoretically the same, whether accomplished up on the nose or some point further back. One must simply adapt oneself to the prevailing oceanic mood, and rearrange one's priorities. In other words—the wave's the thing.

What's more, in tube riding, even the most frantic, maneuver-obsessed shortboarder tends toward that state of tranquility and grace—a melding of psychical and corporeal stillness—that is the ultimate goal of any physical/creative endeavor. One can almost see the tension, the aggression, dissolve as the realization sinks in that for some period of time—perhaps only a heartbeat's worth—*nothing need, or should, be done.* Relax, brother; all's right with your world. (Certain of the strap-on crowd have suggested the possibility of barrel-rolling in the tube—doing an upside down loop in there. I would suggest, say, a short, annual bow-and-arrow season on these tensed-up types.)

A true meditative moment is the tube ride, although it goes beyond that, because of the involvement of the wave—it is not strictly an inner experience. Like the act of riding a wave itself, the tube ride is a unique circumstance, easy enough to outwardly describe, but difficult to analogize. There simply is nothing to compare it to.

In general, I acquitted myself reasonably well that day—copped my share of tube-time—until my last wave, when I must say I outdid myself, and in the process demonstrated that an apparent miscarriage, if executed with a blend of graceful slapstick and wry acceptance of the inevitable, can be an event worthy of aesthetic note. Surfing may not be unique in *this* regard, but I would submit that a classic, balls-to-the-wall, aplomb-ridden wipe-out can come pretty damn close.

As the session wore on I found myself trimming further noseward with each ride, pushing the limits of longboard control and stability, craving that walk-on-water, flying sensation unique to the up-front position. Finally, having caught an outside boomer early, i.e., before it started sucking up over the shallows, I impulsively went right to the tip and immediately secured the added rush of speed and precariousness one gets up there, along with an up-close, unobstructed view of the wave—which was now steepening precipitously before me.

I had taken the high line, as one must do in noseriding, a bit more than halfway up between the trough and the crest. Strictly speaking, where I should have been was a couple feet back on the board and a bit lower down on the wave face, tucked in a crouch and ready to duck the cascading lip as it threw itself out and over my head, meanwhile maybe grasping the outside rail for balance and added edge control.

Within two, maybe three seconds, the ten-foot-high wall of water ahead was approaching the vertical and would very soon go beyond it, into the realm of concave that constitutes a tube, or barrel. When I sensed my surfboard's tail losing its grip and starting to drift, I knew I was indeed pushing the noseriding envelope. The wave was about to throw itself outward, launching me with it into the impact zone. An immediate backpedal to a more control-friendly position aft was very definitely called for—my muscle memory, born of a thousand similar situations, virtually cried out for it.

Well, I didn't backpedal. Not sure why. Perhaps I was just enjoying myself too much up there and greedily sought to extend my position beyond reason. I was for the moment in perfect, speedy trim, with the toes of my front foot wrapped around the tip of my surfstick—an affectation as functionless as a ballet dancer's final flourish, and, in my version of the longboard approach, just as stylistically requisite. Or perhaps my little lunacy of malingering on the nose was a manifestation of obdurate free will—and damn the consequences. Whatever the nonsensical theory, the die was cast, the fate of the ride sealed. I was going ass over teakettle, and soon.

This certain knowledge had a calming, almost soporific effect, and I found my weight had shifted to my back foot, not so much to transfer my center of gravity as to afford a more relaxed posture. Having resigned myself to the coming calamity, and therefore being under no pressure to do anything other than experience the passing here-and-now, I had made the commitment to conduct myself with what I suppose one might term Grace in the Face of the Inevitable.

It was here, in the instant before the wave threw itself shoreward under me and my surfboard and I went our separate ways, that I caught a glimpse of Bart, who was stroking back out from the inside. He was right ahead, no more than a dozen yards distant and in the process of pushing his board through my wave's feathering lip, when we made eye contact. His expression upon taking in my impossible circumstance, and my stoical insouciance in the face of it, was something between confusion and awe. For my part, I had the presence of mind, the instinct (an inborn one to entertain my fellow man, perhaps) to flash him a sort of laconic grin; and then the sea-bomb detonated and I was pitched into rag doll oblivion. It was a nice final touch, that grin.

Now I must own up to the fact that I was in no real danger here. The wave was meaty all right, but not big in the sense of Big. The Hawaiian adrenaline junkies who specialize in Big would have yawningly pegged this near-double overheader as of about five feet—such is their penchant for looney understatement. A wipeout on a wave of that size might keep one underwater for ten seconds at the very most, so there was no risk of a hold-down drowning. Nor was the reef shallow and sharp and therefore a hazard with respect to coral head collision.

Having hit the beach a while later, I was stretched out in my hammock scribbling in my journal when Bart emerged from the water and ambled on by on the way to his tricked-out, near-six figure European SUV, parked in the shade of an almond tree grove. I looked up as he stopped and said, "Very cool move before you ate it."

I nodded and grinned and uttered some bit of surf jive, while Bart scoped out my act: battered though beefily impressive pickup with New York tags and surfy little cottage on back; quiver of two longboards and one short splayed about, the latter sporting a FOR SALE/SE VENDE sign; tattered laundry strung between nut palms; questionable-looking mutt lolling in the shade of the hammock with her tongue hanging out and one eye slitted open to observe the interloper, but too lazy in the midday heat to make a fuss; and so forth.

It was here that Bart came to the Einsteinian conclusion that I was not, after all, a DEA agent—although, as he would later tell me, he had already suspected my innocence through watching me surf. Eyeing the notebook in my lap: "You a writer?"

Yeah, I told him. Writing about my trip down the coast, plus this and that.

"I hear you're looking for someone."

I fished out my photo, meanwhile running down the basics and chronology of Christopher's bolt.

Bart squinted at the photo. "Yeah, I know this dude," he said. "I've run into him a couple times. He came through here maybe five years ago with two dogs."

Mother and son golden retrievers. Sweetpea and Jumbie.

"Old blue pickup truck. New York tags like you." Bart indicated a little clearing just to the north. "Camped over there for a week or so. He caught it good, like today."

"You remember what kind of board he was riding?"

"I do, as a matter of fact. A racy Brewer. Gorgeous board."

"Right. A Brewer rounded pintail."

"I wanted to buy it from him but no way."

Dick Brewer had been one of the major design mavens behind the late '60s shortboard revolution. He'd shaped both Christopher's and my last few boards in '69, including the guns—the big wave boards—we'd paddled out at Sunset the day of the night that ultimate wave came ashore and changed our lives.

Dick had moved to Kauai and I remembered how Christopher had delayed his departure back in '92, waiting for the rounded pintail he'd ordered. He'd gone on about how there was something special about a Dick Brewer surfboard, a quality that went beyond its physical elegance, as if through his hands and his personal history and his shaping art Dick had put into each board he built the essence of the evolution of modern wave riding.

"Then I met up with him again about a year ago down in CR (Costa Rica)," Bart was saying. "What was his name again?"

"Christopher."

"Right. Christopher. It was on the Osa. Camped out on the point at Matapalo."

It was about time I got definitive word of Christopher's still-among-the-living status. As is the case with the more sedentary resident expat, the world of the traveling surfer is a small one. It had begun to worry me that none of the *viajeros* I'd quizzed could recall having run into my friend, and notwithstanding my instinct to the contrary, it *had* occurred to me that Christopher might have somehow come to grief. Plus, back stateside, there'd been rumors and innuendos, some cryptically propagated by Christopher himself, that his run south was related to the two years he had spent in a Cayman Islands prison in the mid '80s, after being interdicted with a boat-load of Jamaican purple bud. The subtext being that someone was aggravated about the loss of the merchandise. It was possible that Christopher rested in a shallow or watery grave.

I knew a bit about the Osa Peninsula, and the adjacent right-hander off the point at Matapalo. The Osa was a true, unfettered wilderness where rain forest descended from interior highlands right down to the wave-rich coast. The jungle track in was marginal, usually impassable during the rainy season. It made perfect sense that Christopher would be ensconced there. The Osa was on my list of places to check out in Costa Rica.

"You say camped out?"

Bart nodded. "He'd built a two-story lean-to and had his perimeter cordoned off with deadfalls and kerosene torches, like a compound."

I thought of Chicho and his wall, up in Baja.

Bart grinned. "A real wild man, your friend. Funny guy."

"This was a year ago?"

"More, actually. It was in late November, early December." Bart anticipated my next question. "I doubt he's still there. He was talking about moving on. The breaks on the Osa need south swells."

December marks the theoretical start of the doldrums of summer in the southern hemisphere, and hence a dearth of groundswell-producing storms between Tierra del Fuego and New Zealand. These distant cyclonic disturbances produce the waves that break on Central America's south-facing reefs. It also made sense that Christopher would move on at that time, to a west-facing shore or perhaps to Costa Rica's Caribbean side, where the winter surf season was just beginning. Or who knew where else? Maybe even back north, to Mexico.

. . .

The following night I dined at Bart's ocean-view villa, which I'll only describe as isolated and well-protected. Its interior was festooned with pre-Columbian artifacts and a score or so of collectible surfboards from as far back as the 1930s, several of which were in the five-figure range. He probably could have named his own price for the mint Tom Blake redwood paddleboard suspended from the living room ceiling.

Bart's Mexican wife, a shy mestiza with some northern European lineage—as evidenced by her striking hazel eyes and light complexion—served paella and broiled grouper while we talked story and drank some rather good, if a bit sweet, Mexican wine.

Bart's career as a pot mover had started about the same time mine had ended, around 1980, and in the same venue, the north coast of Colombia. He moved his operation to Mexico in the mid-'80s when it became apparent that the Colombian growers were unable, or unwilling, to adapt to a changing stateside weed market. Such was not the case in Mexico, however, where various hybrids of sinsemilla had been bred, with spectacular results. Plus the emergence of cocaine as Colombia's chief export had further complicated the already dangerously Byzantine dynamics of the north coast's power elite. Bart, like many of the old guard surfer/scammers, wanted nothing to do with the white drug trade or the highly organized, murderous thugs who ran it.

Bart had also dabbled in the importation of multiton tai stick loads and "still did some things" in that purlieu. A techno-wizard of the first order, he ran his multinational enterprises from his Mexican lair, relying on avant-garde communications technology to oversee logistics and infrastructure. The grounds of his villa bristled with antennas and satellite scoops; the nerve center within was replete with electronic and scrambling gadgetry that he claimed, ridiculously, was so advanced that "it hasn't even been invented yet." He rarely strayed from Mexican jurisdiction—his governmental connections, he told me, went above the top (another oxymoronic classic)—except on surf trips further south, mainly to Costa Rica, where he also had landholdings.

Bart's tales were peppered with hair-raisers from the old days: wild water chases with the law off the Bahamas cays, plane ditchings on Mississippi bayous, shootouts with rivals of his Colombian connection in the outback of the lawless Guajira. The boy could spin a yarn.

If it seems a little odd that Bart saw fit to share all this with me, I couldn't agree more. The thing about Bart that was, in a prima facie way, most impressive—and that also made him a study in contradictions—was his longevity. To be still active in the business after going on two decades, and not to be currently dead or in jail, was a feat worthy of Guinness mention. Such longevity had to have been based on a deep and abiding, borderline paranoiac, caution; and such was evidenced by his quieting right down in his braggadocio when his wife was within earshot. It was one thing for me to ramble on about my own past felonious exploits; they're ancient history, statute of limitations-wise. Not so for Bart, who unaccountably spilled contemporaneous details that could have put himself and his substantial personal wealth in serious jeopardy. Obviously: How could he be sure that I could be trusted? His subjecting me to the specifics of his doings was of problematical motivation. My theory has to do with the endeavor of wave riding, and with the complexly fragile egos of men.

For all his dedication and stoke, Bart was not a good surfer. He was simply not hardwired for the activity. He was at best mediocre in terms of wave smarts, reflexes, and grace under pressure. Combine this with a rather massive and self-conscious ego, and the frustration potential ripens. Which in turn compounds incompetence. And my presence in the lineup further exacerbated Bart's disconcertion, not only through my outsurfing him, but through my habit of continually outpositioning him and hence catching more and better waves than he.

Bart had long since been relegated to a subordinate position in the local pecking order with respect to the younger regulars. He had come to accept his status, I suspect, and could rationalize it via the age difference (Bart was in his early forties). But I was noticeably older than Bart and, to boot, a newcomer at his home break. I was consequently a subtle threat to his self-esteem. And on the second day of our surfing together—the day of the night

I visited him at his villa—Bart managed to humiliate himself on a much deeper level than simpleminded competitiveness.

Here's what happened: after a set had cleared the lineup of everyone but Bart, another slew of waves loomed, a set that was clearly more sizable than the day's average. Paddling back out, I picked up my pace and angled for the takeoff zone, hoping to make it outside in time to grab either the last or second to last wave, depending on what Bart did. He was in the perfect position to take his pick.

Bart started stroking for the second to last wave, then changed his mind and pulled up, presumably when he realized that the last was the biggest of the lot. Having at first figured Bart had committed to the penultimate of the set, I had not prepared myself and so I missed it. Now there was just one wave left and the two of us in position to catch it. With Bart a few yards outside of me, this last wave was his to take.

The wave commenced steepening quicker than either of us expected, building in height and thickness apace. It was a boomer, maybe the wave of the day. I could see that Bart's takeoff would be late, i.e., at the last instant before the wave broke, but it was nonetheless completely makeable. In fact, the rush of the elevator-shaft drop of a late takeoff is one of the joys of surfing, especially in sizable stuff.

Bart sat and waited, facing outside and poised for a fast spin-and-launch, as the wave approached, steepening further . . . and further still, hovering over him now, the wall of water nearly vertical, the razor-straight edge of the lip thinning even as the body of the wave thickened . . . that lip translucent now, trembling just slightly . . . right on him then, that wave was, preparing for the violent forward pitch and now was the time, Bart, to go for it, man.

But Bart didn't go for it, didn't spin-and-launch, didn't do anything. He sat there all frozen up as the wave passed him by and then he was gone from view behind the *really* steep wall now bearing down on me.

I spun my board around and with one quick paddle-stroke was immediately in a near-free fall down the wave face. As late as Bart's takeoff would have been, mine was considerably later, since I was further inside. Plus I was on a longboard, the unwieldiness of which severely compounded the difficulty of the straight up-and-down, very late drop-in.

Of all the fears to which I have lately become subject, fear of a wave like the one in question was not among them. As with the previous day's wipe-out, I felt no fear because there was in fact nothing to fear. Sizable though that wave was, I wasn't going to drown from a hold-down and I wasn't going to get impaled on the reef. Absent these two dangers, there is nothing . . . real . . . to fear out there.

Bart knew this too, intellectually. But he had felt fear anyway and it had gotten the better of him, right there in front of me. And to worsen matters, I had then caught the wave he should have, further inside and on a long-board at that, which threw into still higher relief the white feather he had displayed. Given the type of fellow Bart was, I would submit that these factors colored everything that happened between us from then on. Such as the motivation behind the subsequent invitation to his home.

He invited me to dinner so he could tell me his whole story—a story laced with incidents wherein he'd overcome fear. Consciously or uncon-sciously, and I'm quite sure it was the latter, he needed to set me straight regarding his coefficient of courage.

So this cautious fellow told me things about his life and business that he should never have done. Things he was too cautious to share even with his wife. All because of a moment of unconquered fear in the water.

After our meal, Bart fired up a thick, hand-rolled sample of the source of his wealth, during the smoking of which we waxed flighty and philo-sophical in our chatter. Bart was a UFO buff—claimed numerous spottings of strange lights in the night skies over Mexico. Given his prodigious smok-able intake, I didn't doubt him on this point.

From UFOs the conversation naturally evolved to a debate on the like-lihood that surfing exists on other celestial worlds in this universe we in-habit. Bart figured that if there are oceans up there, along with sentient beings that evolved along their shores, there is sure to be wave riding. I agreed, adding that perhaps the key to faster-than-light space travel lies in some consummate, cosmic version of The Glide, as developed by surfy beings many millenia more advanced than humans. Bart liked my theory a lot but, being wedded exclusively to the shortboard approach, opined that some sort of black hole cover-up was more likely the solution to instantaneous matter transportation. He buttressed his argument by pointing out the structural similarities between a black hole and a deep barrel. It sounded good to me.

Bart kept rolling 'em and smoking 'em. I demurred after a couple hits on the first. Although marijuana used to have the effect of making me blissfully vacant-minded, of late it tends to create in me a sort of thoughtful stupidity—a pointless mental state, in my view. For Bart's part, I could detect no change in his behavior or state of mind, apart from a deliberateness that occasionally bordered on an almost cinematic slow motion.

It was getting late when I broached the subject of our common time and place: 1980, the north coast of Colombia. I was in fact curious about something and thought Bart just might hold the relevant information. Like virtually all the worlds through which I've moved in my life, that of the major pot mover was a small one. I asked Bart the name of his Colombian connection of that long-past era.

The name he came up with was unfamiliar to me.

"You ever hear of a guy named Fredi Calderone?" I asked.

Bart nodded. "Out of Rodadero, right?"

"Right."

"He was your guy?"

"Yeah," I said. "You know what happened to him?"

"Killed in some sort of shootout. When was that? Eighty-three?"

"Eighty-two. Do you know who killed him?"

Bart shook his head. "I think Fredi had a lot of enemies. From what I heard, his problems actually started back in '78, when a ship called the *Ensenada* went down in the North Atlantic."

My neck hairs stirred at the mention of the *Ensenada*.

"It was a couple years before my time," Bart continued, "but I heard about it." He took a long hit, held it then exhaled with a long whooshy sigh. "A hundred thousand pounds of Guajiran Gold buds, gone, down with the ship. Fifty tons. A fucking tragedy, man. Word was, Fredi never really recovered from the loss."

"Neither did Christopher and I."

"What do you mean?"

"We were aboard," I said. "I was the captain of the *Ensenada*."

The only warning Christopher and I had that we were in for a bad time of it was radio reports that a massive low-pressure system was spiraling off the East Coast. *Ensenada*'s position was some 200 miles northwest of Bermuda, her heading just west of true north. The seas had been building for the last 12 or so hours, with the wind rising to a full gale. Just after sundown, I was about to stand in for my trick at the helm when I realized that in spite of the firm handhold I had secured, my feet were starting to slide back across the bridge toward the starboard-side wing door through which I had just entered. Next thing I knew I was wedged in a corner, having half-slid, half-fallen backward as the floor beneath me strayed drastically from horizontal.

My eyes went to the clinometer, a simple pendulum device secured to the bulkhead above the windscreen and which measured degree of list. The ship (being of some 180 feet in length, she truly was a ship, not a boat) was already at 30-degrees starboard list and the pendulum was yet moving in the direction of further slant.

There is what is known as a point-of-no-return in the matter of nautical capsizings, the exact numerical degree of which depends on complex situational factors such as ship design, loaded center of gravity, wave height and period, and so forth. Discounting sailing ships, which are ballasted to right themselves even in 90-degree knockdowns, any list over 45 degrees is generally conceded to be very near that point.

I watched the pendulum swing past that magic number, with no apparent intention of stopping, and as it nudged the 50-degree mark, the helmsman, a young Colombian named Pepe, lost his grip on the wheel and pretty much free-fell across the bridge, slamming into the bulkhead beside me. The wheel, which was hard over to port from Pepe's attempt to compensate for the starboard roll, was spinning so fast back the other way that the spokes were a blur, as the rudder sought to return to fore-and-aft. Lying with my back against the formerly upright wall which, with the ship's tilt, had for all intents and purposes become a floor, I stared at the 55-degree mark on the clinometer, quite sure that if the pendulum reached that point the ship would continue its roll and inevitably capsize, then founder. The needle hovered at around 53 degrees as the conflicting forces that represented the fate of the ship and her crew fought it out mid-Atlantic. Then, ever so slowly, the ship began to right herself.

"Bring us around to a northwesterly heading," I told Pepe, who had crossed himself and returned to the helm. The course change would put the seas more on our bow, rather than our beam. We were within the boundary of the Gulf Stream, which meant that the wind was opposing the current; the worst scenario imaginable in terms of the size and viciousness of the seas produced. I looked out the windscreen at the main deck below the bridge. *Ensenada* had shuddered mightily as she began her roll, so I knew we'd been boarded by green water. I needed to check for damage on deck. I was especially concerned that the main cargo hatch might've carried away, which would mean that subsequent seas would pour into the hold. Many a ship has foundered for this reason; and besides, the whole of our precious cargo was in the main hold and part of my responsibility was keeping it dry. The hatch was secure, I found, but the deck was under a foot of water.

Suddenly, Christopher careened onto the bridge sleepy-eyed, disheveled and annoyed. He wanted to know what the fuck was going on, adding something to the effect that Cookie, our 300-pound Colombian cook, was buried under a pile of galley debris, and that a kettle of black bean soup he had simmering now covered the walls and overhead. Then, looking out at the raging seascape, he said, "Gonna be crackin' down south in a couple days."

I nodded. "Puerto Rico first, then on down." This was exactly the sort of weather system surfers in the Caribbean waited for. As the storm moved east and further out to sea, the groundswell spawned by its northerly winds would traverse the thousand or so miles south and expire on the islands' north-facing reefs, in the form of breaking surf.

Christopher grinned that Christopher grin. "Wild shit. I love it!"

Had these not been the days before real-time satellite printouts and at-sea weather faxes, our exultance might have been tempered by a bit of circumspection. We would have known that the low-pressure system had intensified since spinning offshore. Its isobars had tightened up, were in fact almost touching on the system's western edge, and a well-defined eye had formed. Although of extra-tropical origin, the tempest bearing down on us was, for all intents and purposes, a full-blown hurricane.

Ensenada was a Dutch cargo carrier, steel-built just before World War II. She was a sound vessel, despite her advanced age, although she'd been let go cosmetically. After scouring various Down South ports of call, Christopher and I found her through a ship broker in the Canal Zone in October of 1978. We'd immediately sent our Lear jet to Managua to fetch our engineer, a Nicaraguan national nicknamed Arroyo, who was home visiting his family. Since the near-debacle of *The Fucking Boat* a little over a year before, we'd come to the conclusion that the engineer is the most vital of all the crew of a seagoing vessel, not even excepting the captain. South of the border, engineers (and auto mechanics) are among the best in the world. Unlike stateside, if something breaks, it's fixed—somehow, anyhow—not thrown away. And Arroyo was up there with the best of the best at jury-rigging; he'd raised it to an art form. He was descended from a long line of seafarers and had spent most of his adult life keeping sundry vessels afloat and running, from leaky outboard-powered dories to Nicaraguan coast guard cutters. And Christopher and I both just flat liked Arroyo. In his mid-thirties, he was honest, courageous and of easy, appealing good humor. We pampered him, paid him handsomely and included him in on the profit-divvy when all went well.

Ensenada had raised bows, superstructure slightly abaft amidships, and three cargo holds: a small one right forward that also functioned as anchor chain storage, a cavernous main hold amidships and another aft, which also housed the steering cables and quadrant, plus a walk-in freezer. The engine room lay between the main and aft holds and contained a massive 12-cylinder diesel, a GM 6-71 coupled to an a/c generator, and a well-equipped machine shop.

Arroyo having pronounced *Ensenada*'s machinery well maintained and her hull and bones sound, we coughed up $500,000 for the purchase, then around another $150,000 for new electronics, refinishing and incidentals, plus provisioning; all paid for through an offshore Cayman corporation. After two months of refitting, in early December, we steamed into the blue Caribbean, Colombia-bound.

Three nights later we anchored up off La Peninsula de la Guajira and effected our rendezvous with a fleet of Guajiran Indian cayucas (dugout canoes) that Fredi had hired to transport our mammoth load—as Bart had correctly remembered, 100,000 pounds, fifty tons, of chaffless gold buds. At the time it was thought to be the biggest load ever to leave Colombian waters, which, given Colombia's status as the planet's top cannabis producer, would have likely made it a world record.

Fredi was at the height of his power in '78 and had contracted the Colombian army to assist in transporting the merchandise to the beach. Well over a hundred men were involved in the onload, plus dozens of vehicles and water craft. With *Ensenada* converged upon by a flotilla of 40-foot dugout canoes piled high with marijuana bales, and with her decks swarming with half-naked savages and burp gun-toting *bandidos,* it was truly a wild scene.

In order to avoid recently expanded U.S. Coast Guard drug interdiction ops, we took the long way around, exiting the Caribbean through Anegada Passage, up in the northeast corner of the Windward Island chain. From that point I laid a direct course for New York harbor.

The *Ensenada* enterprise represented a partnership among some diverse criminal factions, from a spooky Dutch industrialist to several big-time stateside wholesalers to Fredi and his cohorts to Christopher and me. It also included a certain New York mafia family, which was to run the offload. We were to sail right into the harbor, first passing under the Verrazano Narrows Bridge, then, leaving the Statue of Liberty to starboard, we'd dock at a commercial quay on the New Jersey waterfront, where the International Longshoreman's Union would unload the cargo into 18-wheelers. (The mafia boys also had a Coast Guard connection who would alert us by radio as to movements of local cutters.) With a fresh coat of paint and a new (non-Hispanic) name painted on our bows and stern (an existing ship of *Ensenada*'s general description, which I gleaned from Lloyd's Registry of Ships), the old *Ensenada* would look no different from the scores of legitimate cargo carriers in New York harbor.

Once we were unloaded, those other union boys, the Teamsters, would transport the merchandise far and wide by truck, from Maine to California and various points between.

Christopher and I had been on a roll since the unlikely success of our Connecticut run in *The Fucking Boat*. We'd branched into aviation and—in partnership with Fredi, who, through his well-oiled connections, had transformed Santa Marta International into our own private airport—we'd made successful runs in a DC-3 and a King Air. We had brokered a seagoing load (acting as middlemen between Fredi and a syndicate of other smugglers) that had landed without incident in Nova Scotia, for distribution throughout Canada.

All of which was well and good, in theory. But the truth of it was that Christopher and I had forgotten who we were. We had forgotten that we were just a couple of surfers, not the big-shot denizens of the Underground Empire we now fancied ourselves. We were getting altogether too big for our britches, and were consequently in for a rude awakening.

Big Blue was about to set us straight, remind us of who was really in charge—and how severely we had betrayed the faith.

Awakened from a dreamless slumber in my cabin, I found myself on the floor, jammed against the bulkhead by the door. I had somehow been catapulted off my bunk and across the room. I extracted my penlight from its little holster and illuminated my watch: it was just shy of 2200, 10 P.M. Agitated Spanish voices issued from the companionway, along with the fast *thump-thump* of sea boots running on steel flooring and the duller thumps of bodies careening off bulkheads, a result of the ship's horrendous rolling and pitching. Then, another panic-stricken voice was yelling in Spanish something along the lines of "All hands on deck! We are all going to die!"

Back in those days, before all the doubts and fears and bouts of self-reflection, this sort of behavior in others had a calming effect on me, not that I ever needed much calming. In this case, I actually almost went back to bed, figuring that Christopher, who was on watch, would arouse me if I were really needed. But seeing as how I was the ship's captain, I decided I should go see what all the excitement was about. I pulled on my boots, donned my slicker and went up to the bridge.

First thing, I checked the anemometer. The device had obviously malfunctioned. Its needle was buried at 100 knots—115 miles per hour, 40 miles per hour above hurricane force—which seemed unlikely. The helmsman, a middle-aged Colombian, had the wheel in a death grip and his face was sheet-white.

"Donde está Christopher?" I inquired. The guy indicated the bridge wing with a jerk of his head, then said he was having trouble holding a northwest heading. The problem was the windage of our high bows, I was thinking, as I opened the bridge wing door. When a gust hit the bow even slightly from one side or the other, as opposed to dead on, the force would push the ship's head off to leeward and . . .

But holy shit!

I'd stepped out onto the bridge wing and . . .

THE WIND!

By which I mean the brute force of it, and the sound of it. The effect of the wind was that of a solid presence pressing against me, rather than the comparatively ephemeral, airy nudge of a mere full gale. It was as if a giant invisible hand was adamantly preventing me from going anywhere but where it bid—as I forced the bridge door shut, I was very nearly blown right aft down the ladder to the deck. I quickly dropped to my knees to get under the protection of the chest-high bulkhead that enclosed the bridge wing area.

And the sound! The dull roar of earlier was now a high-pitched scream that would waver in synch with stronger gusts, changing pitch like an ambulance siren dopplering by, and that I felt as a bone-deep vibration. The ship, too, felt it deep. I could feel her humming under me as for a moment I cowered on my hands and knees. I could feel the resonance of the wind and the sea there in the steel of her.

Christopher was wedged in a corner, looking down on the main cargo deck, his arms wrapped around a support post to keep himself from blowing down to leeward. Staying low, I did a sideways crab-walk in his direction and then slowly stood up by his side, my body canted forward into the teeth of that awful wind and my hands gripping the edge of the bulkhead. Although the bridge wing was some 25 feet above the sea surface, the air was thick with horizontally driven spray coming from high over the bow, which stung my eyes like rock salt shot from a scattergun. I held my right hand a foot in front of my face to curb the impact and grimaced, squinting my eyes down to fierce slits. The loading crane lights were on, illuminating the deck and the spume-strewn sea for 30, 40 yards on either side and some distance over the bow. I looked down.

Someone was on the main deck, I saw, doing some goddamn thing with the cargo hatch. One place you definitely didn't want to be in these conditions was anywhere on the lower deck and exposed to boarding seas. "Who's that!?" I yelled. "What is he, fucking nuts!?" But Christopher hadn't heard me over the roar of the storm.

White water raked the ship longitudinally, covering the man on deck. Surely he was gone overboard or . . . no, there he still was, emerging from under the turbulence . . . then I noticed the lifeline attached to a ringbolt on the hatch coaming and clipped to his belt, which had probably just saved his life.

It was Arroyo; I recognized him by his grease-stained yellow slicker. He had moved aside one of the hatch planks and was pointing a flashlight down into the hold . . . looking up at Christopher and me now, wide-eyed and grimacing and shaking his head and soundlessly moving his mouth. He ran a finger horizontally across his throat in the universal gesture of . . . but what did that mean?

Christopher was yelling something right into my face but his words were lost in the howl of the wind and the roar of the sea. Then I focused on his lips and understood. "Fucking wild! Fucking wild!" was what he was saying. His eyes were glowing in a way that was as if we were sharing something amazing that had to be dealt with immediately, maybe before it was too late.

Then I realized that the wind had dropped right off to what felt like normal hurricane force. The seas seemed to have calmed also, and the decks were clear of green water. For a moment I felt encouraged, but then I saw that Christopher was squinting at something ahead over the bow, something that had shut him right up.

Out of the darkness over the bow loomed a wave so massive that it had created a wind shadow, which had formed the place of relative calm we were now in. It was as if the ship had found the lee of a high island that was affording her refuge from the storm. The difference here was that the island was coming our way at great speed and with plainly belligerent intent. Even as I watched, the apparition was building in height and steepening and I found that in spite of my high vantage point I was craning to look upward at the spectral ridge of its crown, an obscure division between the black sea and the blacker sky beyond.

A true rogue that wave was, the rare but—in the utter chaos of Big Blue's tantrum—statistically inevitable convergence in time and space of two, maybe three watery giants. Which in exponential combination created an offspring whose might was equal to the sum of its progenitors. It was *Ensenada*'s misfortune that the course I'd laid days before intersected with the path of that monster's wanderings. But a ship in survival conditions continually casts the die of fate. A meeting with a rogue would come, inevitably; it was just a matter of where and when. And this was probably our third. One rogue had knocked us down some five hours earlier, another had no doubt been responsible for my violent arousal from sleep, and now this. The mother of them all, as I saw it.

Arroyo, too, had seen the beast loom; in fear for his life he had scrambled from the deck up the companionway ladder to the relative safety aloft with Christopher and me. Meanwhile, as the angle of the incline steepened further, the wave pulled in its gut and the sea surface deep in the protected wind shadow became slick and devoid of chop. With the abated wind, flying spume wafted down onto the water like a filigree of curvy white lace. Seeing the sea surface so smooth I found myself picturing some ultimate big wave junkie taking an endless, suicide drop down the face of the wave the ship was so laboriously ascending—the wave face was that steep, surfable steep. If it were to break on us, catch us inside, we would surely roll over athwartships or even flip backward, end-over-end. Either way, it would be a wipeout of complete, deadly finality.

As we summited that mountain of water, it did break, but only at the very crest. The face itself remained intact, charging off into the void behind us. With the mere crumbling of the wave-lip, though, untold tons of churning white water, followed by a river of unbroken green, inundated the ship stem to stern, sending a thick spate up the superstructure and onto the bridge wing, soaking the three of us in icy deluge. Then for a heartbeat there was a weightless sensation as the ship plunged off the wave's back and down into the trough behind it. The deck below had disappeared underwater and the ship seemed slow in regaining steerage (the brunt of the blow had stopped her dead in the water) and in shedding over her bulwarks the burden under which she had been buried.

Arroyo was yelling something and his grip on my arm was viselike in his urgency, but with the ship's topping of the wave that awful wind once again hammered us and the howl of it blew his words into oblivion. He pulled me down into the lee of the bulkhead and pressed his lips against my ear.

"La cabina carga esta inundada!" The cargo hold is flooded.

Making the perilous pilgrimage down to the deck to see for myself, I saw that our buoyant merchandise was jammed up against the hatch and the underside of the deck. The hold was indeed flooded. A top layer of bales was already water-soaked and seawater sloshed up out of the hatch with the ship's violent movement. The horrendous deadweight of water down there explained the ship's sluggishness and her refusal to properly answer the helm. And Arroyo bore further gloomy tidings: the hold's bilge pump was inoperable, no doubt choked by loose cannabis debris.

I pretty much knew what had happened. The impact of the second wave, the one that had sent me flying from my bunk, had likely sprung a plate in the hull under the cargo hold, maybe more than one. It didn't much matter how severely we'd been holed. Whether the opening was a foot across or ten feet, the result was the same. The hold was flooded and there was no way to pump the water out.

Back in the refuge of the bridge, I dug out *Ensenada*'s specs and found she was designed to survive the flooding of any one of the four belowdecks compartments (the three cargo holds plus the engine room). The good news was that they were all sealed fore and aft by watertight bulkheads. But when I pointed this out to Arroyo, he shook his head and said, "La barca va a hundirse." The ship is going to sink.

To which Christopher, who was reclining by the chart table, joint dangling, replied, "No fucking way, bro. We'll ride this sucker out."

I tried to explain to Arroyo about the specs and the physics of flotation, but he just told me to follow him. Leaving Christopher and most of the rest of the crew on the bridge—everyone was wide awake now and fearing for our fate—Arroyo and I descended to the engine room.

The state of affairs in the bowels of the ship brought me up short. Even with the engine-room bilge pumps going full bore there was already a foot of water over the floor plates. A gasket had blown on the heat exchanger which fed the hot water holding tank, filling the room with a hellish steam.

But the main source of my concern, and the reason for the perceptibly rising water level, was a deluge coming from above. The bulkhead between the engine room and the main cargo hold was only watertight to about three feet below the overhead deck. That upper three feet was mostly open space, designed to keep belowdecks ventilated by ensuring a fore-and-aft flow of air throughout the ship. Under normal sea conditions this was all well and good. The water level of even a completely flooded cargo hold would have been several feet below the ventilation space. But with the oceanic conditions that night, each time the bow rose up to ascend a mountainous sea, a huge volume of seawater from the hold would slosh aft and surge into the engine room through the ventilation gap; some ridiculous amount, maybe a thousand gallons at a clip. The water that had thus vacated the hold would then immediately be replaced by an equal amount through the hole in the hull. The process would then repeat itself until the engine room was flooded, which would then equal two flooded compartments, one more than the ship could survive, even in calm seas.

Arroyo was right. *Ensenada* was going down.

Around 2300, 11 P.M., we began broadcasting mayday calls on our single-sideband radio. Christopher, Arroyo and I took turns at the mike, 10 minutes on, 20 off.

Christopher and I had debated options for a half hour before commencing the S.O.S., although there were no real options left. Fact was, the possibility of losing the load was so unacceptable that we refused to deal with the truth of our circumstances. And it wasn't the money, which was already largely lost. The $30,000,000 wholesale value of the cargo (street value around $200,000,000) had been cut at least in half, maybe as much as two-thirds, due to its being water-soaked. And it wasn't the idea that in all likelihood the ship would be on the bottom by sunrise, all of us dead by drowning or hypothermia. It was the idea of failure. Our-Surfers-Can-Do-Anything balloon was about to burst.

Even as we broadcast our Mayday there was little realistic hope of rescue. We were many miles from the nearest shipping lane and had seen only one other vessel since exiting the Caribbean four days before. Worse, our SSB antenna had sustained wind damage and we were unsure whether our calls were even making it onto the airwaves. In any event, no one was coming back over the squawk box.

Although the wind and seas had abated slightly since that last rogue, we were still in survival conditions. The ship continued to be battered by towering head seas, and with the continued flooding of the engine room putting us further down in the water, we were in danger of losing steerage altogether. If that happened, *Ensenada* would lie beam to the weather, exposed and helpless. Even an average breaking sea would then roll her right over. And that would be that.

Approximately 0100. The eight of us, Christopher, Arroyo, myself, plus our four deckhands and Cookie, were all up on the bridge. Aside from the muffled roar of elements and the murmur of Arroyo repeating the word Mayday into the radio mike, all was quiet. I was at the helm, struggling to keep us bow-on to the seas, with Christopher wedged in the pilot's seat close by.

"We might try running before it," Christopher said in a hushed voice.

I thought I knew what was on Christopher's mind, and it wasn't survival. Running downwind in those conditions, if we were to be overtaken by a rogue like the last one, *Ensenada* would surf down its face. Christopher was in essence suggesting one last go-out, one last surf session.

"Be a rush, wouldn't it?" I said.

"Yeah."

"Problem is, we'd probably broach, then roll over on the way down. And even if we somehow made the drop, with all the deadweight up for'ard, we'd pearl at the bottom." In other words, the bow would bury itself and the ship would flip longitudinally.

"Be a big-time wipeout."

I had the helm hard over but the ship wasn't responding. Our bow was starting to fall off to leeward. Come on, honey . . . come on . . .

"What's our speed through the water?" Christopher asked, seeing we were on the verge of control loss.

"Under three knots," I told him. Barely steerage. And the big diesel was at max revs. With the deadweight of the water in the hold, plus the head wind and seas, the ship was laboring heavily. In normal sea conditions, at max revs, she'd be doing twelve knots and the helm would be lively.

Ensenada finally responded; the bow swung ever so slowly back up to windward.

"I wonder if the engine's under water yet," Christopher said. Not that it mattered. Diesel engines will keep running even when completely submerged, as long as the air intake is clear and dry. One of us could go down to the engine room to check the water level, but what would be the point? Whatever it is, it is, and there was nothing to be done about it.

"I'm more concerned about the generator," I said. "And the batteries." With its lower location, the generator would go first, short out immediately upon the water level reaching the coils. The d/c system, a bank of 24-volt batteries, was higher up, secured on a ledge over the machine shop bench. All the ship's vital operating systems, including the steering gear and the bilge pumps, were run by those batteries. Once they went . . . But by that time the ship would have come to grief anyway.

Arroyo and I had figured we had until no later than around dawn before the ship went dead in the water, and then foundered. It was a rough calculation. Our decreasing buoyancy was a function of the geometrically progressive water intake—the lower we sank in the water, the faster the flooding of the engine room, which would put us down still lower, which would still further increase the rate of flow, and so forth. Overlaid upon this fuzzy equation was the possibility of another fell swoop from a rogue. The end might come considerably sooner than dawn; at any time.

"I wish we could fucking see," Christopher said, referring to the state of the sea out the windscreen, and his words startled me because I was at that moment thinking of my old girlfriend, Candice, on the night the wave came and took our house. I imagined her pointing offshore at the full moon-lit view from that North Shore hilltop; at the sight of the raging seascape that at the time struck me as a glimpse into the chaos of Creation itself. That was a distant view, though, a spectator's view, of the far-removed aftereffect of the real thing. This was the real thing, and Christopher and I both felt that because of the darkness we were missing a large part of the experience. Death was still not a conscious factor in our perception of the future.

At approximately 0430, I was doing my trick at the SSB radio, repeating the word Mayday into the mike and then releasing the transmit button to listen for a response, when I suddenly realized something. I shook my head and almost laughed at my own stupidity. I hadn't switched on the VHF radio, probably because its range was line-of-sight, which in those sea conditions might be as little as three or four miles. Faint, faint hope that another ship would be that close here in the middle of North Atlantic nowhere.

But some hope is better than none, so I switched it on and even before I could reach to fiddle with the gain knob, the bridge filled with a voice asking if we're in need of assistance. I was for a moment struck dumb and so was everyone else, and then the radio voice was saying that his position is right aft of us, and, again, are we in need of assistance?

I dashed out to the bridge wing and there was a ship right there, maybe a quarter mile astern, all lit up like a cityscape. I could see someone on her bridge, could even see that he was looking at us through binoculars.

There was no perceptible dawn, but rather the atmosphere's inky blackness merely faded as the night gave up its opaque ghost to ever-brightening shades of gray. Somewhere beyond a low, scuddy cloud cover glowed the sun, a remote presence in the slowly waning gloom of what was now barely a full gale. But then far downwind a hole in the sky opened and the sea's slate complexion exploded into dazzling azure where the sun's shaft touched down, as if to shout my pet name for the endless presence before me: Big Blue!

As the sky closed up and all was gray again my focus shifted back to closer aboard: a half mile to leeward, *Ensenada* struggled like a drowning man. Down by her head, foredeck awash and stern up, the big bronze prop visibly cleared the sea surface when she dipped low. Intervening ground-swells played tricks with my perception of her founder: now I saw her, now I didn't . . . now I saw her, now I didn't . . . and then I didn't see her any-more, because she was gone.

We were all of us—the safe-and-sound crew of the lately departed vessel—standing on the second-tier deck of the *Atlantis II,* a research ves-sel out of Woods Hole, Massachusetts. *Atlantis II*'s crew was gathered there, too, likewise to bear witness. Nothing was said for a long moment after *En-senada* was gone. The silence among the other ship's people was respectful and perhaps a little awkward, as if they had stumbled upon a tight-knit fam-ily's funeral and were hesitant to address the bereaved.

Indeed, the feel of it was that *Ensenada* was not merely gone in the sense of being out of sight underwater, but that she was gone from this earth, like a soul departed. I could not picture her in her present state, descending into the abyss slowly, or perhaps quickly. The reality of that was not available to me, even as an abstraction.

By approximately 1700 of the day of our rescue, *Atlantis II* was steam-ing through moderating seas northward toward her home port of Woods Hole, and Christopher and I were dining with the ship's crew, mostly sci-entists and graduate students. Arroyo and the rest of *Ensenada*'s *latino* con-tingent were a couple tables away, having amicably isolated themselves due to the language barrier. Christopher and I had come to terms with the loss of our ship and cargo, and realized how close a call we'd had. We were con-tent now merely to be alive.

The "A 2" people were a fun, even raucous bunch and the vibes as we ate were easy. The hair-raising sea rescue was relived with relish, timing and descriptive prose no doubt being refined for the retelling of the tale ashore.

It was no secret what *Ensenada* was up to—two *norte*s and a Nicaraguan on a freighter with an otherwise all-Colombian crew pretty much gave us away—and Christopher and I were grinningly quizzed as to the volume of smokable merchandise we were carrying. As guess-the-weight estimates were spouted, we frowned or shrugged or rolled our eyes as indication of how far from the truth was the guesser. (The highest figure mentioned was a mere ten tons.)

These folks were all young and . . . hip is the word that comes to mind. I suspect that late-night smokes by the taffrail were commonly copped aboard. But toward dessert we were joined by one of the ship's mates, a middle-aged fellow of some girth amidships, massive forearms, close-cropped hair, sunburnt face scarred by decades of wind and weather. With gray in his beard and the sea in his veins, no long-haired, landlubbin' egghead was he. In a word, a salt. He pulled himself up without fanfare and silently set to stoking his boiler.

There came a lull in our laughter and revelry and then the fellow spoke, informing us in his deep gravel that a radio message had just come in regarding a commercial fishing vessel that had gone down in the storm last night some hundred miles to the northeast, with all hands.

The news functioned as a reality check for all of us. The table fell silent and I found myself smitten by a bad feeling that I was at first at a loss to evaluate. Although there was certainly a component of grief for fellow seamen lost at sea, what finally surfaced was guilt. While *Atlantis II* was busy rescuing a bunch of get-rich-quick criminals transporting an illicit, mind-scrambling cargo, law-abiding, hardworking men lost their lives.

Needing to say something, I mentioned what a miracle it was that A 2 had been where she was, when she was (she'd been in that remote sea-place collecting bottom samples when the storm struck), and was therefore able to rescue us from certain doom. I felt blessed, I said, that I hadn't come to a watery end.

To which the salt levelly replied, "You were in no real danger."

A very odd observation, I thought, and, indeed, curious looks were cast in the salt's direction by one and all.

The salt did not at first elaborate, but appeared to concentrate on his vittles. Then, he looked at me. "The man who was born to hang," he said, "need not fear the water."

5.

Two days after my expat surfer/scammer buddy Bart and I dined together in his villa, the surf went down and I decided to get back on the road. Bart showed up as I was breaking camp. He seemed a little tense as we made small talk, Bart recommending what surf spots I should visit further south. As I was about to pull out he leaned in on my window.

"Listen," he said. "If you *are* DEA, come down to fuck with me"—the look in his eyes was something between fear and embarrassment—"you're the best they've ever sent."

There was nothing I could have said that wouldn't have compounded Bart's fear, so I just flashed him a grin, laconic like the one before my wipeout. Then I was gone down the road, leaving him to continue worrying.

DEEPER

Mex 200 deteriorating on a southeast heading in the state of Chiapas after a long, straight, flat stretch of good tarmac, but with a hot dry wind so hard and right on the nose that even with the Ford's big diesel at max revs you have not been able to breach 40 mph; and now, faced with an endless succession of potholes of tiger pit plumblessness, you've abandoned the road entirely and are cruising at good speed over the scurfy desert hardpan with a bit of the old Ludwig Van booming over the Bose, an "Ode to Joy" sing-along.

6.

Sitting on a stoop at dusk at a little truck stop *pueblo* a few miles north of the Guatemalan frontier. I'll overnight here and negotiate the border crossing in the morning. I thumb through my journal entries, reminiscing about my nearly six months in Mexico. So many stories; people, places, roads driven, waves ridden. Experiences strange, wonderful, frightening, unforgettable.

There was Luis, the Roberto Duran look-alike who emerged from the bush onto a remote beach I found south of Lázaro Cárdenas in a full-on wind sprint, toting a smashed-up, finless, unrideable '70s vintage surfstick, tattered shorts barely decent and flapping in the breeze, screaming in Spanish, "My brother my brother we will surf together!" in spite of the fact that the surf was dead flat—and who got so stoked when I gave him a surf-logo decal that tears came to his eyes.

There was the primitive rain forest village of Chacahua—accessed after an endless half-day 4WD low range ramble through ever-deepening bush—where I created a near riot with my Polaroid camera, dispensing images of the kids and the men who fish the estuary.

There was a guy named Joe at Playa Suave in Acapulco, a senior-citizen vagabond who claimed his phony *National Geographic* credentials made by laminating a passport pic onto a cutout of the mag's masthead logo had extricated him from some tight spots in the years he'd been solo on the road, and afforded him free and easy admission to events far and wide.

There was the Puerto Escondido local with whom I came close to blows over ownership of a fat, mean double overhead barrel at the break known as Mexico's Pipeline, while his surfgang buddies converged on us with territorial fire in their eyes.

There was that pack of ragamuffin preteen budding *bandidos* who waylaid me near Puerto Angel by using the smallest one's body as a road blockade and who smashed my right tail light and pretended to blast me with machine-gun fire when I refused to cough up some pesos.

There was that beautiful 15-, 16-year-old Mexican girl waitressing at her family's tidy little beachfront restaurant an hour outside Ixtapa, who stood in the kitchen doorway and pulled her T-shirt up to her neck and arched her back to show me her perfect little breasts while her mother cooked my *huevos rancheros* inside with her back to the door and her father washed the family's Toyota out front, and who never once looked at me directly or spoke, even when she served me eggs that set my mouth on fire.

There is no doubt in my mind that she spiked those eggs with extra *salsa caliente,* to see how I'd handle it.

7.

Tecún Umán, Guatemala, was what I'd expect you'd get if you asked a great movie director who'd been out in the real world a bit—say, John Huston as opposed to Steven Spielberg—to build a set of a small Central American border town and fill it with extras who can get you anything you want but have razors in their shoes for when they meet up with you later.

Much as I was guardedly attracted to the place for the bad-ass bustling chaos of its cratered main drag, its dreggy dirtbag hotels, its dim raunchy bar with the rickshaw out front where Bogart will surely up the ante and turn the plot, much to Greenstreet's dismay—in short, its timeless, almost comical sleaze—I did want to move on down the road, maybe find a beach where I could get wet, put another X on the surf map.

Problem was, I couldn't seem to get out of town. Gave it three futile shots—there were no signs and the directions I got from shifty, choleric street dudes only sent me down various ever-narrowing labyrinthine alleyways terminating in ramshackle adobe hovels or abrupt, dense bush—before a squeamish left made to avoid flattening a very dead dog put me in the wake of a startlingly multicolored bus that seemed to have elsewhere on its mind.

I had been the only *norte* in evidence at the three-hour *mordida*-laced nightmare of my border crossing. (The literal translation of *la mordida* is "the bite".) I hadn't yet met anyone undertaking an expedition like mine, nor had I seen another stateside license plate since Puerto Escondido, more than 600 miles to the north. I made inquiries about Guatemala's general political situation (I knew vaguely about the country's bloody, decades-long civil war), but all I got was a shrug and an offhand "Guatemala is a dangerous country, my friend" from a northbound Salvadoran. Then, in full view of a cadre of amused federal police, I watched as a brawl broke out among a wild-eyed band of ragged Guatemalans competing for the honor of washing my rig for about a buck, leaving one fellow flat on his back and moaning from a blow to the solar plexus from the *malvado* who got the nod—a cripple no less, who used his deformed foot as a kick-launched bludgeon.

Six months in Mexico was just a warm-up for this derangement, I was thinking as I jounced past absurdly overloaded cane trucks and assorted internally combusted, bastardized junk piles out of a Keystone Kops/*Road Warrior* mélange. No more "Deeper" pretensions, I said to myself. This place is as deep as it gets.

I was wrong about that.

I was wrong about Guatemala, as was my alarmist Salvadoran friend. I found the country—and by that I mean its people—to be openhearted, kind and generous almost to a fault. Never judge a country by its border town. And I would find myself Deeper, considerably so, soon enough.

How did I find my next stop, Tilapa? The short answer is that I took a wild, if slightly educated, stab. I had either lost or neglected to pack "The Surf Report" for Guatemala, which in a way was an exhilarating relief. I have mixed feelings about that publication, its dilution of the sensation of exploration I remember so fondly from my younger days, when foreign surf trips were true adventures of discovery.

I deduced from the road map that the country was lacking the rocky points needed to produce world-class conditions. Just across the Mexican frontier, however, I noted a river at whose mouth was likely a silt effluence that could impart some shape to incoming groundswells. At the estuarine terminus of this river, El Rio Naranjo, was marked a little town called Tilapa.

I rolled in late-afternoon and, it being Sunday, found the *pueblito's* dead-end dirt main street a-teem with Guatemalans finishing up their day at the seashore. My rig caused a minor, though polite, sensation. Initial inquiries and comments were made shyly from a distance. Apparently none of the locals had ever seen a pickup as impressive as my jacked-up, off-road–ready F350 4x4 bruiser with its 33 × 12 Goodyears and 16,000-pound-capacity winch out front, let alone one with a little house with a double bed, enclosed head, indoor-outdoor shower, hot and cold running water, four burner-stove/oven and propane-powered refrigerator sitting on the back. One admirer nearly fell over himself in his haste to move his car so I'd have a prime parking space.

Where was the beach? I inquired of a nearby restaurant proprietor after the hubbub had run its course. From where I stood, the little *pueblo* seemed surrounded by deep forest estuary; there was water everywhere, but no sand in sight.

"Take the footbridge," he directed, pointing southward, "and don't worry about your truck. I will guard it." He pulled up a chair.

There is usually a singular physical feature of a place that stands out as definitive of its charm, the image that first comes to mind when fond recollections surface. With Tilapa, I had three to choose from. First was the beach, nut-palm fringed and endlessly deserted to the east and west (Guatemala faces due south), with a cluster of sprawling ad hoc palapa bar/restaurants that were inundated twice daily by high water, much to the squealing delight of young and old. Pigs, chickens, dogs and nonplussed drunks would flow by well-anchored tables and chairs, inland bound.

There was also the rain forest, tendriling outward from the rio that fed it, its surreal, stately arboreal beings passively observant, and its constant avian chatter—warbles, chirps, yowls, yawps, shrills and yoo-hoos—as melodic commentary.

Finally there was that rickety 100-yard footbridge spanning a mangrove marsh to the beach. Man-made though it was—rough hewn from surrounding hardwood and uniting all the elements: village, estuarine forest, beach—it remains my single favorite image of Tilapa.

I crossed the bridge and, toward sundown, surfed a small beach break wave just west of it. Conditions in the water were mediocre at best, but as a traveling surfer you're there for the view as much as the wave. As I sat solo in the lineup with the sea and sky down the coast a shimmering liquid gold, I liked what I saw.

After my session, with Shiner at heel, I padded back across the bridge, taking care to hop the gap from a missing plank I'd almost fallen through earlier in my haste to reach the sea. The village street was deserted, apart from my rig and the man seated by it, Mario. A sunburnt Guatemalan couple was eating at Mario's little open-air restaurant, their young daughter throwing scraps to a pig seated by her feet like a fat ugly dog, while a huge rooster eyed the proceedings from atop an adjoining table. On a small TV inset on one wall, James Bond raised hell and seduced women in sly, guttural Spanish. I bought a beer from Mario, and he would not accept a tip, notwithstanding the zealous sentry duty he'd stood.

I showered at a little *hosteria* down a short side street that petered into a footpath into the bush. As darkness fell and the jungle benignly closed in on the village, I emerged to find the proprietress petting Shiner. Her name was Carlotta and she was of 50 or so years, with kind, expressive eyes. When I asked how much I owed for the shower, she replied that there would be no charge. I would probably be more comfortable parking my rig in her yard, she added, which was fenced and shaded by towering mango trees. There would be no charge for that, either. This was no way to run a business, I chided, but she insisted, and said that I should meet her husband, who would be back tomorrow.

The next day I understood the motive behind Carlotta's generosity. As the rare *norte* in town, she'd wanted me to be there as a diversion, a treat, for her husband, an American expatriate named Teddy Carlton. I liked Teddy almost immediately; his soft-spoken, self-effacing modesty, the way his cherubic face would suddenly erupt in a mischievous, gap-toothed grin, his pale blue eyes closing down in an involuntary squint, the better to contemplate the ironies of life.

Twenty-five years ago Teddy was building nuclear-powered submarines at Electric Boat in Groton, Connecticut. One day he up and bolted, piled a few necessities in his van and headed west, then south. "I had no idea where I was going or what I'd do when I got there," he told me. "I just knew I didn't like where I was and what I was doing."

This sounded familiar, in a personal way.

Teddy had bought a map of Central America and liked the look of a tiny Guatemalan town called Tilapa. It was pretty much a random thing, he said. And pretty much how I'd come to be there, I reflected.

"I drove on down and never left," Teddy said.

I told Teddy about my old friend Christopher, how he'd journeyed south going on six years ago and had not returned, and how I was hoping to track him down. Teddy looked at the photo of Christopher as if he saw something there, something familiar. But he shook his head and said he was sure the fellow had not passed this way, and that if he had he would have remembered.

Sitting in the courtyard of the little hotel he'd built brick by brick on the edge of the rain forest, Teddy and I talked for another hour or so, after which he excused himself, explaining that he was starting a second business in the bush near a *pueblito* a few miles inland and had to get back to work. He'd be spending the night there but would return tomorrow. He suggested we get together again then.

The surf having dropped overnight, the next morning I hired a local fisherman and his dory for a tour of the dense, winding estuary. Around noontime, Teddy and I sat down again. When I mentioned his new business in the bush—he'd been just this side of coy about it the day before—he said, "I'm thinking about calling it 'Centro Erotica.' "

Teddy Carlton was building a bordello in the Guatemalan jungle.

Carlotta was nearby, hanging laundry, and although she spoke no English, I lowered my voice when I asked Teddy what she thought about it, or, come to think of it, whether she even knew about it. By way of an answer, Teddy addressed his wife directly: "Que piensas del 'Centro Erótica,' querida?" which pretty much translated as "What do you think of my whorehouse, dear?"

Carlotta rolled her eyes in the way an American wife might react to her husband's obsession with collecting vintage Spiderman comic books.

I found myself wondering if all Guatemalan women tended to be this understanding.

The next morning something wonderful happened.

As the sun peeked though the mangroves, dappling the shore break in a hard, warm light, I stood on the deserted beach to find the surf had come up overnight. It was about head high but disorganized, the groundswells having been generated by local winds rather than a far-distant storm. The latter is much preferable, as the waves will have had time in their oceanic travels to form long lines and mature, discreet "energy bundles," or sets, comprised of three or more waves, with lulls in between that make the paddle-out easier.

It was a chore reaching the lineup that morning, with thick shifting peaks breaking without letup all across the seascape. And once outside I found virtually none of them makeable. The rides were short, fast, and invariably they ended violently as the shoulderless waves dumped on a shallow sandbar.

But about an hour into my session I got very lucky. With young and confused local swells, individual waves will sometimes merge at just that point of increasing steepness where the shelving bottom pushes them heavenward, the vertical wall of water becoming concave, and potential energy becoming kinetic. The total energy of the new, aggregate wave will then have approximately doubled. It is the same random process that forms a rogue wave in the open sea.

Added size and power without the open door, or shoulder, that allows a surfer to emerge unscathed from the wave's inner recesses, however, is a dubious improvement. Like a boxer seeing an advantage in getting hit with a straight right rather than a left jab.

No. My real luck was in the angle at which the peaks of both waves merged. They were advancing upon the beach from slightly different, and exactly perfect, directions: the lion's share of the energy of both swells was focused on one spot in the lineup—the spot where I happened to be—

creating a big, thick, top-to-bottom barrel with a tapering shoulder of unbroken wave down the line to make for.

It got dark in there.

That's how thick the wave was and how deep within it I found myself. I was in a crouch, which is pretty much instinctive in that sort of situation, but I could have stood up and still not gotten my hair wet. For the three, maybe four seconds before that wave spit me back out into sunlight with my feet still firmly planted on my board, I was exactly and without doubt where I wanted to be on the surface of planet earth. And there was not a drop of water in my universe that was out of place.

I decided to get back on the road the next morning. Although I could have easily stayed a lot longer, I knew I could surf the Tilapa shore break every day for a year—maybe a decade—and not again find myself tucked into a niche like I'd found in that amazing, freak barrel. I did not want to dilute its memory.

From *Webster's New Riverside Dictionary:* niche: "Something, as a position or activity, for which one is particularly suited." A little piece of philosophy gleaned from half a year on the road and in the water in confusing and sometimes dangerous situations: When confronted by chaos, search out a niche. It's there if you know how to look for it.

I could tell Teddy was disappointed that I was leaving so soon, and he subtly tried to get me stay. (He made a point of informing me that his twenty-something, quite attractive daughter was unmarried.) Neither of us was the type who craved company for company's sake; in the few hours we'd spent together, I believe we'd come to see each other as kindreds.

Before I left, Teddy gave me the grand tour of his brothel-to-be, nestled in a remote banana grove on the edge of the deep bush just inland from Tilapa. He pointed out where the beds, hot tubs, closed-circuit TVs and living quarters for the girls would be. Like guys everywhere, he showed considerable pride in the details and refinements in construction and layout he'd come up with. He was especially gleeful about his hand-dug well, which had come in early—a sign of good fortune, he was sure. On the other hand, and considering that "a certain percentage of the human race is comprised of psychopaths," Teddy kept within reach a 12-gauge zip gun he'd crafted from a block of wood and a piece of pipe.

I didn't leave immediately after we said our good-byes, but sat in my rig watching him stroll back down the jungle path to his construction site. There goes a happy man, I thought. A man who'd found his niche.

Late morning and you've left burning cane fields behind, though a sweet stench lingers, scorching your throat and making you sneeze through the damp red bandana covering your face below your tearing eyes—a glimpse in the rearview of the badman mask, damp, bloodshot eyes, surf-shop logo cap, and you cackle uneasily at the broken-hearted bandido yanqui *surf bum fugitive reflection staring back as you tool on through the wilds of Central America.*

8.

It was now late afternoon and James Ortega had been at El Salvadoran customs since 7 A.M., trying to get his truckload of office furniture released and on the road to San Salvador. A U.S. citizen of mixed Salvadoran/American parentage, James was finding his nascent office supplies business rough going, despite his fluent, nearly accentless Spanish. He was in fact subtly rattled, chain smoking and continually mopping his sweat-streaked face as he waited to see if his latest *mordida* payment would loosen up the slimy bureaucrat with the *estampa*—the omnipotent ink seal of corrupt approval. "I mortgaged my house for this business," he muttered.

There was another American at the customs and immigration compound, and I knew his *curriculum vitae* by his gringo-ized español, his baggy, low riding shorts, untied Air Jordans and assbackwards Dodgers baseball cap: he was a Los Angeles gangbanger, probably sent south to set up a drug or weapons deal with a Salvadoran cohort. (By rep, and pound for pound, Salvadoran street gangs in L.A. are more feared than their Mexican counterparts.)

United by little more than our passport logos and familiarity with American sports, we three *nortes*—James in his sweat-stained button-down shirt, disheveled tie and Dockers, the gangbanger with his swarthily naked, muscle-bound torso and crazed, pupil-less eyes, and me in my huaraches and Real Surfers T-shirt—found ourselves in a loose, us-against-those-shit-for-brains-foreigners huddle.

Although James was obviously highly informed about the doings of the country, I avoided asking him about what I could expect down the road, not wanting to be subjected to the sort of gloom-and-doom-you're-gonna-die-real-soon bullshit I seemed to get whenever and wherever I posed the simple query, What's up?

I did ask him, however, how long it would take me to get to La Libertad, the sight of a world-class but rarely traveled-to right point break. James said I could make it in about an hour and a half, then nudged me aside until we were out of earshot of the gangbanger.

Ready or not, here came the gloom-and-doom anyway. "Listen to me," James said, sotto voce but with panic in his eyes. "Don't tell anybody your business here."

A bewildered "Wha-what?" was all I could come up with.

"That guy (the gangbanger) knows where you're going now." James lit another cigarette with a trembly hand.

"I really don't think he cares, James." I said.

"Look . . ." He said, inhaling deeply. "There's a certain . . . tension in this country."

No shit, I was thinking.

Three hours after pulling out of customs, and with a last blush of dusk fading behind me, I found myself yelling out the rig's window as it rumbled down a traffic-less, rutted dirt track skirting a plumb line drop of a quarter mile to the sea, "Yeah, James, it might be an hour-and-a-half drive to La Libertad, IF THERE WAS A FUCKING ROAD TO DRIVE ON!"

I switched on my headlights for the first time in over six months—I hadn't driven after dark since crossing the border at Tijuana. My hard and fast rule throughout the journey had been to find a safe place to stay well before nightfall. Now here I was in pitch-black on a highly questionable road in a country where, over the past two decades, so many people had disappeared without a trace that in local *norte* usage the verb "disappeared" had made the grammatical leap to transitive, to mirror the nuance of the Spanish; as in "José's family *was disappeared* last night, probably by a right-wing death squad." And tens of thousands of others, some U.S. citizens included (advisors, businessmen, nuns, freelance writers; plus a whole Dutch film crew), had been just flat-out slaughtered.

I should have known better. If I'd learned anything in the last few months, it was that no one, *no one,* south of the Mexican border has any idea how long it takes to go from anywhere to anywhere else. And even at best—even had it only been 90 minutes to La Libertad—I'd still have been cutting it close with the dark. I'd been fantasizing about that goddamn point break, envisioning myself in the lineup at first light, when what I should have done was stay at El Salvadoran customs overnight. (Customs stations, along with airport parking lots, are safe, if insipid, places to overnight in a pinch Down South.)

Okay. Lights up ahead. Finally.

La Libertad, El Salvador, was Tecún Umán, Guatemala, minus the humor and perspective of Bogart's phantasmic presence. No, wait. Bogie was there all right, lying in a back street *barrio* gutter with a shiv in his innards under opening credits. Some real Centro Americano film *noir* going on here, except that this rough-cut *mise en scène* wasn't up on the silver screen, it was out my windshield. The extras had run amok on the set; nothing as purposeful or organized as a riot; more a randomly seething mass of hard core, down-and-dirty humanity, blocking my way in garish pools of streetlight, then parting sullenly sideways into the shadows, with individual covetous stares at my little traveling house and the imagined goodies within; and someone's bad thoughts actualizing in the banging of a fist on the side of the rig (perhaps to see what would fall out) as it jostled down a narrow, one-way descent into more of the same.

At some point in my tour through town I started considering my situation borderline serious, verging on actually serious. Even so, I was too tired and hungry and disgusted and pissed off to be fearful—a condition ripe for mistake making.

I considered turning around, going back to *La Carretera Litoral,* the coastal route, maybe find a dirt turnout, but then thought more about that tortuous, suspension-busting non-road that made Bandido Alley up in Michoacán look like the 'burbs of Oshkosh.

No, wrong. Mistake.

How about I power right through this mess, keep on going . . . and what? Drive until I run out of diesel and get waylaid on some bleak stretch of . . .

No, wrong. Mistake.

A gas station up ahead, brightly lit and clear of the worst of the *barrio bajo* chaos, a couple guys busily closing up, it looked like. I pulled in to fuel up and regroup, think this over. But one of the guys was waving me through, saying the pumps were locked and indeed the lights went off. I stopped anyway, offering fifteen colones (a couple of bucks) to park for the night. Twenty, he said. Okay, I said, if you put the lights back on, all of them—I wanted that gas station to look like high noon in Alabama. We settled on twenty-five and I was soon ensconced under a glowing Chevron sign.

The rest of the night didn't go all that well. Leashed to the back of the rig outside, Shiner kept up a continual snarling racket as assorted street goons made tentative forays. It occurred to me that the wash of light I'd cleverly contracted for amounted to a neon arrow pointed at all my worldly possessions, with the caption COME AND GET IT! After two gunshots boomed down the street, I brought Shiner inside, locked up and set my jalapeño spray (nastier than Mace and legal everywhere) and fish billy (with its tighter swing radius in close quarters, better than a baseball bat) by my bunk. I cranked up the *Miami Vice* soundtrack tape I used to play for inspiration when I was writing for the show in its first season—a move I soon abrogated as being ridiculous and embarrassing. What was I thinking? That Donny and whatsisname'd come barreling onscreen to my rescue if the shit hit the fan? Was I that jangled?

With the door shut, not a breath of breeze stirring, and two hot, keyed-up bodies in the cramped space of La Casita Viajera, the temperature rose steadily, no doubt into triple digits. I covered the two of us with towels soaked in ice water, turned on both 12-volt fans and settled in to a long, sweltry, paranoid wait for morning, glad for the steel bars I'd through-bolted over the windows and forward hatch, lock lugs on my Goodyears, and alarm system up front.

There's a certain . . . tension in this country.

Eventually I dropped off into unconsciousness, only to be startled awake by some miscreant banging on the back door and—probably inspired by my Empire State tags—yelling something about "Nueva Jork." He sounded more drunk than dangerous so I ran him off by swinging the door open to give him a gander at Shiner's dentals.

First light came like a reprieve. The coming dawn cleared the streets as swiftly and completely as if La Libertad, El Salvador, were a southern stronghold of Hispanic vampires. I fired up the rig like a man on a mission, which I in fact was.

Find that point break.

By simply making every turn that led downhill, I eventually found myself with an unobstructed water view. And there it was, in the distance to the west, past a long steel pier piled end to end with fishermen's dories. Known simply as La Punta—The Point—it had the jutting rock configuration of a world-class setup. And it was breaking, long lines bending into the bay and peeling across the seascape with machinelike precision. Only two guys out.

There's nothing like your first wave at an uncrowded, warm-water point break to impart the proper perspective on things. In truth, the last twelve hours had rattled me to where I'd been wondering, truly wondering, what the fuck I was doing here. But pulling out of that first razor-edged, shoulder-high zipper at The Point, I was reminded: *this* was what I was doing here. Last night wasn't that big of a deal, I was thinking as I stroked back out. What had been my problem? Spend the night way back at customs? Was I nuts?

What, me worry?

Early on in my first session at an unfamiliar surf break, my habit is to actively chat up the guys who are already there. First, you can, to some extent, shortcut getting the wave wired. Get a more immediate handle on the takeoff area, what the swell is doing, bottom conditions and hazards, if any.

The other objective is more subtle, and more important. By asking for advice and counsel you're in essence acknowledging the other guy's right of eminent domain, but in a way that doesn't cost you any waves. This can be vital in crowded, cranky conditions, especially with certain types who figure they're locals if they've been someplace two days longer than you. Throw in a few respectful "Wow, man . . . no shit . . . really?"s and they're less apt to pull the sort of wave-theft moves that can take the Zen out of the activity. Although I would find this sort of ass-kissing unnecessary at La Libertad—it never got crowded or cranky—Tim from San Clemente turned out to be a wealth of local knowledge and a fun guy to surf and hang with.

As we waited out a lull, Tim warned me of a rock on the inside that was a factor at low water and this swell size. "Listen," he added, "it's best not to wear a watch or jewelry surfing here." This was not the sort of advice you normally hear in a lineup and I quickly sensed it wasn't fashion-related. "Locals 'll hop that wall you have to walk along to get to the paddle-out spot and rob you before you hit the water."

A set popped up and I gave Tim his choice of waves, even though I'd drifted to the preferred inside position. Didn't matter, they were all good, and just one other surfer out, a pistol-hot young guy on a shortboard who was having his way with the place. The kid was plainly gifted; if and when he matured in his approach to the medium, calmed down and let his personal style surface from under the weight of his aggressiveness, he had the potential to be truly special.

Paddling back out together, I mentioned to Tim that I'd had a slightly uncomfortable night parked in town. "Be careful in the *pueblo,*" he cautioned. "Dress as grubby as possible and don't carry anything of value, cameras or whatever. Two surfers got held up last week, one in broad daylight, both at gunpoint.

"Most of the locals here are cool," Tim went on. "But there're also a bunch that'll kill you in a heartbeat. And by the way, your timing is good. There's an election this weekend. Word is it might get a liiiittle tense around here."

We both laughed and I reflected on the contrast between Tim's happy-go-lucky, borderline goofball deportment at the level of tension in El Salvador, and James's, which had amounted to borderline panic. Surfing was the difference. It'll take the edge off almost anything.

Tim had been traveling in Central America for a month or so, mostly by bus. I asked if he happened to run into a surfer from Long Island named Christopher, who had last been sighted in Costa Rica.

"Hangs out with a pack of dogs?"

I perked. "What kind of dogs?"

"I don't know. Mostly local mutts he'd adopted. And a couple golden retrievers."

"Where was this?"

"Town called Puerto Viejo on the Talamanca coast on the Caribbean side."

"When?"

"About two weeks ago."

After my session, walking along the wall the locals hop to rob you before you hit the water, I found myself picturing Christopher and myself on that North African beach in 1970, world map spread out on the sand before us. Christopher standing back and grinning down on it and saying, "It's right there, somewhere, Allan."

Whatever, wherever, Christopher had found, I was about to find it, too.

9.

In the early '70s, a guy named Bob Rotherham had come to La Libertad with a mutual friend of his and Christopher's and mine from Long Island—a good surfer and a certifiable wild man named Eric Penny, now deceased. Bob wound up settling in La Libertad, marrying a local, starting a business, the whole expat nine yards. Bob himself was probably the best-known expatriate surfer in Central America, and I learned that his son Bobby Jim was the kid surfing so brilliantly that morning at The Point. He was in fact the Salvadoran National Champ. While in-country, I wanted to sit down with Bob, drop a few names, shoot the breeze. Plus, given their mutual acquaintanceship with Eric Penny, it was more than likely that Christopher had seen fit to visit Bob on his way down. I was curious about his trip south five years ago, what had been on his mind then.

It took me all of about a minute-and-a-half to locate Rotherham; I'd parked my rig right in front of his restaurant overlooking The Point. Once you eliminate the nonsurfing population, then weed out the uncommitted masses, the world becomes a very small place indeed.

Bob remembered Christopher all right, how he'd come through La Libertad "like a hurricane," raising hell in the lineup and ashore and then quickly continuing on south. Had plans of establishing a surf camp deeper down, Bob recalled.

"Puerto Viejo over on the Caribbean side maybe?" I inquired.

"Sounds familiar," Bob said iffily. "Vaguely."

But then again, Bart up in Mexico had encountered Christopher a year ago on the Osa Peninsula, which was on CR's Pacific side.

We talked about Eric Penny for a bit, and Bob told me about their first surf trip to El Salvador a quarter century back. They'd ridden The Point, then moved on, to Panama. Eric wanted to dabble in drug smuggling to finance further surf travels, but Bob had demurred and, feeling the powerful draw of the wave at The Point, returned to La Libertad.

We had another Long Island friend in common, Ricky Rasmussen, who back in the mid-'70s was rated as one of the top five surfers in the world. Ricky was gone now, too, shot and killed while making a heroin buy in Harlem. He was one of the relatively few of us who had gotten into hard-drug use and trafficking.

"Everybody was nuts back then," Bob said. A trace of nostalgia crept into his voice. "No fear of repercussions."

"We were invincible," I said.

I then asked Bob what it was like in El Salvador back in those days, when Central America was still largely unexplored, by surfers or anyone else from up north, apart from CIA spooks and kind.

Bob waxed rhapsodic about that golden era, when La Libertad was a free zone, a wild and wooly port town of fleshpot guzzleries, brothels and itinerant merchant seamen from far and wide; plus a small, tight-knit cadre of serious *norte* watermen, there for the wave at The Point. These were the days before *el problema. La situación.* The civil war.

Bob had lived here—even prospered here—through all of it; the death squads, the *desaparecidos*—the mass disappearances—the bloodbath of torture and murderous mayhem that had taken the lives of uncountable human beings.

"I learned to live around it," Bob said. He described how the FMLN—the antigovernment guerillas—had stormed La Libertad just before the 1992 ceasefire, and pointed out where mortar emplacements had been set up in the hills to the north. One round had exploded on the beach in front of his restaurant.

"The FMLN don't surf," I said, referring to Robert Duvall's classic line, "Charlie don't surf!" in *Apocalypse Now.*

"Yeah," Bob said, grinning. "It was right out of that. In fact, there was a hotel full of surfers just down the street that took a direct hit from a rocket launcher."

"What happened?"

"For some reason, it was a dud. They found the thing later, embedded in the wall behind their room like some big, nasty dart." Bob shook his head. "You had to laugh at stuff like that."

"Guys just kept coming down to surf The Point, revolution or no."

Bob nodded. "Guys with nicknames like 'Pinhead,' 'Cosmo,' 'Brown Dog.' " More wildmen. "This one guy, Roger something, carted a mess of bizarre radio gear with him. He was trying to contact extraterrestrials." Bob frowned. "Guys that show up here these days . . . most of 'em are light-weights."

Even though the civil war was technically over, I was surprised to learn from Bob that the situation was actually considered more dangerous now. According to the country's attorney general, El Salvador's murder rate since the cease-fire has escalated to the point where the total dead from violent crime over the same 12-year period as the civil war will be well over 100,000, which would surpass the carnage of the conflict.

"Listen," I said, finally getting to another motive behind my talk with Bob. "Where do you suggest I overnight around here?" The quaint little area of seaside restaurants and *hosterias* on the peninsula at the base of The Point had the Nexpa-like feel of a stronghold, but just a block inland the *barrio bajo* began, and spread inland and up and down the coast like enemy territory.

Bob had to think this over. Almost all the visiting surfers at La Libertad flew or bused in and stayed in *hosterias*. Arriving by rig, my dog and I were a rarity. Where to put us was a good question.

Meanwhile, a fellow came over to our table and spoke briefly to Bob. A *norte* in his early thirties, his round, wire-rimmed glasses, pallor and pleas-antly studious mien suggested a teacher, an academic of some sort. His name was Erik. "Not a surfer," I said, as Erik hoofed it across the downstairs patio to the road.

"Nah," Bob said. "An agricultural advisor with some international agency. Arrived from up country a couple days ago."

The guy reminded me of someone.

Bob suggested I talk to a woman who ran a nearby hotel about staying on her property. It was fenced and shaded and would probably be safe. An easy walk to The Point. Great. Although I was pumped by word of Christopher's current whereabouts and at the prospect of our reunion, as long as the swell at The Point lasted, I wasn't going anywhere.

I was sitting on the steps at the town's swimmers' beach a couple days later with a fellow traveler, a French surfer named Tremont. He was a big, strapping guy in his twenties, with blond dreadlocks flowing in a matted tangle down to his butt. His accent was exactly that of Peter Sellers as Inspector Clouseau. "Room" is "rim," "phone," "fun," "bomb," "bim," and so forth. The ac-CENT invariably falls on the wrong syl-LA-ble.

Considering Tremont's youth, I was astounded at the number of far-flung places he'd surfed: Africa, Indonesia, Australia, the West Indies, obscure islands in the Indian Ocean, every island in Atlantic, it seemed. He'd even been to Ascension, where there are about three people.

Tremont was rhapsodizing about Brazil, not so much for the waves, but for the fact that "Zere are twenty wee-MEN for each one of us." He sighed and shook his head, eyes going unfocused. "How zees could be, I wass not unnerstanding, Al-LAN . . . but eet wass very good."

Tremont didn't just go places; he stayed for months. He'd been in Central America for twelve weeks now and was not yet halfway through his trip. He was also very methodical about his choice of destinations. He'd study a world map he cut to remove the far north and south latitudes ("I don' like zee cold wa-TAIR"), cross-referencing it with the type of nautical chart that defines swell-producing storm centers by season. Then he'd cram his act into a knapsack and board bag and go. Like most serious surfers on the hunt, Tremont traveled alone.

Erik joined us on the steps as Tremont was saying, "You must have zee ba-LANCE in your life, no?" Erik had mostly kept to himself since I'd first met him at Bob Rotherham's restaurant. No one would see him for a day or so, then suddenly he'd just unobtrusively show up. Tremont went on: "For six mahnts you do your work for zee mo-NEY to do what you love, zee wave rid-ING." What Tremont did for the other six months was this: he strolled the beach at St. Tropez, selling espresso coffee from a backpack canister. ("Low, how you say, over-head; eet ees all prof-EET.")

"Let me get this straight," I said. "When you're not on the road surfing, you're hitting on topless women in the south of France."

"Last sum-MER I haf to hire a West Indee-AAN fel-LOW so I can haf a leetle more time for zat," Tremont said with a shrug indicative of help-lessness of his plight.

"So, Erik, what did you do last night?" I'd heard enough about Tremont's life. I was also curious about Erik's doings.

"Well, I met four American girls," he said, in his characteristic low-key manner. "We had dinner and went for a swim." This perked Tremont and me up. La Libertad wasn't exactly crawling with on-the-loose women. "It's not as great as it sounds," Erik added. "They're Christian missionaries."

"Shit," I said. "Nuns?"

"Not exactly, but close."

"Ahhh . . ." Tremont said, sensing hope. "So zey haf not yet signed zee pa-PERS, eh. Zees could be Impor-TANT."

"Maybe one of them joined the church because of a problem with nymphomania," I added. "And is ripe for a backslide."

"What does zees mean?" Tremont wanted to know. I told him; he nodded pensively. "Zees would be good, too."

Erik looked at his watch and got up. "I'll bring them around tonight if you want."

"We want," I said.

As Erik strode purposely off, I said, "What does he have, some kind of appointment?"

Tremont shrugged.

"I think Erik's a spook."

Tremont squinted at me in noncomprehension.

"A spy. A secret agent."

Tremont laughed.

"Think about it. What were his last few jobs? A refugee camp in Thailand, screening Vietnamese who wanted to emigrate to the U.S. Then he goes to Indonesia, teaches English there, he claims. Does Erik speak Indonesian?" Tremont spoke some Indo and had thrown a few words at Erik the day before.

Tremont shook his head. "I wass surprised. How can you teach EngLISH if you don' speak zee oz-ZAR lan-GUAGE?"

"And now he shows up in El Salvador as an 'agricultural advisor,' during the week of the first election this town's had since the cease-fire. I bet he doesn't know one end of a cane field from the other."

But Tremont's mind was elsewhere. "May-BE zey kill zee boy ba-BIES, eh?"

"What?"

"Een Brazil."

"Goddamn it, the guy doesn't surf. What could he possibly be doing here? I'll tell you what," I said, speaking mostly to myself and having gotten on a roll. "He's here to help the right-wing-government motherfuckers screw around with the election."

I'd finally come up with who Erik had reminded me of: a guy Christopher and I had run into in Panama while outfitting *Ensenada* for her doomed run nearly 20 years before. Erik was cut from the same mold: same low-key, studious act (the guy in Panama had even worn those round, wire glasses) and shifty résumé. We'd met him through our Panamanian government connection, then-dictator General Omar Torrijos's head of security and liaison to the various spooks, drug runners and all-around miscreants who kept Torrijos's personal coffers flush. The liaison himself was a classic Third World slimeball, an arrogant, dipshit fanfaron whom we called to his face "Manny"; but because that face was so stone-ugly and deeply pockmarked, everyone privately referred to him as "The Pineapple."

At the time, and because of the severely unofficial nature of our dealings with him, I never bothered to commit to memory The Pineapple's last name. However, when he took control of the country a few years later I saw his visage plastered on the covers of various magazines and newspapers. The Pineapple, our Panamanian go-to guy for everything from official protection to clandestine airstrips to head stash to high-end whores, was Manuel Noriega. It was through Manny the Pineapple that Christopher and I were introduced to this guy Erik so strongly reminded me of, who turned out to be CIA.

Erik did not show up that night with the Christian missionary girls. The next and only other time I saw him was on election day, striding determinedly somewhere and looking at his watch. Although he claimed he was in La Libertad for the sun and salt air, he was as pale as the day we first met. I don't recall once having seen him on the beach.

Just before sundown the day of my conversation with Tremont and Erik, the traveling surfers in La Libertad gathered for a little shit-shooting in my niche in the hotel courtyard. Aside from Tim from San Clemente and Tremont, a young Aussie named Andy showed up, plus a newly-arrived SoCal *norte* who'd immediately seen the wisdom of joining the already-entrenched surfpack. There was no snobbish reticence in accepting newcomers, no questions asked, no waiting period while aplomb in the lineup is judged; none of the customary initiation or hazing rituals. You show up here with a board bag, you're all right. Be careful on the streets and watch out for that rock on the inside section at low water. Welcome to La Libertad, El Salvador.

Two Brazilians, Flavio and Luis, also joined us. A fun pair, those two, especially exuberant, wild-eyed Flavio. He and Luis—his perfect laid-back, diffident foil—had bought a beat-up old rattletrap in Panama and were working their way north, with plans to enter California via Baja. We were on reciprocal headings on wave jaunts with identical itineraries: I'd finally found people doing what I was doing, if in reverse.

Flavio spoke no English and I no Portuguese, so we conversed in Spanish. It soon got heated, then crazed, as we each sought to out-bullshit the other with respect to the waves we'd found in our travels (luck in finding surf is somehow ego-boosting, as if the surf gods have blessed you out of respect for your astounding courage and ability in the water) and how the other might do as well. Pretty soon we were yelling and waving our arms. Punctuating his Spanish hyperbole with the English phrase, "I not shitting you, my brahdder!" Flavio extolled the endless, uncrowded tubes of Panama while I countered with southern Mexico, Puerto Escondido and Nexpa especially. I told him about Bart's home break and how to find it.

Flavio, I noticed, skipped over Costa Rica (Hah! I was thinking, you got skunked). He moved on to Nicaragua, where the surf apparently hadn't dropped below head-high since prehistoric times.

I cracked a sweat describing Baja—I was running low on Spanish adjectives—and at some point realized that Flavio was staring at me askance.

Tim spoke some Spanish and had been following the conversation like a spectator at a tennis match. "Todos Santos was *sixty* feet and glassy for a week?" he asked.

"Oh. I meant to say *six* feet and glassy," I corrected, adding lamely, "It was more like *two* weeks."

But it was too late. The mistake had taken the wind out of my sails: I essentially gave up. Flavio's Spanish was better than mine, plus he was younger and had more stamina. He had won Dueling Surf Spots.

Or had he?

As an oh-by-the-way I suggested they stop by at Tilapa, Guatemala. Flavio's eyes dimmed as I described the mediocre shore break wave, but rekindled when I mentioned Teddy Carlton's brothel in the banana grove. It would probably be in full swing by the time he and Luis got there, I said.

There was a beat of silence as Flavio and Luis looked at each other. Then Luis, who had been silent all this time, spoke. "Puedes mostrarnos en el mapa?" he wanted to know. Can you show us on the map?

It was somewhere around 9 P.M. on election night when Shiner and I joined Tremont, Tim and Andy in Tim's four-dollar-a-day oceanfront hotel room balcony overlooking The Point. Tim was busing up to San Salvador in the morning, then flying back home; he'd invited us over for a going-away party. With its boxy, cement layout, tiny, unfinished rooms and slitted, barred windows, his hotel had the distinct feel of a bunker. (An architectural response to the FMLN's mortaring of the town, perhaps.)

The four of us stepped outside and listened to the election-night din rising and falling from the *barrio* like the changing moods of a stadiumful of rabid soccer fans. A wavering flicker of street fires could be seen reflected on the crumbly side of a narrow lane adjacent to the oceanfront street and on the taller buildings to the north. Car horns were blaring, firecrackers (I'm pretty sure) popping; a distant bullhorn warbled incomprehensively to the cadence of some sort of rallying chant.

Notwithstanding the chaos of the streets and a ban on alcohol, Tim went off in search of beer, dragging with him a disinclined Andy, and claiming that he had cultivated "certain connections" in the *barrio*. The alchohol ban was a three-day edict and a serious one, meant to keep election-related strife to a minimum. Not only was purchase forbidden, but even consumption in the privacy of one's home. Anyone caught with so much as a whiff on his breath would be summarily hoosegow-bound. That afternoon, I had been refused the purchase of a few cc's of isopropyl, which I mix with vinegar as an eardrop prophylaxis. (Ironically, the pharmacist had cheerfully coughed up Valiums and codeine-based painkillers, which taken in tandem would have been enough to send me staggering onto the streets yelling for the bloody overthrow of everything in sight.)

The duo returned with a knapsackful of local brew, along with a baggie of pot to go with it, and soon we were all sprawled on the bare cement overhang of a rail-less second story balcony, ooohhhing and aaahhing and uttering monosyllabic hooey of the "Wow!" and "Yeaaahh!" genre (along with the occasional "Heav-ee!") at seaward-flashing sheet lightning and grumbles of thunder like the bunch of stoned idiots that we were. Shiner, God bless her, was curled up dozing at my feet, uncomplaining and non-judgmental. The perfect traveling companion.

Another joint was loosely constructed and lit, more beer guzzled. A light, feathery rain had commenced when this Dutch guy who was staying at the hotel appeared on the balcony. He and his three knapsack-toting buddies were the only nonsurfing foreigners sojourning in La Libertad—apart from Erik-the-possible-spook. "Hey, you guys," he said in lightly accented English, "we can smell that pot all the way out on the street."

"Oh, wow," someone said, then the whole crew of us cracked up laughing. This of course annoyed the Dutchman, who said something to the extent of "All right, it's your problem," then huffed back down the stairs. (Our cohesiveness as foreigners in town did not apply to nonsurfers; we considered outlanders in La Libertad who were not there for the wave at The Point to be idiots.)

"Hey, Tremont," Tim said, squinting through the dim, smokily pungent air. "Look at you. They'd throw away the key." Tremont had a liter of beer in one hand, the fat, droopy joint in the other. He examined the objects affixed to the ends of his arms and grinned through his mane of blond dreads. I was hoping he'd come up with something good in his fractured, Clouseauesque English, but if he did, it was drowned out by an admixtured din of laughter, rolling thunder and a crescendo of hue and cry from the *barrio.*

I'd been thinking a lot about Christopher, now that our reunion at Puerto Viejo on Costa Rica's Talamanca coast was all but a certainty, and I broke the ensuing dimwitted silence by asking Tim what it was like down there.

"It's . . . it's . . . I'll tell you what it's like." Tim took a contemplative hit from the joint to rally his recollection. "It's like the end of the road." Then, with portent exaggerated by my addled faculties: "It *is* the end of the road."

Silence ensued as eyes crossed and brows furrowed (at least mine did) at the weight of Tim's utterance. "There's a serious wave there, too," he added, and the weight lifted.

"What do you mean," I queried, summoning a vague image of cracking green.

"I'm talking *serious,* bro," Tim said, and the bloodshot look he'd cast me was suddenly itself serious.

A serious wave at the end of the road.

. . .

In a fearful late afternoon swelter you're a hundred yards from the no-man's-land between Honduras and Nicaragua when you hit the brakes and spring from the rig to face the walleyed, pockmarked scumbag in the Nike cap who's been banging on your door and persisting that you owe him "money money money more money." When you demand of his ugly greaseball ass just what the fuck he's gonna do if you don't give it to him, he does what he shouldn't do, which is to grab your arm with a bony claw and spittle-spray your face with his money-money-money-more-money litany. Now in your last-straw outrage you've turned the corner on the day's fear and you're thwacking the startled little prick's heaving little chest for the trespasses of a whole country, meanwhile backing him across the road and then up against the side of a northbound bus stopped in the incoming customs line as your dog roars and throws herself against your rig's window across the street.

10.

March 17, a Tuesday, was a bad day.

There was only one good thing that happened that day. Shiner tore up someone, a Honduran, I'm quite certain. She did this in defense of our home. Before her encounter, I did not know for sure that she was actually capable of violating human flesh, although over the course of this journey she has become intensely protective, and, like me, operates under a heightened degree of vigilance.

March 17 was a three-country day. We drove out of La Libertad, El Salvador, in the early morning. By dusk we were in Nicaragua, at customs, where we spent the night. Between El Salvador and Nicaragua was Honduras.

We were on the verge of escape from Honduras when Shiner had her run-in. I'd just spent fifteen minutes haggling with the head man at immigration (a "Badges? We don't need no stinking badges!" kind-of-a-guy) over how much of a *mordida* he'd get for permitting me to leave his shithole of a country and stepped outside the compound to find the rig's cab door ajar and Shiner anxiously pacing back and forth along the bench seat. Missing were my second-to-last camera body (another was down mechanically), my workhorse 20–40mm zoom and the roll of film upon which I'd documented several of my encounters with the previous Honduran lowlifes and thieves—including three of the five separate roadblock *federales* who extorted from me a total of a hundred-and-some-odd dollars using threats of loss of my passport, jail and innuendos of violence as their only justification for lightening my resources.

How the intruder had unlocked the door—I'd only cracked the window a few inches for ventilation—and managed to get the camera while Shiner did her best to stop him must fall into the Where There's a Will There's a Way category. From the crimson arterial drops I found on the Ford's dashboard and driver's side window, it's possible that the piece of garbage died of blood loss on the way home.

The experience rattled Shiner to the core. The ridge of fur on her back was at full erection for a good hour after her confrontation, and her ears, which are the best indication of her state of mind, took even longer than that to return to their normal mobility from being pinned back rigidly to the sides of her head.

I talked to her at length that day, to assure her by my tone and body language that what she did was right. I told her that it's permissible even to kill a human being in defense of our home, and that it's best to do that, to go for a kill, to end a potentially life-threatening situation quickly, decisively, and in our favor. Or even just in her favor, should my safety not be at stake.

What I meant by this was not just that I value my dog's life more than that of a human being who invades our home, but that, further, someone who does so has no right to continuing on living. Even if the motive for his invasion is the need to feed a starving family.

Kill the fucker.

There is no surf in Honduras, making it a useless country to begin with. But I had no choice but to pass through it in order to find another wave to ride and to continue on my southward trek to find Christopher. I wished to accomplish this as quickly and painlessly as possible, to mind my own business and not be preyed upon.

I don't believe this is possible in Honduras.

11.

There being no working public phones in the seaside *pueblo* of San Juan del Sur, Nicaragua, I negotiated for the use of a bar phone to make two collect calls, the first of which was to Denise. Her machine picked up and while I was oddly relieved that she hadn't been home, at the same time, hearing her voice made me feel empty and alone and I found myself missing her terribly.

I'd last spoken to her from southern Mexico, a short, awkward conversation from an anonymous roadside *pueblo* off Mex 200. Jostling locals in line to use the town's only phone glared impatiently while I tried to keep up my end.

"Are you all right?" Denise had asked.

"I'm okay," I replied.

"Are you sure? You sound different."

"I'm all right."

After we hung up I sat on the curb by the rig, stroking my dog, momentarily overcome by loneliness and exhilaration, while the people around me went about their business, speaking a language I suddenly could not understand at all.

I looked around the San Juan del Sur bar. Shiner had slinked unnoticed by the barkeep over to a corner by the patio and gingerly laid down, knowing from experience that a low profile was the best defense against ejection. I'd come to let her shift for herself in eating and drinking establishments, except that, given her less than rudimentary understanding of Spanish, I'd have to interpret with a jerk of my thumb toward the door and an apologetic "Out" when her presence was requested to be elsewhere.

As I placed my second call, I craned to take in the sunset view out the front window. It was three days short of the vernal equinox and our local star at that far southern latitude bore nearly dead west as it dropped perpendicularly through pellucid pink to the sea horizon. The spring twilight is a fast fade so close to the equator; it would be all but dark in a half hour.

San Juan del Sur was situated on a stunning, nearly enclosed bay peppered with moored commercial fishing craft and a few unostentatious yachts, foreign voyagers from their bleached but seaworthy, no-nonsense look. The *pueblo's* main drag was lined with saloons, restaurants and *hosterias,* ranging in style from Early Hovel to Downright Quaint, and catered to a mostly local tourist crowd, along with a handful of itinerants and expatriates of various nationalities. Picturesque. Problem was the town's beaches were surfless. I'd be gone south come morning.

"Allan! You all right?" my surfbuddy/defense attorney Joe Giannini was saying in his thick Brooklynese. "We were startin' to worry about you." I could hear Joe's wife, Nikki, in the background calling out for him to ask when I'm coming "home." Before he could relay the question—I didn't want to deal with it—I launched into an abbreviated account of the past couple months, mainly surf-related. I also revealed that I'd pretty much located Christopher and was closing in fast on the sonofabitch.

"Are you planning . . ." But Joe's voice had faded over a bad connection. Looking up, I spotted a *norte* expat I'd met earlier in the day, Dale, who had breezed in and was making his way to the patio. Dale was about my age, a surfer, sailor, and from the smooth, understated and competent vibe he exuded when we'd talked a bit of story, an all-around waterman with some hair-raising tales to tell.

"Say again, Joe?"

"Are you planning on stopping at Tamarindo?" Tamarindo was a surfy town in northern Costa Rica.

"Hadn't thought about it."

"I heard Robert August is there." August was one of the globe-trotting surfers in *The Endless Summer,* the movie that had changed everything about my life thirty-odd years before. "Yeah," I said. "I might stop and look him up." The idea of maybe sitting down with August had a definite sentimental appeal.

"Listen, Allan." Joe's voice surfaced through static that sounded like brittle paper crunching. "A coupla things've got to be dealt with."

"Oh, boy."

"Your New York State driver's license has been revoked for letting your truck's insurance lapse." Months before, from somewhere in Mexico, I'd faxed the DMV a note saying that since my NYS insurance was invalid Down South, I saw no reason to continue paying it. I'd included a copy of my Mexican insurance as proof of continued coverage. Apparently, none of this had impressed the computer up in Albany. "Not only that," Joe went on, "but they're fining you five dollars for every day you're lapsed."

"Well, hell," I calculated. "That's already going on a thousand bucks."

"I called them and explained the situation but didn't get anywhere."

". . . Fuck 'em, Joe."

"Your Writer's Guild Health insurance has lapsed also, due to insufficient employer contributions." In other words, I hadn't worked in the movie business in a while. "They also say you're arrears in dues."

"Fuck 'em, Joe."

"And listen: your credit card bills are piling up. You've got enough money left to keep paying the minimums for a while but . . . I don't know."

I had to think about this one.

"Ahhhh . . . fuck 'em."

"And listen—"

"I thought you said 'a coupla things.' "

"The IRS . . ."

"Fuck 'em!"

There was a bit of a silence during which I believe both the friend and the lawyer in Joe were analyzing the drift of the conversation. Finally, in a much muted tone, he said, "Nikki wants to know when you're coming home."

. . .

Home. Wow. What a concept, I was thinking as I approached Dale's table. He motioned me to take the adjacent chair. The two of us had some acquaintances in common: a couple hotshots from the old days in Hawaii, as well as Bob Rotherham, up in El Salvador. Dale had run into Christopher, too, although it had been several years before and his recollection was vague. Maybe somewhere in Costa Rica while Dale was running surf charters on his trimaran. As with most of those who recalled Christopher, it was the dogs Dale had initially remembered, and then that he'd liked my old friend. Dale was now semi-marooned in Nicaragua after being dismasted in a blow while trying to get an injured crewman ashore.

I've come to loosely categorize the nonlocals (generally *nortes* and Europeans) I encounter in my travels. In ascending order of commitment to the alternative lifestyle the Down South world offers: Tourists, Travelers, *Viajeros* (Travelers with a bit more backbone) and, finally, Expats—those who have chucked their former incarnations and made the ultimate commitment to life south of the border. Among these categories are subcategories based on my perception of the motivations behind the individual's presence down here.

There are the Big-Fish-in-a-Little-Pond types; those who, for psychological (or psychopathological) reasons, have sought a simplified Down South social hierarchy in which they are dominant figures, a standing not possible in the more intensely competitive world stateside. These types reveal themselves through surface swagger, boisterous horn-blowing and the cultivation of an acolyte entourage more than through any real accomplishments.

There are Fugitive/Outlaw types, who are holed up or on the run for legal and/or business/interpersonal reasons. This group includes severely wayward spouses and thieves who would be sued or blown away if located by their former stateside associates.

There is the subcategory of Lost Souls—sub-subcategorized as Veggie-Hippy-Dippies, Space Cadets and Flat-Out Idiots—types who, for reasons of disorientation or stupidity, simply can't seem find their way back to their stateside existences. Closely related are the For Sure, Dudes (pronounced in Airhead SoCalese as "Frrr Shrrr, dewd"), the stateside waterhead version of which has given surfing its dumbass image. (Think the Sean Penn character in *Fast Times at Ridgemont High*.) This type is identifiable by his low-riding surf trunks, slack jaw, and tendency to sway slightly in those rare moments when he's upright and involved in abstract thinking.

The most interesting is the Born-Too-Late type. These truly committed expats are subcategorized into Homesteaders and Explorers. The former has traveled south in a legitimate search for a better, more independent life; for physical and psychological freedom. He/she (often a couple) has invariably found a niche, a little piece of Paradise, and has created something where before was little or nothing.

Although both Homesteaders and Explorers are serious risk-takers and worthy of healthy respect, the Explorer is my emotional favorite. Profoundly rootless and intensely interested in the world around him in all its facets, the Explorer type often has a passion that gives added meaning to his wanderings (the vast majority are solo males). Surfing is the quintessential example here, for there are very few endeavors that so perfectly combine travel/exploration with a creatively satisfying relationship to the environment.

Homesteaders are often former Explorers who have stumbled upon their destined niche and/or have ultimately tired of the itinerant life. Bob Rotherham is an example of an Explorer who became a Homesteader. Teddy Carlton, who beelined for Tilapa, Guatemala, and essentially never left, was a Homesteader from the get-go.

I had quickly come to see Dale as a true Explorer. Having combined the surfing life with that of the itinerant sailor, he was a deeply committed, long-term apostle of Big Blue. I envied him this, and in talking to him found myself waxing wistful over certain of my life's decisions.

Dale and I ordered a round of local brew with rum shot chasers. At the next table, a German—call him Adolph—was making me grimace with his sonorous, interminable ramblings about how savvy and seasoned he was in the art of traveling skinflintism; how much he'd cannily saved (a couple of bucks) via endless hunts for cheaper *hosterias* or more favorable currency exchange rates. Adolph was big and burly, mid-thirties, with a shaved head and thick, tattooed biceps. His entourage was a mixed bag of Europeans, an effete collection of psuedo-adventurers hanging on Adolph's every word.

Based on the hydrant-pissing drift of his drivel, it quickly became apparent that Adolph was the most annoying of all the hyphenate types—a Big-Fish-in-a-Little-Pond—Tourist—Flat-Out Idiot. Now, having switched conversational topics, he was going on about the types of travelers who visit Nicaragua. "The Americans don't come," he said with a grand scowl. "They are afraid because they hear about revolutions and violence."

My own nebulous status as Viajero or Expat or neophyte Explorer or future Homesteader or Fugitive or whatever the hell I was notwithstanding, I wasn't about to let this barb aimed at both my country and myself slip by uncountered. Excusing the interruption, I asked Adolph in a congenially disarming tone by what means he'd arrived here.

He'd flown, he replied.

"You took a bus from the Managua airport to the corner down the street?" I said, jerking my thumb toward the nearby bus stop. "Then you walked the block or two to your hotel, and here you are. Right?"

Adolph opened his mouth to speak, but I didn't let him get a word out. "There are two Americans here tonight." I indicated Dale. "He's here because he got shipwrecked in a storm. I drove here, my dog and I, put over 20,000 kilometers on my truck. And some of those kilometers," I continued, "were through some shit."

It would perhaps have been nice to somehow slip in a reference to the Normandy Invasion or the firebombing of Dresden, but as it was I simply added, "That's how we Americans got here."

All Adolph managed was a feeble hand-flutter as an attempted gesture of dismissal. I turned back to Dale, who shrugged as if to say, Good point but why bother? Then he said, "The Germans are a strange bunch. They're either *complete assholes* or guys you'd very definitely want at your back when the shit goes down." Although Dale was soft-spoken (another trait of the true Explorer), his words were clearly audible at Adolph's table. And it was absolutely obvious that Dale was defining Adolph as being in the Asshole subcategory of the Teutonic scheme of things.

It was a showdown moment, no question. Not only was Dale insulting Adolph and in front of his entourage, but, by doing so in such an offhanded manner, was further defining Adolph as a nonentity in terms of being a physical threat. This in spite of the fact that Dale was maybe 5 feet 8 inches and at best wiry, closer to thin. Adolph had him by half a head in height and at least 50 pounds, plus he was a good 15 years younger.

The tension was palpable but brief. Having my back to Adolph, I kept my eyes on Dale, knowing that if Adolph made a move, Dale would instantly react. In which case I'd be up and ready to deal with either Adolph himself or anyone else at his table who saw fit to get rowdy. As silent seconds ticked by, Dale had another sip of beer then glanced over my shoulder at Adolph, as if to say, Time's up, pal. And it was. Violence-capable types tend to react that way very quickly, and after three or four seconds Adolph still hadn't done so, nor had he come up with a verbal sally. As I'd suspected based on his lowly placement in my hierarchy of Down South dipshits, he was a lightweight, a windbag with nothing behind his bluster. He and his Eurotrash toadies quieted right down, then casually left, as if nothing tense had occurred with the two Americans in San Juan del Sur.

Dale and I knocked back another round and ordered dinner. The barkeep/owner produced a bowl of water and scraps from the kitchen for Shiner. As we ate, Dale started in about the advantages of wave hunting by boat. There were untold Central American breaks accessible only by sea, he said, especially off Panama, which boasted numerous islands, many uninhabited. Multihulls like his trimaran were ideal for such work, in Dale's opinion, due to their ample deck space and accommodations, shoal draft, beachability (not only for landing but for hull cleaning, painting and repairs) and speed in light airs.

"Yeah, but if they capsize, that's that," I countered. "No coming back." Multihulls have always made me nervous for this reason, at least for serious ocean voyaging. Monohulls, with their deep ballast, will eventually right themselves, even if knocked completely upside down.

The mono-versus-multihull debate is a time-immemorial one amongst seagoing types, with true believers copping an almost religious fervor in maintaining their position. And so it was. Further powered by beer and rum, our discussion waxed lively, then heated.

"Multihulls're level in a seaway," I was saying a round or two later. "Until a night squall hits you broadside aback and next thing you know you're upside down with your thumb up your ass, if can find your ass in the inverted chaos. Meanwhile, in a mono, you loose your sheets and she'll right herself—"

"If she doesn't sink first!" Dale interjected.

Sinking. Hah! There's a subject I know something about, I thought, as Dale ridiculed the nonsensicalness of filling the bottom of an object meant to float with lead or pig iron (as ballast), two substances the essence of which is that they sink.

"Yeah, well, I expect sinkablity in my vessels," I said. "In fact, I *demand* it."

"Huh?"

"Sinking is the natural and inevitable corollary to floatation," I said, serenely philosophizing. "A yin and yang deal. A matter of dramatic tension."

"Yeah, well I'll take the yin, pass on the yang," Dale said. "And fuck the dramatic tension. Last thing you need at sea is dramatic tension."

"Plus it comes in handy under certain circumstances," I said, ignoring Dale's self-evident wisdom.

"What comes in handy?"

"The sinkability factor." I told Dale about *The Fucking Boat,* explaining how tough she'd been to put down, due to her all-wood construction and lack of ballast. I described *Ensenada*'s final moments, which seemed relevant in the yin-yang, dramatic tension context. The ship being of steel construction, I rambled on, she'd gone down decisively, once the weight of deluging seawater surpassed that of water displaced by her bulk: Archimedes Principle in action.

Then, over our last round, I told Dale about my last nautical command, a pot-laden motorsailer named *Rana*, which Christopher and I scuttled after having been intercepted, then followed for three days by the U.S. Coast Guard, in international waters off the north coast of Puerto Rico in 1981. The yacht, which was steel built, also carried more than three tons of lead ballast bolted to her keel.

The Coast Guard cutter had launched a lifeboat to try to prevent the sinking, or to at least secure a piece of our illicit cargo as evidence. They managed the latter, to Christopher's and my chagrin. While we watched from our life raft, the C.G. boys broke into the cabin and pulled out a bale just as *Rana* slipped from sight enroute to the abyss. She'd gone down quickly all right, but not quite quickly enough.

The two-day voyage back to Puerto Rico was wet and all-around un-comfortable, with Christopher, myself, and our two hired hands chained to the cutter's windward rail near the bow. Although the vessel had ac-commodations for prisoners below, I'd aggravated the skipper mightily dur-ing the time he'd been following us. In retrospect, I can hardly blame him for a measure of payback. With the cutter's cannons and 50-caliber machine guns trained on us at close range day and night, I'd retaliated by having my crew relieve themselves over the taffrail in full view of our pursuer's crew—many of which were females. At unpredictable intervals after dark, we'd shine our million-candlepower spotlight on the cutter's bridge to tem-porarily blind whoever was watching us with night-vision gear. Plus, on the second day of our little cat-and-mouse game, I'd gone aboard the cutter for a face-to-face with my opposite number, the Coast Guard captain. Stinky, disheveled and cranky from two weeks of sleeping, eating and living on damp marijuana bales (*Rana* was cram-packed with our 9,000-pound cargo), I'd called him—among other things—a fat fuck (he *was* overweight) in front of a wardroom full of his subordinates.

Thing was, I had forgotten something: *we were the bad guys.* The Coast Guard was merely doing its job out there; my anger at the interdiction was a function of the extent to which I had lost perspective.

As it was, however, with the whole fiasco having taken place in inter-national waters, there was no proof that we were stateside-bound; the bale they'd secured was not enough to bring charges. After a lengthy onshore interrogation by a cadre of cranky DEA agents, with the salvaged bale sitting on a table in front of us as a reminder of our transgression, they had no choice but to turn us loose.

The *Rana* debacle was pretty much the last straw for my career as a pot smuggler. Since the loss of *Ensenada*, Christopher and I had been beset by one catastrophe after another: bad debts, outright rip-offs; a load we'd brokered got busted off the Carolinas; our DC-3 was stolen from a Bahamas airstrip, a load of supposedly high-grade Jamaican turned out to be nearly worthless dreck, and on and on. Plus our operating expenses—the Learjet, the limos, the chartered helicopters, various safe houses, our increasingly deranged lifestyles—often ran into six figures per month. And as if the loss of *Rana* and her cargo wasn't enough as a capper, upon returning stateside unexpectedly early from the ill-fated voyage, I found my then-girlfriend in flagrante delicto with my then-attorney.

Although Christopher would continue on to new and even more disastrous escapades, I decided to hang it up, try something different. Bidding my unfaithful lover adieu, I checked into a Manhattan hotel and started writing a movie script I'd been thinking about for a while, although I had never written anything before. It was during this time that I went south to inform Fredi of my retirement from the pot trade.

The script finished, I hopped a plane for the West Coast and dropped in on the only person I knew out there, a TV producer I had met a few years previously. Within a week of my arrival in Tinseltown, I'd gotten an agent and producer/director Michael Mann had optioned my script.

With nary a transitional beat from my life as a criminal, I found myself in show biz.

12.

I had visitors the afternoon after my dinner and drinks with Dale in San Juan del Sur, which surprised me—the beach I was now camped upon was about as remote as any I'd encountered since Baja. According to the map, there were no settlements within 10 miles in either direction up or down the coast, nor for a similar distance inland. It had taken an hour of slow going on a bad road for me to just reach the *really* bad road—a jungle track that showed no signs of recent passage—that led to that sweepingly majestic piece of southern Nicaraguan shore.

My visitors were two surfers in a rented jeep, fresh off the plane into Managua. They were Basques and were astounded that I not only knew their country's location and a bit of its history and culture, but its waves as well, mainly a rock reef break called Chambre de Amour (Room of Love; a perfect name for a surf spot) just south of the French frontier on the Bay of Biscay. Chambre was their home break.

We talked for a while, using Spanish as our common language, mostly about the European surf scene, what it is now compared to what it was back in the golden era of the early '70s when I first experienced it, then the boys bolted. As beautiful as that beach was, the surf was poorly shaped from a too-high tide (I'd ridden a decent little peak at low water) and they were in a hurry to get wet.

I had another visitor very late that night, albeit of quite a different sort. The nearly full moon was at its apex when Shiner commenced an uproar, so it was within an hour of midnight. I emerged from La Casita with fish billy and jalapeño spray in hand to see a tall, rangy figure sprinting southbound down the beach with Shiner in hot, yawling pursuit. She slowed, then stopped as the trespasser opened the distance from the rig, though her snarling racket continued for a bit before commencing a gradual ebb, like a windup toy with a tiring spring. Finally, after a final wan woof, she fell silent, but did not return immediately to the rig. She stood on the beach a hundred or so yards to the south, dead still, tail extended like a bird dog on point, staring after the intruder, who had veered into the bush after a long run down the beach.

I sat down on a nut palm trunk and stared at my dog's stock-still silhouette in the moonlight, with my new friend the Southern Cross twinkling down the beach low to the left and my old buddies, the Dipper Brothers, Big and Little, struggling up north to stay above the horizon, as my southward movement across the earth's surface put them ever closer to disappearing beneath the rim of the world.

Shiner had run off nocturnal prowlers three times that I knew of for sure over the course of our travels. Many more times I'd be awakened by a brief flurry of barking, which I took to mean she'd caught wind of a potential invader early and warned him off at a distance. The would-be thief tonight had no doubt been stealthy enough to get very close before she'd sensed him, hence the outraged pugnacity of her defensive reaction. Between the B & E encounter at Honduran customs and tonight, she'd been a busy girl over the past few days.

Shiner was given to me ten years ago by a girlfriend. I can still clearly picture Debbie standing outside my porch door holding this goofy little puppy with a black eye patch and white blaze and boots, severe underbite and cocked ears slightly out of alignment. "I've decided you don't need a woman," Debbie said, only half jokingly. "You need a dog." She was right. I was then and still am the most tiresome sort of male cliché.

I'd been going through a difficult period then, personally and professionally. I was drinking constantly, not surfing much and not writing well. I don't know for sure if there's a connection, but within three months of adopting Shiner I'd quit drinking altogether and written a screenplay that saved me financially and restored my faith in my writing ability.

One other thing, among many, about my dog: absent her companionship I would not have embarked upon this southward journey. There is no question of that.

Dawn broke clear and cool over the jungle to the east, with a light offshore breeze and a wide, trackless, pearly-hued beach as my backyard. As was my habit in the mornings, I'd already been up for an hour or so by sunrise, puttering and scribbling in my daily journal. When Shiner finally arose—she's blear and droopy in the morning—I took her for a beach walk and a bracing early swim. The water in southern Nicaragua is a good 10 degrees cooler than just up the beach to the north. The air, too, is fresher and more temperate; for the first time since central Mexico I'd don a light jacket at night and in the early morning. My guess is that the vast presence of Lake Nicaragua 15 miles inland is the cause of this phenomenon. The land breeze is cooled from blowing across the lake's surface, and the rivers that drain westward (the lake also feeds the Caribbean to the east), along with underground seepage, likewise cool the torrid sea.

After our swim, I sat on the nut palm trunk, sipping my second coffee and contemplating my situation and options. Since leaving Mexico I'd found my journey south accelerating. There was a foreshortening effect, a quickening of the pace of events and intermediate destinations—the next surf break, the next *pueblo,* the next frontier, the next problem or confrontation. Indeed, I found that once in Central America proper, it's possible to transverse each country in one dawn-to-dusk run.

Now in far southern Nicaragua, the northern reaches of Costa Rica were clearly visible in the clear, sweet early light, in the high, undulating form of La Peninsula de Santa Elena, which juts some 20 miles into the Pacific from its base adjacent to the Nicaraguan frontier. Although Costa Rica is only marginally larger than El Salvador—the smallest of the Central American states—it loomed that morning like an unexplored continent, vast, portentous and mysterious; an equivocal, though deeply seductive draw.

The stories of other surfers who had gone before me were mostly paradisiacal. Costa Rica, they said, was a country of almost unlimited surf, with vast unexplored potential beckoning, like the blank regions of sea charts of yore. And although few of my wave-hungry fellows had tarried inland, there were also tales of still-unsullied cloud forests, outlandish endemic wildlife, and raging pristine rivers.

Costa Rica's reputation as the ultimate surfers' paradise no doubt had its basis in fact, for the proof is in the staying, and many had stayed. Including, apparently, Christopher, whose severance of ties from back where he and I used to live proved to be final. He had terminated communication with his physical and psychological roots, lifelong friends put aside as irrelevant to his new Down South incarnation. What had he seen to precipitate such a profound rupture? What sort of ultimate perquisite did his exotic niche offer? Would it be the paradise I myself sought?

And what of Christopher himself? Would I uncover a surfy Lord Jim, revered by Talamancan natives? Or a wild-eyed Kurtz, holed up in a fortified covert, a warrior/wave rider of unsound method? Would our reunion be of the Stanley and Livingston sort, formal and clipped? Or would it simply be Christopher and Allan, a casual beach reunion of guys and dogs?

Although the Talamanca town of Puerto Viejo on the Caribbean side was catercorner to the Pacific's northern frontier—I would have to traverse both the length and breadth of the country to get there—it was no more than 12 hours of driving time from where I sat, and suddenly, after half a year of dawdling, I felt a pang of impatience to get on with it.

One way or another, instinct told me, my journey was likely coming to an end.

But not so fast. My next big, unexpected problem waited a few hundred yards from the beach. Rounding a sharp bend, I stopped the rig short, and a feeling of dizzying unreality swept over me, as if I'd suddenly found that the rest of Nicaragua had dropped into a bottomless void and I was looking down not at a track through jungly terra firma I remembered from the day before, but at blue sky and feathery cumuli in the abyss beneath me.

Goddammit, I was thinking, this was supposed to happen in Mexico.

Then came fear, engendered not only by the inescapable logic of the situation, but by the many warnings I'd been subjected to about the m.o. of road bandits Down South. Staring at a tree stretched across my path, I numbly awaited the inevitable, completely unable, for the moment, to come up with a course of action.

Well, now wait . . . maybe the tree just fell there, trees do fall in the forest all on their own, with no one around—there's even a saying of some sort about that.

No, uh-huh, one in a thousand that a big healthy hardwood 'd come down over a 24-hour span and after a clear, windless night and just happen to topple onto the road and around a sharp, blind bend at that. And check out those fresh axe-bite marks on the trunk . . .

All right, here they came, materializing like a magician's nasty jungle trick. There, the smaller guy in ragtag nondescript, and over there, the tall, rangy one in drab green. Tall and Rangy was the guy from last night, no question. But no guns, that's a positive; just machetes, hanging loose and casual by their sides.

The question was, *What now?*

How about . . . maybe bolting, throwing the Ford into reverse and jamming back . . . back where? The beach was hemmed north and south by rocky points.

No, wrong, mistake . . .

How about . . .

Shut up, Shiner! I'm trying to think!

My two new friends were standing there immobile, 20 or so yards from the rig, artfully positioned and somehow unreal, like wax figures in a museum exhibit of jungle predators. Trying to shake me up, right, boys? Give me a minute to think about all this . . . or maybe, just maybe they're also unsure of their next move.

"*Que suerte!*" What luck! I blurted after piling out of the rig with a loopy, coat hanger-stuck-in-the-mouth grin. "I sure need help here," I continued in fractured Spanish, trying my best to conceal my rattled faculties and the jalapeño spray in my clinched, sweaty fist. If things didn't go real well from the get-go, these sumbitches were gonna get treated to a facial, *muy pronto, sabes tú?* Then maybe a cranial hello from the fish billy under the seat.

"Tengo un problema," I rambled on. And the problem is . . . that I have to get to the bank in Managua before it closes today. To . . . to get money on my credit card, mi tarjeta de crédito. All I have is 20 dollars, U.S., but you can have it if you help me with the tree. "Por favor, es una emergencia."

Whaddya say, fellas? I was thinking, 20 guaranteed bucks, no worries or repercussions, and if you believe my farfetched rap, that's all you'd get anyway. (I in fact had a couple grand cash money well-stashed in La Casita.) Maybe they wanted everything, all my worldly possessions, along with the truck and little house to cram their tatterdemalion families into, but I was betting that these guys weren't pros—their lack of firepower would indicate that—and really didn't want to deal with either a dead *norte* or one on the run to the authorities with tales of *bandidos* in the bush.

Tall and Rangy thought about it while the other guy looked to him for the decision. If I have to use the pepper juice, I was thinking, I'll let Shiner out of the truck while I go for the billy under the seat and they're stumbling around blind and disoriented. I stayed close by the truck door, as if at any moment I'd throw it open and let my snarling dog have her way, although I had no intention of doing so except in the direst of eventualities. Her inch-and-a-half canines would be no match for two 3-foot-long razor blades unless the wielders were first incapacitated.

Tall and Rangy nodded. It was as easy as that. He and his buddy melted back into the bush for a few seconds, then reappeared with axes and went right to work. The transparency of their scam was of course laughable, but I stayed in character, maintaining my demeanor as the hapless *norte*, grateful for the miraculous appearance of these folksy *campesinos*.

The work took maybe an hour. Then, having forked over the U.S. 20, I was rumbling up the jungle track, profoundly relieved yet wondering if I could've gotten out of there with an outlay of, say, 10 bucks. Maybe those characters had never intended to do me physical harm. Possibly all along their plan was to simply extort a sort of toll, via the clearing of the road.

But when confronted by a tree across your path and flanked by machete-wielding *malvados* in the deep bush of Central America, penuriousness would seem to lie in the far distance on the behavioral spectrum from prudence, or even simple sanity.

13.

Four hours later I was in Costa Rica, parked on a dirt turn-out on Central America Route 1, contemplating the Tamarindo turnoff, thinking about that call to my buddy Joe. Thinking about Robert August, who was apparently down at the end of this road.

August was in his mid-fifties now. Maybe the *Endless Summer* image I've always had of him—carrying his big old longboard toward a virgin surf break in Tahiti in 1963, proclaiming to a bevy of lithe, obviously smitten local beauties in a high-pitched, barely postpubescent sing-song that the flower behind his left ear indicates "I'm not married!"—was best left unupdated.

On the other hand . . .

Empty road . . . another crossroad . . . turn west or continue on south?

You're on the coast road to Puerto Viejo now, just below the port town of Limón on the blue Caribbean. Negotiating a narrow, rail-less cement bridge over a swirling brown river like café con leche stirred by a huge invisible spoon, you dig out the tape your surfing DJ buddy Conrad made for you years ago and a wave of nostalgia sweeps you 800 nautical miles east to the island of Tobago as Calypsonian David Rudder asks

Can you hear a distant drum,
Bouncing on the laughter of a melo-dee?
And if you hear it, come come come,

It calls so sweetly, like a symphonee!
. . . Calyp-sooo . . .
. . . Calypso Muuuu-sic!

And now lush, low-lying banana groves and neat rows of nut palms of long-gone copra plantations cast into shade the loamy fringes of trackless white beaches; and scattered hutches of pink-like-conch-recesses and aquamarine-like-shoal-water-over-sand jounce by left and right; and Big Blue turns impossibly bluer in radiant patches as low, cottony trade wind clouds part and the sun bursts through. This right here could be Tobago, that other home you've abandoned for the road life Down South.

Long, rough road, you're thinking, as you stop dead with all four wheels in potholes of varying depths to let your little traveling house settle down in its athwartships roll, back and forth, back and forth, like a tender yacht wallowing in a quartering sea. And then up the furrowed track another bridge looms, rust-flaked steel and narrower and ricketier than the last. You watch as the first traffic since Puerto Limón crosses that bridge and you imagine its unsupported span buckling under the weight of the load: a sleepy mulatto in a straw hat atop a swaybacked, bony gray horse the color of the flotsamy river beneath the animal's clop-clopping hooves. The horse and man glide on by and a wary eye peers birdlike as the hat tilts up.

You inch forward and the clash of falling dishes in the back makes you wince and then curse the diabolically arranged ruts and rents and fissures and craters of this moonscape passage, the likes of which you haven't seen since the worst of off-road Baja; then rounding an axle-busting curve you pull up your creaking, grumbling rig, thinking No this can't be right; they, whoever They are, can't be thinking you're nuts enough to cross this bridge. So you pull out your limp, pawed-over map and down in the far southeastern corner verify that the thin red line you're on indeed terminates at the dot labeled Puerto Viejo, Talamanca, with the blank, unmapped jungle wildness of Panama then Colombia beyond. Christopher is no doubt still here, you're thinking, he'd have to cross this bridge to get back out, then AAAHHHH-UUU-UUUUUH! a monstrous horn blares, dopplering through your skull, and a huge blue bus packed with blurry faces hurtles past at 40 mph minimum and choogles casually over that bridge like it was cruising Fifth Avenue.

Well that was nuts.

Two bridges later, and mystified that every river on the Talamanca coast has its own unique cast—cafes of various flavors to horsey grays to lime greens to sangre reds—flowing into the cerulean offshore, creating new and unnamable hues there in the shore break mix, you wonder further what sort of magic mottled lost land lies in the jungle upstream that its discharged detritus could create that varied palette.

"Puerto Viejo 6 ks," the sign says.

The pavement gives up to a jarring washboard and you find you've slowed to a creep to keep your house and your fillings in place; then as the next sign way further down this carnival ride from hell repeats mockingly, "Puerto Viejo 6 ks," you cackle at the metaphor of the Unreachable End of the Road, already having secreted the Many Bridges to Cross beauty for later contemplation.

Now, past the sweep of a coal-black beach juts a palmy point with scattered habitations a couple miles to the south. You accelerate down that last stretch with a queasy gut then pull up short at the last bridge: though solid cement over a mere trickle from the dense inland bush, you're thinking how perversely fitting would be its collapse under the weight of the load you've carried behind you for so many weeks, months, miles, kilometers, now that you're within whispering distance of the edge of the town at the end of the road.

14.

As I crossed that last bridge my thoughts were of the lightest, airiest sort, as if I were trying to stretch an iffy toes-over noseride one more section down the line. To my ridiculous relief, the sturdy span held without incident.

I bore quickly left to stay on the waterfront, though the straighter route revealed what I took to be the meat of the town—a lushly variegated succession of one- and two-story, motley-hued wooden structures ending a few hundred yards further on at a cluster of palms, with a hint of the blue Caribbean beyond; the curvy coast must sweep back west from the jutting point at the town's north boundary.

The thoroughfare was ungraded dirt, barely a lane and a half narrow and trafficless, with little of permanent construction on the seaward side, and the waterfront saloons, shops and *cabina*/hotels to landward a quaint mélange of sun-faded pastels. I paused adjacent to an old wooden two-story edifice. Lolling on an elevated porch was a sprinkling of sunburnt itinerants with knapsacks and a pair of suspiciously surfy-looking dudes, brews in hand.

Thus reminded, I squinted seaward for a wave check. I'd seen nothing to get excited about while negotiating the road south from Limón and the conditions off the town were likewise small and dismal, although there were encouragingly mottled, shadowy shades of pale aquamarine offshore. The barrier reef that formed a placid inshore lagoon off Puerto Viejo was obviously rich in the irregularities of depth that would sculpt breaking waves to ridable shape when a groundswell arrived from the expanse of blue to the east. Where exactly out there would peak the *serious* wave promised by Tim

From San Clemente I could only guess, the variables that create the phenomenon being so complex as to border on the preternatural.

As I rumbled on, my little traveling house was getting extended once-overs from what I gradually came to realize was a predominantly black local population. Arriving at an intersection with the straight stretch I'd eschewed for the continuing water view of the coastal track, I came upon a quaint little common with hippie types of various shades of skin color and degree of dishevelment selling arts and crafts by a palm and almond tree-shaded strand. Beached *lanchas* and a rustic cantina rounded out an altogether charming tableau of a sleepy but not comatose little Down South seaside hamlet. I liked the look of Puerto Viejo.

I was soon forced to pull up to avoid running down a nondescript hound that had settled in the dust for a spirited bout of scratching. (Dogs in the road and oblivious to or contemptuous of vehicular traffic are always a good sign, I reflected.) While Shiner perked and whined, leaning precariously out the window for a better view of the bedraggled pooch's style of flea dispersal, I accosted a passing black fellow of Rastafarian affectations—hangin' dreads, B. Marley t, badass Walkin'-Down-the-Road-with-a-Pistol-in-Your-Waist, Johnny-You're-Too-Bad, gait—and told him, "Busco un amigo que se llama Christopher."

"Mon, If you be lookin' fo' Christopher," he replied in the mellifluous inflection I'd come to know so well from the islands to the east, "you go up dot way to de Hogfish Ronch." He briefly raised a long, bony finger to indicate a dirt track that ran inland toward the towering fringe of the rain forest some quarter mile to the west.

Pulling a tight turn, I left the water behind and proceeded as directed.

Hogfish Ranch. The obvious influence of Peter Beard at work. His Kenya retreat, where Christopher had stayed back in the '80s, was known as Hog Ranch, for the wild warthogs that ran rampant on the property.

Idling my way inland, I came across nothing resembling a ranch. I pulled up by an elderly black woman in a full-length flower print dress that made me blink and thick glasses that made her eyes look large and surprised.

Leaning past Shiner, I called out to her in English if she knew where the Hogfish Ranch was.

"Christopher livin' ovah dot way," she replied with a sweeping gesture to the right. Negotiating another tight turn, I was thinking how simultaneously disorienting and comforting it was to find this enclave of the Caribbean culture I'd come to know and love, deep down in Central America. I also found it comforting that Christopher was not only here, but obviously well known. This would no doubt be to my advantage in shortcutting acceptance by the locals, both on shore and in the surf lineup.

But meanwhile, still no ranch, Hogfish or otherwise, just a few clatter-shacks of less meticulous attendance than those more to seaward, their yards a dense panic of vegetation gone back to its jungle state. The road, too, had deteriorated, to barely one rutty lane. I'd reached the inland terminus of the town; up the steep sloping hillside above me loomed the Tarzan country of deep, primary-growth rain forest.

By now long used to the inexactitude of direction-givers Down South, I stopped at the next intersection to await a subsequent passerby, for some still further zeroing in on Captain Zero.

The face that almost immediately appeared in my window was an affable one, if a bit cadaverous, and the fellow's smile looked familiar. Then it struck me. The guy looked much like an older version of Christopher.

But it had been going on six years and it was of course Christopher his very own self, grinning that conspiratorial thick-as-thieves Christopher grin, yet stupefied beyond utterance at my sudden appearance.

Even as I sprang from the rig for a giggly embrace, I was reflecting that my old friend didn't look all that well. A pasty glaze glistened under his pink tropical sheen and his naked-to-the-waist frame seemed to have shrunk from the leanness of yore to wizened. His face angled acutely from a wispy pate to almost a point at the chin, with brow, cavernous orb sockets, cheekbones and jawline starkly etched, as if skin and flesh and sinew had been peeled away and the exposed head bone beneath given an impromptu paint swabbing.

But in the heat of the moment Christopher and I merely backslapped and laughed and Shiner bounded from the rig into the midst of a tail-wagging, butt-sniffing frenzy of dogs. Sweetpea and Jumbie were safe and sound, although Jumbie'd lost an eye to some Central American adventure and looked quite the dashing canine corsair.

"Allan, Allan, Allan," Christopher said in head-shaking wonderment and, I fancied—or was it just a play of the harsh midday light?—a moistening about the eyes. "It's really you, isn't it?"

"Lock, stock and fuckin'-A barrel."

As we stood there, having backed up a step, the better to take in the overall view, my overriding emotion was one of relief that I'd actually made it here in one piece. It had been such a long way for both of us to have come to meet on this dusty little Down South intersection, this little X on the world map.

Christopher broke the silence with a sigh, then uttered the words that, for complex and conflicting reasons, would come back to haunt me. "God sent you to me, Allan," he said with a beatific smile. "Everything's going to be all right now."

PART 3

The Town at the End of the Road

My plan, so far as I have one, is to go through Mexico to one of the Central American ports . . . Naturally, it is possible—even probable—that I shall not return. These be "strange countries," in which things happen; that is why I am going.

AMBROSE BIERCE

Bierce disappeared without a trace somewhere Down South in 1913.

He had come to a place of great beauty but it had taken the waves and the act of riding them to grant him communion.

KEM NUNN, from *The Dogs of Winter*

/.

"I'm smoking crack these days," were the next few words Christopher spoke to me upon our reunion, after saying that God had sent me to him, and that everything would be all right now.

I stood there looking at him and the silence wore on.

"We're going to make millions," he said then, as if the gobs of coming money were a corollary to, a result of, the fact that he was smoking crack.

"We'll have to put a stop to that," I said, in reference to the crack smoking.

But we were on different wavelengths now. "It's all about my Hogfish Philosophy."

Hogfish Philosophy?

"You were the last of everybody I figured'd show up here," Christopher said as we rumbled down the dirt track toward the beach, with six dogs, Shiner plus Christopher's pack, trotting behind.

"Really. Why?"

"You? Mister Hollywood? What would you be doing here?"

Mister Hollywood? Notwithstanding my relatively modest successes in the screen trade, "Mister Hollywood" was definitely not how I'd ever thought of myself. In fact, if anything, quite the opposite. I'd always considered myself an outlander on that coast. "Well, buddy," I said, "Hollywood done ran me out of town. So here I am."

"You still got your connections there, I bet," Christopher said as we pulled up to the polished hardwood facade of the Puerto Viejo Hotel.

"Who cares?" Even with the money I still had coming in from screenplay options and TV residuals, that part of my life was the last thing I wanted to think about.

As it turned out, Christopher cared. Sitting in the hotel's rustic little eatery sipping some much-needed *café con leche*, I listened with feigned interest as he rambled on about what he called his Hogfish Philosophy, which he said would form the basis of a full-length animated feature film that would not only make us millions, but very likely change the world as we know it.

"Show me Hogfish Ranch," I interrupted, mainly to change the subject.

I'd gone right by the place in my initial search for Christopher. It was the most run-down of the shacks on the track that formed the inland border of the town. Suspended over a rickety, cockeyed little gate was a rough-cut, oblong chunk of hardwood, upon which was emblazoned a grotesquely surreal but not unamusing pig's head, the body trailing behind that of a fish. *"Hogfish Ranch"* proclaimed a flourished, fading legend. Tendrils of jungle vine and a maze of creepers had wound around the gate supports and were reaching upward toward the weather-beaten artwork as if straining to snatch it. My initial impression of Hogfish Ranch was that it was on the verge of assimilation by the jungle itself. But perhaps, once I crossed the threshold, the grounds out back would open up to reveal the surf camp Bob Rotherham had mentioned: a sprawl of *cabinas* or platformed tents, surfboards scattered about, shaggy dudes swaying in shaded hammocks, poised for the arrival of a groundswell that would set the offshore reef to cracking with that object of great desire, the heralded but currently elusive serious wave of the Talamanca coast.

"All right," I muttered at my first look at the interior of Christopher's abode. "Wow." I mean what *do* you say when after nearly six years an old friend proudly displays his digs, apparently unaware that it's a filthy hovel reeking of cat piss and foul bedding, with a pair of ratty, askew chairs as the only appointments, the hanging and wall decor a zoomorphically motile disarrangement of darting mini-saurians along with fist-sized arachnids and their flossy nets.

I stepped to the back door and surveyed the grounds of Hogfish Ranch. A lawn of some long-gone era was a waist-high tangle of underbrush and rotting vegetation. Dead leaves, thin and brown as old parchment, hung limp and forlorn from a cluster of untended banana trees.

The air inside was heavy and fetid; not a breath was stirring. "You have a fan we can fire up?"

"No electricity at the moment. The bank fucked me up over the bill."

I scanned the shack for surfsticks but there were none to speak of, just a lime-green old monstrosity in the eaves overhead; a virtually unridable relic, jaggedly dinged and filigreed with cobwebs.

"Where're your surfboards?" I asked. "The Brewer."

"Don't have one right now."

"What do you mean?"

"I mean I don't have one."

"Where's the Brewer?"

"Sold it a few months ago."

"Wait . . . You haven't had a surfboard for a *few months?*"

I still hadn't gotten the picture.

2.

I spent my first night in Puerto Viejo parked in front of Hogfish Ranch, retiring early after dinner with Christopher, who, in a state of edgy impatience bolted from the restaurant (I still had food on my plate) with the words "I'm a man on a mission," after hitting me up for five thousand *colones* (about $15) and assuming I'd pick up the check, which I did. The mission he was on, I suspected—no, I *knew*—was to score crack.

Odd thing was, although we had both occasionally done cocaine recreationally back in our pot smuggling days, it had been Christopher who was the more temperate in consumption. In fact, he'd often abstain altogether and retire for the night, while I, and the party, roared on.

Over dinner, I had tried to sound him out on the evolution of this apparent change in attitude and habits, but he'd waved me off, saying he'd rather not discuss it, adding with an odd finality that *he'd learned a lot about himself through crack cocaine.* When he then asked to borrow money, it occurred to me that the reason he had, upon our reunion, almost instantly brought up the fact that he was smoking the stuff was that he was hoping I'd suggest an immediate buy; he was broke and looking for a toke. When I failed to take the hint, the subject was no longer of any interest. The depressing point was that his first thought, the very first thing that occurred to him, when I'd finally tracked him down after well over half a year of searching, was, *here's someone who can finance my next high.*

The one thing I knew for sure about the situation was that I had to somehow help. It was with this thought that I finally drifted off into fitful sleep, somewhere around midnight.

Chaos commenced about 4 A.M., when two girls, one whom I'd met through Christopher that afternoon—a slinky *gringa* named Wanda—began pounding on his door and yelling for Christopher to come out. The pair banged and blabbered incessantly for a good half hour, unable to grasp the obvious fact that no one was home.

Christopher finally pulled up, riding shotgun in a vintage Dodge ragtop. The driver was a scraggly fellow with shoulder-length hair and one leg; he was shirtless and his slug-pale skin was bedecked with a swirling mass of tattoos. The tattered cuff of his vacant pant leg dragged the ground as he hopped sprightly toward the gate, using his crutch to keep himself upright and on course. Through my back window, I watched as all four entered Christopher's shack.

The edgy cackling of a crack party began as first light spread its soft, clement blush over the high reaches of the rain forest above the road, although the coastal plain upon which sprawled the town remained in deep, lugubrious gloom until dawn itself.

"You a friend of Christopher?"

It was about 9 A.M. and I was sitting on my back-door stoop sipping coffee and yawning when the kid appeared. Diminutive, fragile, with a wide, open face and astonishingly long eyelashes, he looked to be seven or eight years old. A local kid, a black kid.

"Yes," I said. "I've known Christopher a long time."

"You shouldn't be stayin' heah at night." He looked over at Hogfish Ranch; it had been quiet in there for an hour or so. The crack had run out, I assumed, and the party had deteriorated to a squirmy group jones.

"Why not?"

"De stone men come at night," he said. "Dey steal, mebbe killin' your dog."

Pieces of crack are called stones. Stone men. Crack addicts. "How do you know this?"

He pointed up the street. "I livin' dere. I see dem at night."

"What's your name?"

"Werner. But Christopher callin' me Kiko."

"Is Christopher a stone man, Werner?"

Werner's direct gaze wavered in discomfiture. "Christopher my bes' frien'," he said.

Werner was right; I had to find another place to stay. Aside from his warning about theft and possible violence, there were bound to be replays of last night's obstreperous debauch and I'd been having trouble sleeping lately as it was. And anyway, I needed the perspective of an ocean view campsite. I fired up the rig and headed for the beach.

"Dónde está la ola seriosa de cual he oido aqui?" I asked Andrés Sánches, the proprietor of a little nest of oceanfront *cabinas* on main street. Where's the serious wave I've heard about here? Andres was in his mid-twenties, an expat surfer from Barcelona, Spain. There was a little niche by his row of *cabinas* into which my rig would fit perfectly. It was fenced and shaded, and water and plug-in electric were handy.

Andrés pointed straight offshore to the outer reef. "Es Salsa Brava," he said. *Salsa Brava.* Brave Sauce. A good name for a surf break. I'd have a direct, if distant, view of it from La Casita for the dawn patrol checkout. I made a monthly deal, pulled in, and told Shiner to get comfortable. This would be it for a while.

I liked this place I'd come to, for its physical beauty, its remoteness and the easy feel of it. If only a wave would appear on the dormant outside reef, maybe, just maybe, I'd stumbled upon my little piece of paradise.

3.

A call to Denise was the last of a flurry I'd finally gotten around to making, from a little communications center off main street. I'd first called my mom, then Joe, then Tony C, the mutual friend of Christopher's and mine who'd rekindled my interest in longboarding a decade earlier and who owned a surf shop back at Montauk. I'd wanted to discuss Christopher's current situation with him. These three, plus Denise, were the last of the remaining connections I wanted to maintain with my old life.

"I've been so worried, Allan," Denise was saying. "When I didn't hear from you for so long . . . I didn't know what to think." I'd heard that quavery edge in her voice before; she was holding back tears. "It's been over a month. Are you all right? Allan?"

"I tried calling from Nicaragua, but you weren't home."

"I'm sorry." She was crying now, but trying to conceal it. I could picture the tears welling up in her eyes and then spilling over and running down her cheeks. She would be gamely trying to control herself.

"Don't be sorry," I said. "And please don't cry."

"I'm not."

"It's so hard finding a phone down here."

"Do you love me, Allan?"

I told her I did, and it was true. I also wanted to tell her that she should go ahead and live her life, that there was no future with me, in me. But I didn't.

I had abandoned her and my fear was that she would abandon me.

. . .

Shiner and I hoofed it back to the rig to find Christopher and Werner waiting by my back door. "Thought we'd drop by and see what you have cookin' for dinner," Christopher said.

"A bunch of leftover spaghetti," I said. "Should be enough."

The three of us sat at the settee, Christopher and I on the ends, Werner in the middle. The settee table came up to about his chin. Turned out that Werner was 10; he was small for his age.

I put on a Mozart tape, then served. Although Werner had never heard classical music before, he began conducting, waving both arms in very close rhythm with the symphony. After a bit, he seemed to anticipate where Mozart was going; he wasn't reacting, he was flowing.

As I was about to dig in, Werner lowered his hands and folded them on the table: "Wait! We mus' be sayin' grace." He shot me an exasperated look, then closed his eyes, blessed the table, blessed Christopher and me and thanked God for everything.

I spoke mostly to Werner, asking about his family and school and so forth. His responses were articulate and lively. "You speak Spanish, too, right?" I asked him.

"Sí, por supuesto."

"And patois?" The patois of Talamanca is an amalgam of English, Spanish and various African dialects, thereby reflecting the multicultural background of the locals: the English of the era of slavery on the islands to the east (mostly Jamaica), the Spanish of Costa Rica and the African of their genetic roots.

Werner nodded, shoveled in the spaghetti.

"Tri-lingual. Not bad." I turned to Christopher. "Y tu debes hablar español muy bien después de seis años aquí."

"Huh?"

"Your Spanish must be pretty good after six years here." Christopher had always let me do the talking when Spanish was called for during our smuggling days, but I figured that now, having lived in Central America for so long, he'd mastered the language.

"I get by."

As I would realize over time, Christopher spoke almost no Spanish at all.

Werner finished his meal and asked if he could be excused; he had to get home. When I said "Sure," he started clearing the table, saying, "I clean dee dishes firs'."

"No no," I said. "Leave 'em, but thanks for the offer."

Werner thanked me for the food and left.

"What a great kid," I said.

"Sure is."

"He told me you're his best friend."

Christopher nodded.

"So listen," I said, getting serious. "I spoke to Tony a little while ago."

"Yeah?"

"I told him basically what's going on down here with you and we both agreed that you should go back up north for the summer."

Christopher laughed.

"Look. He'll fix you up with a place to stay and a summer job. You could come back here in the fall with at least five thousand dollars. With that kind of money you could really fix your place up, maybe build some *cabinas,* properly launch Hogfish Adventure Tours (he'd been talking about this). But mainly, you'll never kick this crack problem down here."

Christopher's eyes were bright with amusement at my charming but misguided naiveté.

"I'll spring for your plane ticket."

"Do you really think I'd go back there, anywhere, to *work?*"

"Just for the summer, then—"

"My life is fine here."

"You're a dead-broke crackhead, Christopher, goddammit."

"That's what you see."

"What else is there to see?"

"I'm well loved here." This particular notion would turn out to be the blindest of Christopher's many denials.

"Really? By who?"

"The local people, and the other *nortes* that live here."

"You know Mister Patterson?" He was my neighbor across Andrés Sánches's fence. A neat old local guy I'd chatted with the day before.

"Sure. We're close friends."

"He told me that crack is destroying this town. Ruining the young people. Making thieves and liars of them."

Christopher shrugged.

"I asked him about you." My voice was getting shaky with anger. "He said you are part of the problem. Part of the problem that is destroying the place he's lived for sixty years. The man does not like you."

Christopher shook his head. "You've been here a few days. You don't know anything about me. Talk to Miss Sam or Miss Dolly about me. The matriarchs."

"Okay, Christopher," I said. "You come, too."

The following afternoon, Miss Dolly squinted at Christopher from the porch of her well-kept cottage across from the Puerto Viejo Hotel as we walked up. Christopher greeted her effusively, like a favorite aunt. Miss Dolly was a wise and kind old woman, Christopher had told me. She would sit on the Hogfish Council when the world saw the wisdom of the Hogfish Way, its deep regard for children and their salubrious upbringing; its respect for the elderly; the world as benevolent extended family.

As Christopher introduced me, Miss Dolly glared at him, eyes burning angry and intent from the pulpit of her porch steps. She indicated a packet of candles in Christopher's shirt pocket. "What those fo', Christopher?" she exclaimed, "To light dee pipe gonna send your soul to hellfire?"

4.

The banging became part of my dream—a squirrelly, nonsensical montage—shaping it until someone, somewhere was banging and banging and banging and calling out my name.

I awoke with that hollow, scattered feeling I'd lately found taking control, directing my thoughts in melancholy directions, preventing me from writing or sometimes even talking normally to people. After little more than a week in Talamanca, I'd begun to withdraw from my surroundings, as surface-beautiful as they were.

I was now sitting on my bunk in La Casita and someone was hammering on my back door. Christopher's voice whispering, "Allan. Allan!" His pounding was enough to wake the dead, let alone the insomniac I'd become, yet he found it necessary to whisper. I looked at the clock: just shy of 3 A.M. Although I knew exactly what was going on, when I stepped to the back door, I said, "Whaddyawant, Christopher?"

"I just need a thousand *colones.*"

Even in the feeble ambient light, Christopher was a sight. Having retreated to the depths of their sockets, his eyes were nevertheless so wide and unblinking as to appear lidless. His lower jaw moved side to side on its own, as if it had come unhinged from the glistening dome of his shiny pink skull, and I could plainly hear his molars grinding from two yards away.

Damn, I was thinking, he looked just like the Crypt Keeper. "Let me guess," I said. "You've run out of crack and need another hit or two."

"Listen," Christopher said, but since his lower jaw had clamped to the upper to arrest the sideways grinding, it sounded like "Lisshen." "There'sshh a woman involved." He'd stretched out the "o" in "involved" to an elongated "aahhh" and canted his head to one side, peering at me askance. Like some Groucho Marx from hell, he hoisted his eyebrows as an indication that salacious doings were afoot.

"I've been having trouble sleeping, Christopher. I told you that."

Christopher shrugged, and as if it would explain and excuse everything, said, "Crack goessh right to my dick."

"Sounds romantic." I looked around. "Where is she, by the way? Let's have a look at her."

"Come on, Allan. Please."

"Does Werner get to see you like this? You're his best friend, you know. He looks up to you."

"I just need a thousand *colones.*"

"According to the Hogfish Philosophy, children are the most important thing in the world, am I right?" Christopher just stared. "If you want the money, you better answer."

"Yessshh. Children are everything."

"If Werner follows the example of his best friend, which is likely, he'll become like you, won't he?"

"It's his decissshion."

"His what?"

"His . . . decision."

I picked up a thousand *colones* note and extended it out the door. "Don't come around here at night." I said. "Ever again. In fact, I'd prefer not to see you at all for a while."

Christopher, a man on a mission, trotted off.

5.

Two days later the surf came up and by God did I need it, although my oblique angle of view from a burry lava outcropping by the channel was from behind the breaking part of the wave—predominantly a right-hander, it appeared—giving little indication of how big and fast and thick and hollow—in short, how *serious*—were the conditions out there.

The reefs were alive with charging lines of white water, their relentless high hiss underscored by a sonorous boom of green water breaking further outside. A fine mist of rarefied seawater wafted wraithlike over the lagoon and fringes of the town, broken water having been spewed heavenward and dissipated in a vaporous state after its downward collision with the reef. From the glimpses I caught of the drop-ins of a handful of guys already out, the swell was obviously a healthy one, head-high, maybe better. Still, I could not get a sense from where I stood of this wave called Salsa Brava.

The paddle-out was a bit unnerving. Although I'd been assured that the channel was some 30 feet deep and would not break no matter how big the swell, the chop was huge and disorienting, a result of incoming waves clashing with a current flowing seaward from the inshore lagoon. The channel was narrower than it first appeared, a scant five yards separating scabrous volcanic crags between which had formed swirling, sucking vortices; I felt their nasty pull as I stroked for the outside. But the outflowing current was strong—four knots at least—and I was quickly seaward of the channel turbulence and paddling side-shore to the lineup.

The first thing I noticed was that of 11 guys congregated in the takeoff zone, four were wearing helmets. I'd not seen a single helmeted surfer in the whole of my half-year journey along some 4,000 miles of surfable coast, so finding better than a third of those out equipped with head armor gave me contemplative pause. Just what was the problem here, fellas, nogginwise?

There were a few familiar faces bobbing in the lineup, guys I'd seen in town, including Kurt Van Dyke, to whom Christopher had introduced me soon after my arrival. The nephew of big wave legend Fred Van Dyke, Kurt was owner of the Puerto Viejo hotel, which largely catered to visiting surfers. When we first met, Kurt had been, well, curt. As I would soon learn, the theory that my friendship with Christopher would shortcut my acceptance amongst the expat surfers in Puerto Viejo was assbackwards; such was Christopher's negative image. Kurt and I would eventually become friends, but it would be in spite of my history with Christopher, not because of it. As it was, on this, my first Salsa Brava go-out, Kurt vouchsafed me no more than a sour nod when I said "Hi."

This was a tight-knit group, I sensed; my presence was pointedly ignored. The boys were no doubt waiting to see how I'd handle myself out there, both in terms of wave riding élan and in respect owed to those already entrenched: the usual treatment of a new guy. So be it.

The first set was an eye-opener, an adrenaline pumper, a pulse quickener. Angling in from the east, it at first didn't seem like much, a head-high peak with maybe some moderate juice under it. Then, as the lead swell started to feel the drag of the shelving reef, its shoreward progress slowed dramatically. Its energy was not lost, however, only redirected into building height and in concentrating volume. (It is in fact this deceleration of a wave as it approaches shore that causes it to break. The front part reaches shallow water first and therefore slows first, causing the back part to pile up behind it. The water has nowhere to go but up, increasing the wave's height and the steepness of the face, until the whole shebang disintegrates in a forward pitch. The more precipitous the slowing—in other words, the steeper the shoaling bottom—the more pronounced this effect, and hence the bigger and more powerful the breaking wave.)

Following the pack's lead, I stroked mightily for the outside. All chatter had ceased as the set suddenly loomed then stacked, meticulously arranging itself in ascending height and increasing thickness. Someone picked off the first wave. I got a nice down-the-line view of his takeoff and quickly realized that my head-high estimate was off by about a hundred percent on the under side—and that first wave was the smallest of the set. Charging headlong out of the deep water offshore into the shallows over the reef, the wave at Salsa Brava was doubling up and pitching forward, with the verticalness then concavity of the face coming at the last possible instant before Big Blue turned herself inside out in a booming, rip-roaring, top-to-bottom, full-blown stand-up barrel the likes of which I hadn't seen since Backdoor Pipeline in Hawaii, when I was considerably younger and a whole helluva lot more out of my mind than this.

Imagine a 50-pound child doing a 40-yard dash. Imagine that under the tape at the finish line some twisted practical joker has loosely strung a big rubber band at ankle level. The kid hits the rubber, keeps going for a bit, then trips and falls forward. Not much weight behind him, plus he wasn't moving very fast to start with; and the stretching rubber has allowed him to slow down further before he falls. This is a small wave, "tripped" by a gradually sloping bottom. Not too much kinetic energy results from the falling water.

Now imagine a 300-pound-plus NFL lineman—say, William "The Refrigerator" Perry—and imagine that his severely demented teammates have strung a drum-taut piano wire across the finish, again at ankle level. Imagine the violence of the forward pitch of the top of The Fridge's body as his feet stop short but the rest of him doesn't. This is a double-overhead wave at Salsa Brava, tripped by the suddenly shelving reef.

They just kept on coming, each bigger, fatter, steeper, meaner and ornerier than the last, with the takeoff so late that you pretty much just launched yourself over a vertical precipice of avalanching sea—which was just what that second guy was doing now, but I lost sight of him as I pushed myself through the thick, straight-up-and-down feathering lip of his wave and he free-fell into the "pit" behind me. Good luck, pal.

From everyone's mad scramble toward the horizon, this was obviously a "sneaker" set—bigger than expected. Getting caught in the impact zone of one of these beasts would be no laughing matter. I veered off toward the north, making for deeper water, and noticed that a couple other guys were doing likewise . . . Whoa! there was a ballsy move, a turn-and-burn take-off, a last instant spin and launch, very late, the thick curling lip raking the guy's back as he tried to slip in under it. But again I lost sight of him behind me and didn't really give a hoot as to his fortunes anyway. I had my own problems—like deciding whether to take that next loomer or paddle over it.

I looked around. The pack had scattered, some having gotten waves already; others were further outside or down the line this way or that. No one else was in position, so the wave was mine if I wanted it.

My instinct said take it, not only because it was my, well, my *job* out there to take waves, but also out of a measure of fear: Although I could not see it for the blue-green wall bearing down on me, the next wave outside was likely still bigger and may have had designs on unloading on my sphinctering butt—the idea of hurtling shoreward therefore had a certain appeal, in the lesser-of-two-evils sense.

One thing I learned in big waves in Hawaii my younger days is that if you're going to go, go. Don't sort of go, or pretty much go, or halfway go and figure you'll decide later whether you should really go. Just fucking GO.

So I WENT, spun my board toward shore and stroked for all I was worth until I felt myself sharply rising; and then suddenly I was on my feet—a quick and flawless transition to standing is absolutely vital on a wave like this—and for a split second contemplated the view of the 12-foot drop I'd be presently making, like it or not, either standing up or somersaulting, board flying, into the impact zone.

You're pretty much weightless for the first third of the way down on a wave at Salsa Brava, and unable to make adjustments. Pursued by some ridiculous volume of cascading seawater, you stoically just hope for the best until you reach the trough, whence you project yourself in the logical direction—away from the freight-training breaking part of the wave, which, thankfully, you can't see because it's behind you.

I was more or less hoping that my first Salsa wave would be a peak, that is, a drop then a quickly petering shoulder. I could thus sort of break myself in gradually to the bodacious conditions out there. But no such luck. I quickly found myself tearing across a straight-up-and-down wall of ocean that appeared to be on the verge of closing out, dumping across itself in one mighty heave for 40, 50 yards down the line. I was in the correct position (not counting sitting on the beach with a beer in hand), halfway up the wave face or a little better, where the speed lay, so I tucked myself into a crouch and awaited further developments.

Truly, in the few seconds between when I stood up and when the wave folded over me in one gargantuan heave, extinguishing the sight of the thick, almond-shaped eye of the curl way up ahead, I rather enjoyed it. Such is the lunatic nature of an adrenaline high.

My wipeout was a minor one by Salsa Brava standards. Still, I've never been partial to collisions with sharp coral reefs and this one very definitely got my attention.

Human skin is very sensitive to touch and texture, and as my right shoulder and the upper part of my back bounced along the reef, I realized that the sea bottom in the Salsa Brava boneyard was of identical configuration to that jagged lava outcropping I'd gingerly walked out upon to get to the channel. I also knew that the holes and fissures down there were, like the outcropping, bristling with sea urchins. I tumbled shoreward like a load of laundry in a dryer, instinctively protecting my head with my hands and forearms.

I surfaced and checked myself for injuries, noticing that I'd suffered only superficial scratches on my shoulder. The logic behind the helmet phenomenon was now obvious. I'd alighted fairly softly and on a fleshy part of my body, but in the violent, disorienting turbulence I could just as easily have come down hard and on my head. A concussion, unconsciousness and subsequent drowning would then be a possibility, if not a likelihood.

A wave, like any animate entity, has a personality, frequently of some complexity. A break's appellation, which usually surfaces by unremembered, even mysto means, often reflects the dominant trait—the one most easily agreed upon. Salsa Brava. *Brava*. Brave. The other translation to English, depending on context, is *vicious*.

As I reeled in my board (half expecting it to be broken; it wasn't), the exhilaration of the ride faded. With a decision as to whether I should paddle back out my next concern, I suddenly found my stomach doing a bit of fluttering. I'd ridden waves as gnarly as this before, with just as nasty a sea bottom, but that was over a quarter century ago. I was still in good shape, no question. My weight and body fat were about the same as in those days, plus I'd spent a fair percentage of the past seven months in the water, but . . . but . . .

I looked outside to see Kurt Van Dyke tucked into the last and biggest wave of the set, an immense open-ended barrel from which he emerged unscathed onto a wonderfully flat, innocuous shoulder (my wave had no makeable shoulder), his board decelerating from some absurd velocity to a slow plane right in front of me. Falling in beside him for the paddle back out, my voice broke into an embarrassingly high squeak as I yelled, "I want one of those!"

"Go for it, bro," Kurt replied, my enthusiasm for his accomplishment breaking down the first barrier between us. "Sit in the pit and catch a fat one."

I surfed for about two hours that day and rode a dozen or so waves. After conditioning myself to the fact that everything happened exponentially faster than on a "normal" wave (which cost me two more wipeouts, along with the inevitable encounters with the reef), I found my rhythm and had a memorable session, which included two major barrels from which I escaped upright and unscathed, that malicious reef benignly below me.

The tube ride at Salsa Brava was, however, for me, a bit different from that of other breaks I surfed on my southward journey, and for many years before embarking upon it. If the essence of a meditative moment is the suspension of concern with causes and consequences—the past and the future—then my moments were technically flawed. Although causes were of no concern—I did not dwell on how I'd come to be in that remarkable hurtling niche—consequences tended to be. This had not previously been the case—not at, say, Bart's home break, nor even at Puerto Escondido, which I had caught big and mean. Puerto, Mexico's Pipeline, was as hard a breaking wave as Salsa, coming out of deep water onto a shelving, very shallow bottom with which collisions were frequent. But that bottom was sand, not sharp coral. It was the Salsa reef that put the fear of consequences into me. At the very time when my mind should have been devoid of reflection, I would find myself consciously thinking about making the wave. Really, *really* wanting to make it. To some extent this was a failure of spirit on my part, a malfunction in the arena of grace under pressure. My thoughts were a distraction and a source of internal embarrassment.

It was a problem I would work on, I told myself.

6.

On my third day in the water at Salsa Brava, I was late getting into the lineup—I'd had a fitful night—and quickly realized the swell was peaking. The set waves were a good couple feet bigger than the day before and there were a lot more of them.

Kurt was out, lurking deep in the pit at first point to the south of the pack, just outside the swirling boils that mark the shallowest point of that jagged, treacherous sea bottom. The southern lineup point is the real deal at Salsa, where sneaker sets and unmakeable rogue walls make wave selection difficult and critical. I approached from the channel to the south, so my view was back-door—from behind the peak—as Kurt launched himself over the edge of a fat, nasty one, a near mutant. I winced, thinking no way he'll make that, but then he popped out over the shoulder 40, 50 yards down the line with a hoot and both arms raised, indicating he'd been deeply barreled. Kurt was fearless here; he had been surfing Salsa for 10 years. In fact, I found all dozen or so guys I surfed with at Salsa to be pretty much fearless, and skilled way beyond any previous group of regulars at any break I'd encountered on my journey.

For my part, I was able enough—I would get my share of deep tube rides and concomitant hoots from the pack—and I dealt with my apprehensions through conscious suppression: I pretended not to be afraid. The problem with this sort of fear management was that it diverted my concentration and hence my judgment, which at Salsa can be outright dangerous. I'd occasionally not take waves that were perfectly makeable. But on the other hand, and perhaps to offset some previous timidity, I'd sometimes stroke into some malevolent beast, too far back, too late and with near-zero chance of success, in a mental state somewhere between mindless nonchalance and petrified Zen. My last wave this day was of the latter sort, a savage piece of oceanic work that I handled improprietously.

Aside from Kurt, out that morning were Craig From San Diego on his twin-nose thruster (which looked like it should've been hanging under the wing of an F-16), Chris From Florida on a balsa beauty, Mike From Santa Cruz in a blue helmet, Mack From SoCal in a white helmet, and Big Bill From Delaware. Within an hour of my tardy arrival, one by one the rest of the boys, who had been at it since dawn, picked off their last waves and went on in. Suddenly it was just me out there.

Unbelievable. Plunk this wave down on Oahu's North Shore and there'd be 40 young international hotshots all over it, looking to build reps, the beach swarming with surf paparazzi. I still had not gotten used to the idea of this break being uncrowded, that with so many surfers in the area it was just the dozen or so expats and two or three *Ticos* (Costa Ricans) who actually surfed it.

Bobbing solo in the lineup of this world-class wave waiting out a lull, thoughts of Christopher's abysmal descent, along with the failures and fears I'd begun to see as my own life's motif, were displaced by a serene sense of accomplishment. I *had* come this far, via a route few others had the intrepidity to take, let alone solo; I *had* ridden the wave here successfully, having overcome the sort of fear others found insurmountable.

Damn, I was all right, wasn't I?

There *was* something about surfing a wave like Salsa, alone, at some obscure, far-flung corner of the globe, that was . . . significant. Right?

Isn't that what life is all about?

At that moment, Salsa Brava correctly issued a wake-up call to my somnolent, self-congratulatory musings. The set that appeared, angling in from the east as all the serious Salsa sets did, at first seemed simply big, like the others I'd dealt with for the last hour or so. But the one gathering itself out the back, probably the last, was . . . well, it had the look of something else altogether. I could have turned and taken any of the three or four initial waves. Fine, meaty suckers they were, too, but something possessed me to stroke for the outside to see what that last one had on its mind.

When you're paddling a surfboard you're very low to the water, so your view is severely limited. When a wave is in front of you, you see little or nothing of what's behind it. Until I pushed through the steepening lip of that second to last wave, all I had of the last one was a vibe . . .

But holy shit . . .

One instant I was stroking madly up the face of the biggest wave I'd seen on my journey, motivated only by the deep desire of making it to the safety of the other side; then I found I'd spun my board shoreward and done a turn-and-burn that was so late, with the wave so steep, that no paddling was necessary, or indeed, desirable. I was already too far inside for a safe entry, so to paddle further in that direction to gain board speed would only worsen my circumstance.

The problem with a no-paddle takeoff is that you have very little initial forward momentum and must rely strictly on gravity to "drop in" down the face of the wave. Sometimes gravity isn't enough to get you started down before the top of the wave goes concave and with a vengeance pitches itself plus you and your surfboard into the impact zone.

I hung there in the feathering lip of the wave for a period of time that a shoreward witness later described as "forever," unable to force my board down the face, while the wave thickened and steepened and rose up and up past double overhead to near triple, gathering itself like some humongous, oceanic version of Nolan Ryan winding up for the explosion of a fastball delivery.

At a certain point I knew I'd made a serious error in judgment—this wasn't going to work out *at all*. Seeking to get as far from my board as possible (surfboards become deadly projectiles in violent wipeouts), with an adrenaline-assisted standing broad jump I launched myself to the right across the wave face. I skidded on the upwardly rushing wall about halfway down, then plunged into the trough.

With a wave of this size, power and top-to-bottom breaking configuration, it's interesting what happens next in a fuck-up of this magnitude. There is what feels like a long moment of actual tranquility. What's happening is that the wave is fairly gently lifting you up—actually sucking you back seaward a bit—preparatory to throwing you down, along with many tons of churning white water.

I slammed onto the reef with the whole left side of my body from my shoulder to my lower leg, thus distributing the brunt of the impact over a wide area. Still, I believe I lost consciousness—I recall the dull, painless shock of the collision but nothing more until I surfaced, breathless and disoriented. The surrounding swirl of sea seemed canted at an odd angle and I was at a momentary loss as to where I was. My surfboard was within reach, which was good. I definitely needed something to hold onto, to keep me afloat while I hyperventilated to reoxygenate my blood and gather my faculties. I immediately looked to the outside; I was in no condition to bear the brunt of another wall of charging white water and sustain further contact with the reef. To my relief, the expanse of water was all but dead-flat right to the horizon, bereft of energy, as if Big Blue too were catching her breath after some enervating effort.

The paddle to shore is a long one at Salsa Brava. By the time I reached the shallows off main street, I had pretty much recovered from the trauma of the experience, at least mentally. Physically, I wasn't so sure.

Although I didn't sense that any bones had been broken, a dull ache in my left shoulder indicated some serious bruising. My left leg was numb and probably bleeding—upon mounting my board back in the boneyard, I'd noticed a red tinge to the surrounding foam. Thing was, I really didn't want to know how bad the lacerations were. I was squeamishly putting off a visual examination.

As soon as I stood up, the numbness in my left leg dissipated and became a throb. A swollen, purple splotch the size of an apple had bloomed on the fleshy part of my left shoulder. My leg was bleeding all right, but more from a profusion of cuts than from their depth. There were no gaping rents, no cavernous gouges, just numerous ugly scratches and contusions. What did make me wince was the sight of two sea urchin spines protruding from my calf like knitting needles. Still, I had been very lucky—

I'd just experienced my worst wipeout in thirty-some-odd years of globe-trotting surfing and had come out of it relatively unscathed.

There were a half dozen surfers congregated on the waterfront over-looking the break, guys who'd come in prior to the spectacle I'd made of myself with my misconceived over-the-falls-and-onto-the-reef freefall. No one said anything as I approached; then Craig From San Diego, sitting on the hood of his pickup, shook his head. "Dude," he said, "from here that went down in slow motion."

From a distance big waves seem to break slowly, a function of the time it takes for the crest to reach the trough—or, for that matter, a falling body, such as mine.

"Fucking no-paddle takeoff." Craig shook his head again. "And on a longboard. At *Salsa.*" Since my first Salsa go-out I'd been thinking about the equipment I was using, and this incident underscored my misgivings. Salsa was very definitely a shortboard wave. I'd sold my shortboard up at Puerto Escondido.

"Hey, man," Big Bill From Delaware said, "you don't want to fool around on a wave like this."

"I figured I had a shot at making the drop," I said. "Less wind and I prob-ably would have made it." I also probably would have made the drop had I been riding a shortboard. With less surface area to catch the wind flow-ing up the wave face, a shortboard likely would have dropped in before the lip-launch that had sent me flying.

"It was the wave of the day, man," Craig said. "He did the right thing, went for it."

Grunts of assent all around. Even Big Bill nodded.

I very much wanted to make friends with this crew, somehow break through their well-earned elitism. Most of these guys were serious, long-time expats, true Explorers and Homesteaders. They'd given up careers, friends, *lives,* and settled on this wild piece of foreign coast for the wave at Salsa Brava, a move you had to respect, not only for the commitment to a lifestyle it represented, but for the sheer balls it took to surf that wave day in and day out.

Over time, it became obvious that the other thing about the boys at Salsa was that most of them had . . . histories. This was nothing new; I'd run into sundry fugitive types from Baja on down. But there was a subtle intensity about these guys that was different. "There are two types of people who come here," Alan From Maui told me, once we'd gotten friendly, "The 'Wanted' and the unwanted." "If you're going to write about this place, don't use my last name," was a refrain I'd become familiar with. "As a matter of fact, don't use my first name, either," one guy added.

With the one notable exception of Christopher, all the local expat surfers had done well in Talamanca, owned hotels or cabinas or restaurants or farms. No mean feat as immigrants to a poor country with an unfamiliar culture and language. I respected them also for this.

Standing in a spreading pool of my blood, I contemplated how best to capitalize on having gotten the attention of a good portion of the Salsa crew. In theory, it was a perfect moment to shake some hands, maybe extend the surf jive to solidify the inroads I'd made. But calculatingly opting for the casual, no-big-deal approach, I shrugged and looked back out at the reef. "Tell you what," I said, with a commingling of the awe and humility I truly felt as a result of the wipeout. "This is one serious wave you guys have here."

It was the right thing to say and the right way to say it.

Carrying my longboard back to my niche off Main Street, I found myself picturing Christopher's Brewer, that racy little rounded pintail, on the January day in '92 when he came to my house in Montauk to say goodbye. I remembered hefting it for weight and balance, examining its elegant lines, caressing its transitional curves, admiring the symmetry, the art of it.

A perfect Salsa board.

I stopped in front of Andrés's cabinas and sat down on a nut palm stump by a beached *lancha*. Looked out at the distant lineup. It was empty out there now. Salsa continued to crack, a classic hair-raiser going off unmolested.

Christopher. Where was Christopher?

"I haven't had a surfboard in a few months."

My mind roared through the past, a montage of Christopher's fearlessness, his outright lunacies in the water and out.

Surfers can do anything.

What had happened to Christopher?

What had happened *to us?*

7.

I slept late the next morning, right through first light and dawn and beyond. Then, feeling refreshed and rested, I wandered down to the little beach
in front of the *cabinas* to check conditions at the hazy specter of Salsa Brava
on the outer reef.

Although the swell had dropped a bit, it was still booming. The set waves
were well overhead, burnished smooth by a light offshore wind. It occurred
to me how deceiving the wave at Salsa is from the distant, shoreside view.
You truly had to be there, in the pit, to understand.

A fluttering in my stomach indicated what I was thinking about thinking about before I actually thought it: I was thinking about thinking about
going back out. The previous afternoon, while cleaning and patching my
cuts and extracting urchin spines, I'd decided to take a day or two off from
surfing to let my wounds heal. But now I was remembering certain waves
I'd locked into over the past three days.

I've been told that skydiving is scarier the second time than the first, the
reason being that the second time you know from experience what a ridiculous, stupid act jumping out of an airplane really is. It's not just ridiculous
and stupid *in theory.* You've done it, so you *know.* And you also know just
how fearful you're going to be when you get up there and you're in the open
door looking down.

Your fear is now a fear of fear.

Paddling out, I found a full dozen of the boys spread across the lineup.
Most were down at second point, leaving vacant for the moment the

lineup at first point, by which I'd have to paddle to join the group. As luck would have it, a set and myself converged on first point simultaneously; I had only to redirect my stroke shoreward to pick off the best wave of the set. First point, being adjacent to the shallowest spot in the impact zone, is considered the real pit at Salsa Brava, and the wave I took was about as mean and twisted as they came. I handled it well enough to get yodels from a guy paddling out and another in the lineup at second point who had a good view of my takeoff.

No one had been outright hostile to me in the time I'd been surfing Salsa Brava, but neither had any of the crew been solicitous with a word or even eye contact. Today, however, I got grins, waves, nods, thumbs up; one guy I'd never spoken to before stroked over to say, "Heard about your wipeout yesterday. Go for it, man."

But the real revelation came when Craig From San Diego edged over on his twin-nosed speed machine. "Some of us were wondering if you'd show up here again," he said, smiling.

So that was the deal. Flinging yourself into the maw of the beast wasn't enough. You had to go back out for potentially more of the same, presumably the sooner the better. That first wave, from deep in the pit at first point while dripping blood from my wounds of the day before had been the capper. I was now one of the guys at Salsa Brava. I was from then on included in the lineup chatter; chance meetings on the street would result in extended confabulations rather than an offhand nod or monosyllabic grunt. And after a few more sessions, I would be invited to the crew's shoreside gatherings; to their homes.

One thing I quickly came to realize about the boys who rode Salsa Brava was that none of them was involved in the local drug scene. Although joints were smoked and beer-bingeing not unheard of, white drug-taking was shunned. It just wasn't done. This, as much as their dedication to the wave, set these guys apart from the general population of Puerto Viejo. And it set them apart from Christopher.

Christopher had fallen from their ranks.

8.

Don From Orange County was an expat who was building me a new surf-board, one better suited to the wave at Salsa Brava than my longboard. We were in his shaping bay in the basement of his house on the edge of the rain forest. A polyurethane foam blank lay on the rack between us. Within its rough-cut form resided the elegance of a new surfboard. If Don could find it.

I had been hesitant to commit to the commissioning, partly because Don was new to the shaping art; he'd so far built only a dozen boards. There was another problem with Don, however, and I considered it just as serious as his neophyte craftsmanship.

In the three weeks I'd been surfing Salsa Brava, I had never seen Don in the water there. There were other waves to ride along the Talamanca Coast. Waves that did not have the power and speed and the shallow, jagged reef that Salsa had. Waves that were not dangerous, like Salsa. There were many surfers in the area who didn't surf there. This sort of thing is a touchy issue between men, who hangs his ass out and who doesn't. You didn't go on about your day in the water at Salsa Brava with a surfer who didn't surf it; it was bad manners.

But Don was building me a board to be ridden at Salsa—etiquette was no longer an issue and I was within my rights to sound him on his views of the wave. I asked him if he ever surfed Salsa Brava.

"Not for a year and a half," he said, avoiding my eyes. He fired up his power planer and put it to the foam. "I lost my nerve for the place."

9.

Late one afternoon Christopher introduced me to a *norte* I'll call Cranky Bob, who was having a brew down by the waterfront on the northern edge of Puerto Viejo. Christopher claimed that Bob—early sixties, with long, stringy hair, a taut pot belly and spindly legs—was a good friend of his and an interesting character.

As Cranky Bob and I shook hands, Christopher pointed out that all three of us were from New York. Cranky Bob and I had common interests, he added, then bolted, using his "I'm a man on a mission" euphemism for a crack score. Seated at a picnic table on the shore side of Main Street, with beautiful views of the sheltered lagoons to the south and the stunning, curvy sweep of a black-sand beach to the north, Cranky Bob scowled after Christopher as he hoofed it up the road, his pack of dogs trailing behind.

"Useless crackhead, what does he know?" Cranky Bob murmured, but it was unclear whether he was doubting Christopher's assertion that we were all from New York or that Cranky Bob and I had common interests. It was already a given that Christopher's claim of good friendship with Cranky Bob was a delusion. Cranky Bob was yet another in a seemingly endless parade of Christopher's buddies who in reality not only disliked him, but had no compunctions about airing the fact in public.

I asked Cranky Bob how long he'd been in Puerto Viejo.

"A hundred and three days," Cranky Bob said.

"I guess you like it here."

"Hate it. Nothing to do. Crackheads everywhere."

"Then why stay?"

"I'm lookin' for a place to retire to. Figured I'd give it a chance."

The sun hovered over the verdant undulation of the rain forest. An easy trade wind rustled the nut palms along the shore. Cranky Bob drank some beer. Scowled. "How long you planning on staying?" he asked. The query seemed an effort.

"Thinking of leaving soon," I said, although that wasn't true. I hadn't been thinking of leaving at all.

"That's what I keep saying," Cranky Bob replied.

10.

"Look, I don't know what happened to Christopher," Alan From Maui was saying as we waited out a Salsa Brava lull. Alan was the only one of the Salsa crew close to my age; he was, in fact, like Christopher, probably a few years older than me. And like Christopher, he was a Vietnam vet. The two had come to Talamanca at about the same time and for a while were close. "But I can tell you this," Alan went on hesitantly. "Some people come here to die. I know. I've seen it." Alan paddled off, as if he'd said too much, spilled some deep and dark secret. Thing was, what he'd said had already occurred to me, and it frightened me.

11.

I assumed there was no one home at the Hogfish fucking Ranch. True, the top half of the Dutch-type door was open, which generally meant Christopher or one of his reprobate cohorts was in, but I knocked and yelled the usual "Anybody Home!" warning before going inside. I wanted to retrieve the surfboard I'd left for Christopher to use in case he ever got up the constructive energy to get wet.

I scanned the squalid living room. Aside from that lime-green relic in the eaves, not a surfstick to be seen. It must be in one of the two bedrooms. I stuck my head in the first, which was door-less. No, not much here; a mattress, you could grow turnips in the loamy foam; a cat glowering, the reek of its spray.

The other doorway had a sheet hanging from the overhead, white gone to moldy brown and gray. I slipped through with a minimum of contact. My surfboard was there—I was aware of it out the corner of my eye, leaning against the wall—but I found myself staring at the spectacle on the bed and it was like a quick-cut montage from a horror movie in my head, the way I was registering details.

I hadn't seen a pussy in a while, never mind from the sort of gynecological angle I was afforded here, but that very definitely was an example of the phenomenon in all its gaping glory, propped and jutting as if poised to strike.

Just to the north of that dark, furrowed, theoretically fertile copse, along the olive-hued belly of the reposing female to which it belonged, lay what appeared to be a gargantuan slug, such was its oblong shape and deathly white cast, obscenely phallic yet so outsized in proportion as to be beyond fathomable sexual function. Truly, to picture it so employed would be a twisted dabble in the imagery of the blackly occult, of human sacrifice, of certain, horrible death.

And there was a male there, too, or parts of one: a whiskery cheek, a furry ass bedecked with a constellation of pimples, tessellated blue-black patterns on a lean, well-muscled back, a big, grimy foot hanging limply over the bed frame.

Then the beastly slug moved, a shiver of life on the female's inert belly, and by God I was out of there like a shot. Dragging my surfboard out of that house and on down that rutted road at a fair trot, the sweetly nauseating redolence of burnt crack followed me like some bad-ass sylph, and the images returned and shook me up again.

But other details, connective traces, surfaced also. It had been Wanda the Crack Slut and the tattooed fellow with one leg on that bed, and it had been his stump—unrecognized as such—laid across her belly that had given me such a fright.

The realization that my horror had been based on an hallucinogenic misapprehension calmed me, and my lingering revulsion was quickly overlaid by guilt. As for Wanda, I'd caught wind of enough of her ways to feel no conflict in perceiving her as the trash that she was, but the fellow—I'd never met him—thinking of him made me sorrowful. To lose a limb was a trauma and a tragedy beyond my comprehension. Almost as much of a tragedy as to be gone to a cocaine coma in the middle of the afternoon in paradise.

12.

"... What to do? Leave! Yes! Yes! A thousand times yes!"

Christopher had kept a journal of the year he first came south and had given it to me about six weeks into my stay in Talamanca—a thick, leather-bound volume with water stains and yellowed pages and tattered bits of clippings intriguingly peeking out. The idea of journal-keeping, and indeed the motif of adding photographs, doodles, clippings, rubbings and renderings to the daily entries, was another influence of our mutual friend Peter Beard, who first and foremost bills himself a "diarist."

The above entry is from January 19, 1992, three days before Christopher bolted from Montauk. As the words imply, his last days up north were rife with enthusiasm, tempered by just a shade of doubt—as would be mine, five years later.

The next entry is from two days later, January 21. "Stopped by Allan and Diana's" are the opening words.

The 21st of January happens to be my birthday. This—along with the fact that several times over the course of my travels I'd thought about that last time I saw Christopher—resulted in my being beset by a weird, almost queasy, feeling. Christopher's written take on that day was succinct and similar to my recollection:

Showed Allan my new Brewer.

Then, under that:

Allan and Diana arguing so I didn't stay long.

On the next page, which was undated, were these words:

Think the unthinkable
  Imagine the impossible
    Pursue the imagination's limits!

When I read this, I must confess my own imagination took off. I envisioned that the pages that followed would be a cryptic though decipherable chronicle of a good man going wrong, seduced and beguiled by some execrable heart of darkness between the jungle and the sea; all that happy mythical horseshit.

I'd perhaps inevitably come to see Christopher as a sort of cartoon version of Joseph Conrad's Kurtz, with me as the intrepid Marlow, a traveler through strange and hostile lands, come to find the object of his quest a twisted version of the good man, the good friend, he once was, now giving reign to unholy desires, soul ravaged if not extinguished altogether via the pipe that would send it to the oblivion of hellfire.

The reality was that Christopher's 1992 diary disclosed little about his coming decline. On the contrary, his early days on the Talamanca coast revealed an altogether different sort of "man on a mission" than I would discover five years later, that man's mission being one of making a home for himself and becoming part of a community. And the mission of surfing Salsa Brava.

There were sundry little observations about the day-to-day doings of his new life on the Talamanca coast; notes describing the people he met, the marveled exploration of the surrounding rain forest, and so forth, but many of his entries concerned the wave at Salsa. It was eerie how his respect for, fear of, and obsession with, that profound force of nature echoed my own. My impression from his writings was that he had surfed the wave at Salsa that first year even more compulsively than I did when I'd come upon it.

What had happened to Christopher's relationship with that wave? Was the crack abuse a cause or a result of his abandonment of Salsa Brava? Had he lost his nerve for the place, like Don From Orange County, then sought to fill the ensuing rush-vacuum with a chemically induced high? Or had the crack come first, robbing my friend of his wave riding hubris, as it had of his erstwhile mettle?

When I queried him on the chronology, such was Christopher's state of denial that he insisted he still surfed Salsa, on borrowed boards. Yet over the three months I rode that wave and lived within sight of its lineup, I never once saw him in the water there.

According to his journal, in those early months when he wasn't surfing, Christopher worked on his new home, rebuilding, painting, cleaning, landscaping, putting it all right. He wrote of his "eloquent appreciation for the kindness of others" who had helped refurbish the shack, which was evidently a shambled derelict when he moved in.

When I pointed out that he'd let all that good work go to naught by not maintaining his home, his response was, "When I get some money, I'll have girls in to clean, hire some guys for the yard work . . . there's only so much a person can do."

Christopher's journal was gut-wrenching reading, but I saw little of real significance in it, until near the end. The entry for December 16, 1992 reads:

Thinking about Allan, wondering what he's up to. Thinking about the old days, our old quest. Should write him and tell him I found it. IT.

Then, underneath, in bold, calligraphic script:

paradise

13.

I should have known better about this woman with whom I had my first
date in Puerto Viejo: when she walked by my niche off Main Street one
morning, dragging her feet and looking downright disconsolate, and when
I asked her why the chopfallen display on such a fine day, she replied, "Because I'm dead broke."

Mid-thirties, in spite of her apparent financial woes, Karen had a pleasant, if distracted, demeanor—a not unattractive female. We talked for a bit,
then agreed to meet that night at Bamboo, a rustic little cantina on the
waterfront.

Karen showed up at about 11, an hour late. She spotted me at my table
on the patio, waved, then stopped at the bar to talk to a guy I figured to be
German. Then there were a half-dozen other people scattered about she simply *had* to greet and blab with. She flopped down next to me a half-hour
later, breathless and glowy-eyed.

"I guess you've been in Talamanca for a while," I said, referring to her
many goddamn acquaintances.

"I've been here for a couple years," she said. "It's my home. I love it."

"It's truly one of the most physically beautiful places I've ever been," I
said. "But not without its problems."

Karen, as if she were reading my mind, but simultaneously apropos of
nothing, said, "Christopher told me you're a writer."

"You know Christopher, eh?"

"Not very well. We partied one night about a month ago."

Uh-oh. Wait a minute. The words "There's a woman involved" echoed in my head, along with "Crack goes right to my dick."

"You have a late night that night?" I had to be sure.

"Oh, yes," Karen replied breezily. "We hung in there till way past dawn."

I believe I have what amounts to a rheostat connected to my libido, with which women are constantly fiddling, sometimes knowingly, often not. Since her tardy arrival, Karen had been doing a gradual counterclockwise turn with the thing. Now, struck by the image of she and Christopher (looking like the Crypt Keeper) "partying" on my thousand colones, the knob flew off and out of sight, my voltmeter stock-still at dead zero.

The German guy with whom Karen had been talking at the bar soon appeared, cigarette dangling, rum and coke in hand. With his sallow complexion, sweat-stained Banlon shirt, belted polyester pants and gold chain, he looked about as troppo as Nanook of the North.

To my surprise, the guy had come over to talk to me. "So you're a writer," he said in a fairly thick German accent.

I looked at Karen, who nodded and said, "I told him."

I made a mental note to quit telling people that I'm a writer, although it was apparently somewhat too late.

"Are you writing about the ecological problems of the Talamanca coast?" The German's tone had the decided ring of a challenge—like I'd *better* be writing about Talamanca's ecological problems—but I didn't take it as such. It's tough to maintain an even, let alone friendly, tone when you're wired to the gills on cocaine—let alone a German wired on it. The place was buzzing with the shit, I suddenly realized. Everyone was just so bright-eyed and intense.

"So, are you?" The German reiterated. I gazed at him thinking I might wind up having to knock him on his ass after all.

"We have real problems here with the rape of this country," the German added, inhaling deeply on his cigarette. In spite of a fresh sea breeze blowing through the place, a huge bead of sweat hung from the end of his nose, fed by rivulets snaking down his forehead. His twitching jaw muscles, jugular pulse and the vibration of the ice cubes in his highball were in jagged, palpitating syncopation. This guy was cooked.

"No," I said. "I have no interest in ecology." This wasn't true but I said it anyway.

The German shifted his weight from one foot to the other and back again in an apparent search for equilibrium. Then suddenly he was gone to the dance floor, where he was soon moving in perfect rhythm to music I'm sure was playing somewhere.

Now someone was yelling in my ear. Karen. She wanted to tell me about the night she and Christopher partied.

So let me get this straight, Karen. You ran out of crack at about 4 A.M., you and Christopher, right? (I'd given Christopher the 1,000 colones at 3 A.M., I was thinking, so that gibes—up in smoke by 4.) You're desperate now . . . crack gone, no money. I understand. So Christopher did what? . . . Found a gold watch at your place . . . your father's, whom you loved and who committed suicide, and Christopher pawned it for a baggie of stones, just before dawn.

And that was fine with you? Oh, it was actually your idea . . . I see.

And now you feel guilty and want to buy the watch back, is that what I'm hearing? But you're dead broke . . . right . . . you told me that . . . ohhh, I see what you're getting at.

Great, dear, and good luck with *that* quest.

Christ. I tried distracting myself by scanning the joint for a familiar face. Came up empty, except for a local surfer I'd never seen out at Salsa.

Karen again. What? You've licked your drug problem, you just dabble now and then, like that night with Christopher . . . I see.

Dabble, dabble, huh, Karen?

Me? No. I haven't done cocaine in years. Nope, no dabbling for this guy tonight. Sorry to disappoint you.

Gotta rush off so soon? Okay, 'bye Karen.

Lemme out of here.

Walking back to my little niche off Main Street, I recall that the night was clear and balmy, but then again most nights on the Talamanca coast were of that sort, so I could be confusing it with a different clear and balmy night. The palms and almond trees rustled, I'm sure, as they do on such nights, the mix of sea breeze and jungle scents an ambrosia brew in the gentle air, and the lagoon no doubt lapped hushed upon the shore.

Shiner, bless her, was waiting by the back door when I walked up sometime around midnight. I rarely went out at night, but when I did, I'd tell Shiner to stay by La Casita in case of a stone men incursion upon our perimeter. In spite of Werner's warning that they might "be killin' you' dog," I wasn't worried about her. She'd sent more than one of the species hightailing up Main Street after misconceived forays. She had, I was sure, a rep with the stone men of Talamanca.

I unlocked the door, then squatted on the stoop. Shiner sat down, as usual with her rear end on my foot. She does this, I think, to be made aware of any movements I might make, should she drowse or be distracted by her thoughts and otherwise not notice.

Shiner and I were about the same relative age, I reflected. She being ten and I going on fifty, we were both about two-thirds of our way through the bullshit.

I massaged her behind the ears. "It's you and me, babe," I said to her.

14.

Mike From Santa Cruz—he wears a blue helmet at Salsa—had his parents visiting from the states and I was at his house for a sundown drink. High up on the fringe of the rain forest, Mike's property overlooked the town, the inshore lagoons and the blue Caribbean to the east. I'd taken to visiting one or another of my Salsa Brava surfbuddies whenever I could find an excuse, to be around people I could relate to. Mike and I had gotten pretty friendly since my wipeout. Weeks later he'd bring it up, grinning, shaking his head. Dubious, true, but it was my claim to fame, a minor act of local heroism.

"Imagine this," Mike's father Ralph was saying. Ralph was a scientist whose area of study was the phenomenon of sleep, and, peripherally, the nature of consciousness. "Imagine we are able to construct a dream within the mind of a sleeping surfer—a dream of a perfect tube ride." Okay, I was thinking, a big Salsa Brava barrel. I'd had such dreams. "Now imagine we transport him to the reality of that dream. In other words, we are somehow able to physically put him on a wave identical in every detail to the one he is dreaming about. Then, we wake him up. The question is . . . the question is, would he notice the difference? Would he know he'd gone from the sleeping state to the waking?"

"The problem for me in thinking about this," I said, "is that the memory of the dream of a tube ride and the recollection of an actual tube ride are qualitatively the same because they're both memories."

Ralph smiled and nodded as if I'd made his point for him. "I tend to believe the surfer wouldn't know the difference," he said.

"A very Eastern notion for a Western scientist."

"And not verifiable."

"Row, row, row your boat," I intoned

Ralph looked out at the expanse of Big Blue far below. "Life is but a dream."

15.

I was having a beer late one afternoon at the Parquecita cantina when this guy, Gary, pulled up a chair and said, "I think we have a problem with your friend."

"If you mean Christopher," I said with a short laugh, "no shit."

"Looks like he raped my girlfriend."

I was absently watching a new female itinerant with a pair of running shoes hanging from her knapsack browse the trinkets, dope pipes and gimcracks on a dreadlocked dude's table in front of the cantina, but Gary got my attention with this latest bulletin from the edge of the forest primeval. I turned to him and tried to remember who his girlfriend was.

Ah, yes, Wanda the Crack Slut.

Gary and Wanda had descended upon Talamanca together from the states about a year before. Gary sold cheap jewelry, hustled tourists with tarot card readings, and probably did some small-time dealing. Wanda just hustled. Gary was black, by the way, Wanda somewhat less so; she had the olive skin of a local *mestiza*. A pretty girl, but for the cold, rapacious eye of a Dachau dentist on speed.

Across the street, Christopher had just arrived with his canine entourage and was shmoozing a local dealer of more affluent means.

"Have Christopher and Wanda had sex before?" I asked.

"No," Gary said without hesitation and I found myself believing that that was the case.

"When was this supposed to have happened?"

"Last night, at his place."

I had at first had trouble connecting Gary and Wanda probably because I'd never seen them together. I did, however, recall Christopher's remark that when times got tough and the crack ran short, Gary would put Wanda's well-turned little butt out there for the highest or any bidder.

I my-own-self had of course gotten an eyeful of the merchandise. I briefly wondered if Gary was aware of Wanda's tryst with the one-legged, tattooed fellow, if in fact he'd middled it. I would have bet not. I would have bet ol' Wanda had been out there freelancing.

Thing was, I also realized, I had pertinent information about the case. I had seen Wanda and Christopher together that very morning, no more than a few hours after the alleged rape. Listen to me. The *case*. The *alleged* rape. I was starting to sound like my defense attorney buddy Joe.

I'd passed by Hogfish Ranch earlier to find Christopher and Wanda arguing on the porch steps. Wanda was incensed that Christopher had sneaked into the bedroom in which she was unconscious and lifted a crack stone from her stash. Christopher had countered that she'd been smoking *his* stash all night and he was merely trying to balance the scales, as it were. No mention of Christopher having surreptitiously copped some bonus 'tang in the process.

"Wanda accused him, right?" I said. "Is that the deal?"

"Said she woke up this morning all leaky with semen, and Christopher was the only one there."

"She got raped and didn't wake up?"

Gary shrugged. "She'd been partying for a couple days."

Nah. I wasn't buying this.

Gary must've sensed my skepticism. "I just left her. She was all in tears, nearly hysterical."

"Just now, huh?"

"I've never seen her cry before."

A weepy Wanda. It was a tough image to conjure all right.

I told Gary about the scene on the Hogfish Ranch porch, averring that Wanda hadn't seemed upset about any rape. It wasn't logical that suddenly, hours later, she'd gotten all bent about it.

"But I've never seen her cry," Gary repeated, as if, out of all this bizarre shit, that aspect was the most amazing.

"Well," I said, "just go over and confront Christopher, see what he has to say."

Gary nodded, took a breath, then got up and headed for the door. He wasn't a big guy, or a tough guy, and besides, Christopher was his main crack connection. There were considerations to be weighed before accusations were made.

Across the street, Christopher was all wide-eyed with arms spread, talking a streak. Gary was nodding, wanting to believe him, and that his girlfriend had lied.

Just outside the cantina, local kids gamboled on the unpaved, trafficless playground of Main Street, climbing trees in the little common, laughing and frolicking in the shallows of the lagoon. A local fellow in a straw hat and with huge, callused feet was perched on a stump by a cluster of coconuts, opening one with easy swipes of his machete, then drinking the sweet water. A smiling woman in a flower-print dress and turban glided by with a stalk of bananas balanced on her head, holding hands with her barefoot child; a floppy-eared puppy followed behind, trotting to keep up.

Shadows lengthened as the sun dipped low over the cloud forests in the Talamanca Range to the west. Another day would soon be done at the town at the end of the road.

16.

After three false starts, and going on two months after I'd commissioned it, Don From Orange County had finally finished my new board, and although the results were far from what I'd requested, I'd agreed to accept it. Don had been in Talamanca for some four years and like several of the expat surf crew had married a local girl; he now had a young child to support as well. This was partly the reason I'd taken delivery of the board: Don needed the money.

Now we were sitting in the Parquecita having a beer in celebration of the birth of a new surfboard, design flaws and all.

Early on in our friendship, Don had told me about how he came to Talamanca; about his wild and precarious drive south with a fugitive from the law up north. Don's buddy only lasted a few weeks in Puerto Viejo before the DEA caught up with him, swept him off Main Street in his surf trunks. Poof. End of surf guy.

Knowing the how of Don's move to Central America, I now thought to ask him of the why.

"This is one of the last places they'll get to," Don said.

"Who?" I inquired.

"The vanguard of Satan's warriors," he said, in the same laid-back, reasoned tone he'd used to discuss surfboard design.

I stared at Don, giving him time to grin and say "Gotcha!" but his gaze remained level and serious. He picked up his bottle of Pilsen and ran a finger along the edge of the label. "See that bar code?"

I said that I did.

"There's no Mark of the Beast on that bar code yet."

"I'm not following you," I said, but I was starting to get the general idea.

"Six-six-six. The Mark of the Beast," Don explained, ever patient and easygoing. "It's not there. They haven't infiltrated this far south yet."

"What do you mean?" I asked and immediately regretted it. I didn't want to be subjected to any more evidence that this guy I'd known for more than two months and liked very much was in fact out of his mind.

"Up in the states they're already implanting the chips."

Computer-chip implants in the brains of the unsuspecting multitudes, perpetrated by the satanic conspiracy of multinational . . .

Nah. Sayo-fuckin-A-nara, Jack. I was out of there.

17.

Tell you what. Bill Clinton looked older.

I hung up the phone after the fourth ring, before the machine could pick up, stared at the TV. Not only did Clinton look older, but what was the deal with the cane he was hobbling around on?

Aside from sidelong glimpses of soccer matches and dubbed movies from the murky recesses of local bars from Baja on down, I hadn't seen a TV set in nearly eight months. No English newspapers, *Times* or *Newsweeks*, nothing of U.S. or world events. *Nada.* Until now.

I was in San José, Costa Rica, in a hotel room, watching CNN.

I looked at the phone, calculating that it was just after 9 P.M. two time zones eastward. I'd give it another half hour and try again.

I hit the TV mute button and surveyed my 2,412 photographic slides—minus a couple hundred first-edit rejects littering the floor—stacked in accordance with the north-south progress of my journey on the makeshift light box I'd constructed by laying pieces of typing paper on a glass end table and placing a lamp underneath. Two rolls were from all the way up in Baja, my last Sea of Cortez campsite before embarking on the ferry. I'd gotten friendly with some *pescadores* at their remote fish camp. And there they were.

Although I'd kept my exposed film refrigerated whenever possible, I worried about having waited so long to process it. I didn't like the looks of the labs I checked out in Puerto Vallarta and Acapulco, plus the incognizant answers the vacant-eyed technicians had given to some simple questions made me nervous. But these San José people seemed okay, their premises spotless like a clinic, their little white and green Fuji caps.

Sixty-seven rolls here, added to the 40-some-odd from Baja I'd had processed and edited at Cabo San Lucas. What's that? A little more than a hundred rolls. Not much. *National Geographic* photographers will shoot that in a week or less.

One roll, thirty-six minus a half dozen that weren't sharp, was spread on the table. I bent over and put the loupe to one for another look. Denise, her back to a yellow adobe wall by a blue-framed doorway up near Puerto Vallarta. Beyond her model's instinctively perfect posture, the elegant carriage of her head, she seemed thoughtful and sad, looking camera-left down the road.

I bent to a chrome I'd culled from another roll, the candid I'd done at dinner that last night before I put Denise on the plane out of Vallarta and headed south toward Bandido Alley. I'd just told her the story of the *norte* expat and his Mexican wife who were dining across from us; how they'd lived together for 12 years with no common language.

I looked closely at Denise's expression, her eyes.

She was on the verge of tears. I didn't remember that. She'd cried at the airport but . . . no, I didn't remember that.

I did another go-through, flicking the junk onto the floor, making marks on the corners of the selects. Many of my favorites were simple portraits; straightforward, direct. I'd mainly just been there and the people had said yes and the light had been good, the background uncluttered. With certain people, certain shots of a series, there had been that combination of serendipity and connectedness that creates the magic of a good photograph—a story, wordless and open, my interpretation so much blowing in the wind.

I picked up the phone again and dialed direct. Denise picked up on the second ring.

We talked for a while before she told me in so many words that she'd found someone else and was involved with him.

I was silent for a moment then said it was probably for the best, under the circumstances. She asked if I'd found someone else. I said I hadn't. She hoped my life would work out and I'd be happy.

After we hung up I looked at the TV, sound off.

CNN.

Christ. Had all this crap been going on all this time without me? I mean, was it like this *every day?*

Goddammit.

I went back to my editing. I had to finish the work tonight so I could get to a FedEx office early to send the selects back to the states, before my bus left for Talamanca. I wanted my photographs to be safe in case something terrible happened.

18.

"Let's smoke some crack," I said to Christopher around sundown one day in early June, some two and a half months after my arrival in Talamanca. I'd run into him on Main Street and the words had just come out.

"Why?" he wanted to know, though it was clear that the wheels were turning, and the why was irrelevant.

"I'm celebrating," I said, lying through my teeth. Truth was, when not in the water at Salsa Brava, I was in the throes of a deep depression. I had a desperate need to feel better, if only for a few minutes, and I knew cocaine would do this for me.

"Okay," Christopher said. "Gimme some money. I'll come by your place in an hour."

19.

"That's not a gram," I said to Christopher as I dumped the cocaine onto a plate on my settee table and started drawing lines with my Visa card. "That's *maybe* half a gram."

"Really?" Christopher said, cocking his head in surprise. "I don't know what a gram looks like."

Right.

Christopher had brought powdered coke, not crack stones, claiming smoking the shit wasn't as "sociable" as snorting it. Sociable. Truth was, I knew, that not only was it easier to short the weight on powder, but stones could not be cut as this powder undoubtedly was, from the look of it. I wondered if I'd even gotten a quarter gram for my money.

"Where's my change?" A gram of powder was 4,000 *colones,* and that included his middleman profit. I'd given him five.

"I bought dog food with it."

"No, you didn't," I said matter-of-factly as I laid out four thick, two-inch rails. "It's Sunday. The stores are closed."

Christopher shrugged. The lies were along the lines of a formality between us now.

Out of my 5,000 *colones,* and what with his various subterfuges, he'd probably made 3,000. He'd bought some stones with the money, stashed them for later, something like that. Maybe stopped off at the Ranch for a toke—a quick, legitimate rush—on the way here. Plus he was planning on putting half my buy up *his* nose.

I huffed two of the rails then passed the plate to Christopher. Watched as he sucked the shit up through a straw.

I sat back, impatiently waiting to feel better.

20.

"No no no no," I was saying around midnight, tapping the straw on the settee table. "It was '78. It was definitely '78." I bent over and huffed another rail.

Christopher and I were reminiscing about our pot-smuggling days, one-upping each other with tales of lost loads, sunk ships, overloaded antique aircraft landed on altogether the wrong islands by harebrained stoners, the overall hilarity of plans gone awry.

"No no," Christopher insisted. "Was '77, a few months after our run on *The Fucking Boat.*"

We'd gotten word through a Bahamian connection that a plane crash had littered one of the outlying Abacos Cays with loose bales and the locals were having an impromptu tag sale.

"F. Lee Bailey's Grand Banks forty-two."

"It was a Hatteras."

We'd chartered Bailey's yacht out of Lauderdale, using a phony corporate front for what we thought would be an easy overnight run.

"I'll tell you what that deal was."

"Fucking surreal."

We'd gone ashore to find the schoolmistress, the constable, grandma and the kids, everybody on that remote little cay dragging waterlogged bales onto the village common.

"Then it gets tense."

"Remember the fucking *mayor.*"

"What was he, an albino?"

"Yeah. An albino black man."

"Adventures in Paradise meets *Deliverance."*

"The little fucker puts a number on our heads with the local buckaroos."

"Fucking *tense,* is what it got."

I bent for another huff. Passed the coke to Christopher.

"Wait, wait. The time you fell off the roof."

I was back at Montauk in 1972. Christopher had lowered himself off a boarding house roof in an attempt to watch a buddy of ours have at it with his girlfriend in their upstairs bedroom. The rope parted and he'd fallen two stories onto the porch. A lounge chair had broken his fall; he came up unhurt.

"Roland and his girlfriend, buck naked, looking down at you from their window."

Our laugher was high-pitched.

I laid out more lines with my Visa card. "See this?" I said, cackling, referring to the credit card. "The fucker's *burnt."*

"Morocco."

"Omar."

"That time in the Rif Mountains . . ."

"Casablanca. You stole the visa stamp from Immigration."

"Us dispensing fresh visas to the other surfers and scammers."

"The roadblock in Colombia."

"That was a close one."

"It was our *attitude* that got us through."

"The North fucking Shore, sixty-nine."

"The wave that night."

"Biggest ever."

"Summer of seventy-one, Montauk, my friend."

"The prodigal son's return."

And so it went. After nearly three months with hardly a word about our history together having been uttered, we were suddenly obsessed with reliving every moment. At some point I sent Christopher off for more cocaine, nursing the last bit to maintain my head. Not having done the drug in so long, my high was razor-sharp and crystalline, my thoughts heady and giddily optimistic.

I was *fearless.*

And it had always been that way, hadn't it?

21.

Where would I go?

What would I do?

What had my life come to?

First light found me face down, moaning into my pillow in the throes of an abject cocaine crash, and listening to the booming of a new groundswell on the outer reef at Salsa Brava.

I would not surf that wave, this day.

I was just another paralytic cokehead in paradise.

PART 4

Beyond It

. . . for it is my belief no man ever understands his own artful dodges to escape from the grim shadow of self-knowledge.

JOSEPH CONRAD, from *Lord Jim*

I *am* nature.

JACKSON POLLOCK,
when asked how he utilizes nature in his painting

1.

The ring of Christopher's machete up ahead resounds metallic and unnatural under a primary growth canopy so dense that the effulgence of this cloudless noonday sky is attenuated to a misty, crepuscular gloom. The air is still and sweltry and heavy with an admixtured redolence of new life, old death. Some hours ago we veered off the coast toward the interior, following a footpath now obscured at our feet by vegetation of a green so thick and rich it seems to tint the air itself with fecund verdancy.

We left the rig behind early this morning, nosed in by a little cantina just short of the true end of the road, which I've found to be some few miles beyond the town of Puerto Viejo and at the mouth of still another Talamanca rio, one the color of thick beef bouillon. The road I embarked upon months ago at the Tijuana crossing in Baja has ultimately shriveled to the serpentine footpath trickle into the bush we are now following—my compass course is yet south, that natural direction of vanishment.

From the political technicality of the Panamanian frontier just a few miles further on, marked by the flexuous flow of the Sixaola River, the rain forest perdures, densely uninhabited until the brief break of the Canal. Still further south looms the Isthmus of Darien of Colombia, wild and vicious and little explored. Of those few from civilization who have ventured there, some have never returned. Being completely roadless, that narrow neck of land separating the two great American continents represents the practical limit of southward land travel.

To the west of us, inland, there is likewise little in the way of marks of modern man until some scattered coastal towns of the Pacific side. From seaside Talamanca the land rises steadily to the pristine cloud forests of a jagged cordillera of the same name, new mountains geologically, some still grumbling and belching in the throes of creation, rising to in excess of 10,000 feet and peopled by Bribri and Cabecar Indians—remote enclaves of which are stone age cultures to this day.

Although Christopher claims we have a specific destination in mind— a headland on the blue Caribbean called Punta Mona, Monkey Point, where, he says, lives in solitude a wise old fisherman—in my gut I feel no goal to our ramble up ahead, just deepening bush. And now, absent the infinite perspective of Big Blue, and with the sure knowledge that inimical, feral eyes mark our progress, I am having bizarre, paranoid flashes that there is evil at work here.

All is not well with me. Since the episode of cocaine abuse nine days ago, my state of mind has deteriorated; I'm shakier now than when in the worst throes of my next-morning misery.

I look back on our drug-ridden reminiscing with disgust and anguish. The past that Christopher and I reveled in that night suddenly seems an illusion, an apocryphal tale. Perhaps a story told around a beach fire somewhere on the long road down the winding coast leading here, and which I've fraudulently taken as my own.

Adding to my despair, Salsa Brava went dead flat immediately following the one-day swell to which I awakened the morning after the debauch. I have not surfed for many days.

Salsa, flat. Eight days and counting. Salsa is so flat that, staring out at the lineup point as I do each morning come dawn, the Caribbean conjures in my mind the bewildering illusion of concavity. Big Blue is beyond slumber, it seems. She's dead: no wave will ever break upon that reef again.

How I miss Salsa's benefaction of speed, beauty and fear.

In my intensified tirades against Christopher's continued drug use, I have taken on the evangelical fervor of the newly reformed. Three days ago, in a toe-to-toe shouting match on Main Street—we drew quite a crowd—I outright accused him of cowardice in his abandonment of Salsa Brava. Even then, in the heat of my outraged moment, I knew I had gone too far.

And something in Christopher changed at the moment my attack took this nasty turn. His eyes went from wild to cold and hard, as if some inner light had been doused. I saw violence there.

It's perhaps significant to note that it was Christopher who suggested— no, *insisted* upon—this *caminata por la selva,* this jungle walk. Last night he appeared at my door and succinctly explained that we were going into the bush in the morning. I hadn't seen him since the argument, and perhaps still guilt-ridden at my wicked assault, I submissively assented. It was only later that I began to wonder about the motives behind his proposal. In my darker, more irrational moments, when truly unbalanced, bad thoughts arise, the possibility flashes before me that Christopher means to do me some ultimate harm; to dispose of me without a trace in this primitive place.

Crazy? Yes, no question, but as he guides us deeper into the bush beyond that last bridgeless river, I am keeping watch on my friend, my ex-friend, whom I came so far to see.

2.

The meandering jungle path has snaked back to the coast where a shallow stream empties into a wide, secluded bay. We'll rest here by a deserted, Spartan *pescadores'* camp with a rough-hewn table and a beached dugout canoe and have lunch before continuing on. The dogs, Shiner, Sweetpea and Jumbie, have wandered up a streambed to a little waterfall to drink their fill and cool off.

I watch as Christopher rummages through his knapsack—*my* knapsack, actually. Indeed, everything we're carrying is mine, for Christopher owns nothing of any practical use or monetary value.

"I can't believe that guy," Christopher says, still miffed that he'd been searched by a lone *federale* with an M-16 who'd been lurking at the edge of the jungle back by the river. "He's known me for years."

"Maybe he searched you *because* he's known you for years," I say.

"What do you mean?"

"Everyone on the Talamanca coast knows you're a crackhead," I say, unable to refrain. "He was looking to catch you with some."

Christopher glares at me for a moment but says nothing. He extracts from my knapsack the *Tico Times,* Costa Rica's English language newspaper, and ruffles it open.

Meanwhile, I'm wondering what else he's got stashed in there or perhaps concealed on his person. I'm wondering what he did with the 1,000 *colones* change he shorted me from the grocery money I gave him just before our departure this morning, wondering if he scored crack with it to sustain him during our time in the bush.

3.

After lunch I'm drowsing in the beached dugout canoe, stretched out with arms folded across my chest as if I were about to be launched into *mestizo* Valhalla, when the air erupts with a sound so deep and resonant, so starkly disquieting, that my initial reaction is wholly physiological: a quickening of breath; a flush of heat in the extremities as muscle fiber engorges with oxygen-rich blood; a sensation of nonspecific clarity; a tingling of the scalp and neck as that which—in some prehistoric incarnation of me—used to be fur stands erect to make my aspect larger and more frightening; all fight-or-flight reactions. My body is arming itself for the life-and-death struggle that, based upon the strident outrage of the gargantuan carnivorous beast out there, is surely to come.

I remain supine and still as jungle deadfall, although my eyes have blinked open to scrutinize my immediate surroundings for an escape route or a place in which to make my last stand. The ocean! The canoe! Of course! Launch the canoe and . . .

Christopher. Why is Christopher still sprawled casually on the edge of the beach, perusing the newspaper, yawning, apparently oblivious? And Sweetpea and Jumbie, snoozing and scratching respectively, the very picture of canine quiescence. And speaking of dogs, where's Shiner? Got to get her into the canoe and . . .

RAAAAAAA-OOOOO-AAAAWW-AAAHHHH! is my lettered interpretation of the appalling bellow that shakes the firmament once again, but it's as feeble and insubstantial an exemplification as trying to describe a cataclysmic earthquake by rattling dice in a cup. So: imagine a lion's roar in the closest of quarters, a small empty room with perfect acoustics. Imagine that lion, that lioness, has discovered you in the act of disemboweling her newborn offspring and her roar is an announcement of immediate intent. Imagine that sound and, further, now imagine that it is the mewing of a newborn kitty over the phone from two oceans away—compared to the feral yawl of the monster in the jungle that day.

I exaggerate only slightly.

And now a clamorous splashing approaching from up the stream bed, heavy breathing, a charging four-legged creature, unconcerned with stealth, closing at a dead run . . .

It's my dog, wild-eyed with fur erect, ears pinned back, looking to me for comfort . . . an explanation. What was *that sound,* she wants to know; what sort of mess have I gotten her into this time?

RAAAAAAA-OOOOO-AAAAWW-AAAHHHH!

"Christopher!"

Rattling the newspaper, unconcerned, his dogs both snoozing: "Huh?"

RAAAAAAA-OOOOO-AAAAWW-AAAHHHH!

Shiner spins clockwise, scouring the dim emerald recesses of the surrounding bush, lower jaw agape, panting.

"Whatthefuckisthat?"

"Howler," Christopher says, eyes furrowed at some tidbit in the back pages of the paper. "A monkey."

"Monkey? Areyounuts? That's a fucking dinosaur!" Yes, that's it, that's what it is, something out of *Jurassic Park,* a T-Rex, really pissed off or in heat or something.

Christopher rises, stretches, looks around apathetically.

"It's not some sort of big cat or . . . monster or something?"

Christopher squints at me, smiles thinly. "Good thing I'm here to point out that it's just a monkey, right?" he says. "I guess I'm not totally useless."

We stare at each other for a moment. I look away first.

4.

They're all around us now, these demented howlers, bellowing like demons, as we make our way south through thick bush, having left the coast behind again. The path has narrowed further, is nearly nonexistent, really. Christopher got us turned around a couple miles back, led us to a dead-end escarpment and we had to retrace our route halfway back to the fish camp, using his machete cuttings as trail markers.

The howlers, possibly sensing our disorientation and therefore weakness, have increased their numbers and the viciousness of their bellowing. And now they are obviously closing in, although the dense secondary growth below the primary canopy allows them to stay easily out of sight.

"They're very territorial," Christopher says, scanning the canopy overhead. The dogs have closed ranks and are staying by us. Although Sweetpea and Jumbie have gotten used to the sound of the howlers' roar over the years, they are now on alert, with Shiner keeping a close eye on them, presumably for cues as to the gravity of the situation. I've picked up a stout, seasoned piece of hardwood to hold onto.

"How big are these things?" I ask, voice lowered. I've noticed that when we speak the monkeys seem to take it as a challenge and increase the volume and bluster of their bawling.

"A big one might be about Shiner's size," Christopher responds, also sotto voce. "With a similar set of teeth."

"Is this the usual thing, I mean, following us?"

"I've never had them come this close before," Christopher says. "There's also a lot of them."

"Are we going to have a problem with these animals?" I'm trying to keep my voice casual.

"I've never heard of them attacking a human being," Christopher says, and turns to look me in the eye. "But if they do, we go back to back."

He stares at me until I nod. We then continue on southward, Christopher swinging the machete in downward swipes across his chest, carving Xs in the air.

5.

I'm up to my right knee in mud, trying to work my foot loose from the suction without leaving my shoe down there. *Sssshllluuurrrp,* out it all comes, intact. Great. *Slap, slap.* Goddamn mosquitoes.

The narrow path I'd followed after getting separated from Christopher and the dogs has descended from a series of hilly switchbacks to this slurpy bog, then petered out. Just how *had* we gotten separated, I'm wondering, vaguely recalling that I'd stopped to tie a shoelace and have a sip of water. Next thing I knew, I was solo. The son-of-a-bitch left me to shift for myself, even lured my dog from my side. Fucking power trip he's on, that's what all this is about. Follow me into the jungle and we'll see who's got his shit together. That talk of the jungles of Vietnam back there before the howlers' retreat, how comfortable he felt there, and now likewise here in the bush of Central America. Making me edgy with tips on hand-to-hand fighting in case of primate attack. All a response to my jabs at his miscreant lifestyle and constant denials. This is retribution, this little jungle walk.

Well, I've got some news, I'm thinking, as I unstick myself from the mire. I've got some jungle time under my belt, been goddamn shot at, too, in the bush south of Santa Marta that time back in '78. Forgot about that, didn't you, motherfucker? Where were you then, anyway? Back in the states, if I remember correctly, while I did the dirty, dangerous work. We'll see who's got his shit together.

I look up, searching the canopy for the sun. I'll get a general fix on which way's east, plow through the undergrowth to the coast (of course, he has my machete), then turn south. I'll beat his ass to Monkey fucking Point.

"Hey."

I wheel around to find Christopher somehow right there behind me, maybe ten feet away, absently tapping the machete blade on his leg.

"Where've you been?" I ask, trying to conceal how deeply he's startled me.

Tap-tap-tap goes the blade against the flesh of his leg. "You took the wrong fork, buddy."

"Where's my dog?" I consciously calm myself. And a thought strikes me: Christopher ditched me so he could have himself a hit of crack.

"Down on the beach with Sweetpea and Jumbie." he says. "We're there. Monkey Point."

6.

The jungle ends and the beach begins so suddenly and precipitously that one moment I'm plowing blindly through the shadowy gloom of dense bush and the next sliding on my ass down a slick loamy berm into dazzling sunlight. My legs are caked with brown mud flecked with sparkling bits of beach, a sprinkling of icing on chocolate.

I remain seated, thinking nonspecific negative thoughts about Christopher and, come to think of it, about my dog, who also abandoned me in the jungle. The sweep of flotsam-strewn cove is deserted. Where did Christopher go? He was here just a minute ago, leading me out of that mud hole.

Okay, there they are, four dark dots on the unruffled waters of the inshore lagoon, Christopher and the three dogs gone for a swim. Beyond them but still close inshore rises a massive, humpy island flecked with green scrub. I remember it from the map as being just north of Monkey Point. So this *is* it. Okay. Good.

I call out for my dog to come, using the tone that indicates she's in deep trouble. She hears me; even from a distance I can see the telltale perking of her ears. But she turns and swims the other way.

I find I've stood up, hyperventilating slightly from the heat, exhaustion and general aggravation. I slide off my knapsack, strip down and wade into the lagoon, shedding caked mud, sand, and bad thoughts in a swirl of brown. I submerge and float just beneath the surface, face-down like a corpse, cooling my superheated system.

7.

The first thing I notice when Christopher and the dogs and I round the headland of Monkey Point is a volleyball net on the beach, which itself sweeps ever southward in an endless, pristine, palm-fringed ribbon toward Panama and beyond.

A volleyball net?

Set back on the fringe of the rain forest a good distance from water's edge are two shacks set high on stilts. They appear lived-in, but not at this moment. Hanging on posts adjacent to the volleyball net are the nets of a fisherman, presumably the wise old one of Christopher's promise.

"What the fuck is a volleyball net doing here in the middle of nowhere?" I ask Christopher in irritation, as if the play-net's jarring presence was somehow his doing. Does the asshole think I've hiked half a day through the sweltering bush with crazed furry creatures screaming for my blood to play some fucking *game?*

"It's for Steven's guests," Christopher says, unriled by my hostility. Steven runs an eco-tour operation out of Monkey Point, Christopher has told me, and we'll be ensconced in his compound for the next couple of days. Steven is apparently stateside at the moment, being treated for a severe case of a tropical malady known as papalomoya, caused by an insect-born microbe. The symptoms are painful boil-like eruptions.

"Padi must be out fishing," Christopher says. He breathes deep, as if taking in the panorama in front of us aspirationally. "Beautiful, isn't it, Allan?"

Christopher's words and rapturous look beg a response but none is forthcoming from me. I'm wondering if the smile on his face right now is in fact a by-product of coke, not scenery.

8.

"Gimme the cigarettes," Christopher says as we approach the larger of the two shacks on the headland. Although it's only late afternoon, the sun is gone, lost behind a towering tangle of rain forest to the west. To the east, a dugout canoe, which was not there an hour ago, is beached upon the shore. A gathering overcast has erased Big Blue's translucent hue, laying on her surface a heavy slate gray in its stead.

I hand Christopher the four packs of cigarettes he bought with my money this morning as a gift for the old fisherman he has been telling me about, this man who has lived by and worked upon the waters here for many years in solitude, and who Christopher claims has achieved a state of insight and grace the mere proximity to which will no doubt help with what he refers to as my "attitude problem."

The two of them are, of course, close like brothers.

Christopher has told me that the old fisherman is well into his sixties. But when we mount the rickety stairs to a tiny porch overlooking an expanse of sea and sky, the black man we find seated with his thin, knotty legs propped on a scarred, cluttered table wedged into the corner by an inner door seems younger, although his face is deeply creased and his wizened frame appears stooped and tired even in repose.

Christopher places the cigarettes on the table with a flourish and says, "For you, my friend," implicitly taking credit for the gift. His rationalization for the purchase had been that it would be an introductory gesture from me.

The old man looks down at the cigarettes, then his gaze bypasses Christopher and falls upon me. He smiles in what I take to be acknowledgment, as if he has seen through Christopher's mild deceit and is on the verge of laughter at the harmless absurdity of it.

It is just now that I realize why I thought him younger than his visage and bearing would seem to indicate: though reddened by sun, wind and weather, his eyes are those of a young man, credulous and trusting yet astute. There is a tranquility about him that has somehow come to terms with the hardship and personal trauma he has undoubtedly experienced over decades of living the uncertain and perilous life of a man who goes to sea.

"Padi, I want you to meet a friend of mine, Allan," Christopher says, then rambles something about my being a writer, but his words are lost to me as Padi and I shake hands. I'm thinking I'll have to find a way to sit down with this man without Christopher around, talk a bit of story, maybe find out some things.

9.

The eco-compound appears unlived-in, as Christopher said it would be. Its main structure, an aging but sound old two-story house right out of *The Addams Family,* is set back from the beach on a well-tended lawn a little to the south of Padi's shacks. Behind the house are a couple of outbuildings and a checkerboard of neatly arranged and numbered but vacant tent sites. Tendrils of surrounding rain forest encroach from the north, west and south, feelers seeking irresolution in the holding of the ground. Here again is a place with the overall feel of a stronghold.

It's late afternoon and I'm at the dining table in a communal living area under the house, adding up the prices of the groceries Christopher bought. Here, in this man-made structure, my wariness of Christopher eases. It's only when we are alone in the bush, it seems, that twisted visions surface.

Suddenly, a guy, a good-looking towheaded kid in his mid-twenties, appears in the back doorway.

"Hi," he says affably.

"I figure there's a thousand *colones* missing," I tell Christopher, then say "Hi" to the kid.

"How do you figure? There're no price tags on anything."

"Yeah, you peeled 'em off."

"I'm Jason," the kid says. "I'm caretaking the place while Steven's away."

Ignoring him, I say to Christopher, "You're a thief. That's what you've become."

"You're hassling over a couple of dollars," Christopher says through clenched teeth. He is now not denying the theft, he's pointing out my pettiness in calling him on such a small amount.

I know I'm on the verge of going too far with him again, but I see an opening and go for it. "A two-bit thief," I say. "You bought crack with it, didn't you?"

Jason just stands there.

Christopher's eyes go cold and hard.

10.

The light from three kerosene lamps hanging from raw hardwood beams overhead casts conflicting shadows, throwing into fuddled relief the darting little gravity-defying creatures with which we share this sheltered space on the edge of the velvety shroud of deep night. The floor beneath us is humusy dirt, the primordial stuff of the jungle, and Jason warns us that last night a terciopelo, the deadliest of the Central American vipers, slithered right through the kitchen in the beam of his flashlight. A slick and electrifying visitation, truly, he testifies with a wordless shiver.

We sip tea sweetened with dollops of the rum Christopher uncovered in his rummaging of the premises, which I found distasteful, given the owner being absent. I'm glad for the tingling warmth of alcohol, though, after a tiring day of physical exertion and bad thoughts. Whether it's simply the rum or something else, I don't know, but I'm feeling much better.

Monkey Point is named for the profusion of howlers that inhabit the area, though Jason says they have not been much in evidence lately. And they are quiet tonight. "A few times, early in the morning or toward dusk, I'll spot them hanging out in the trees on the edge of the jungle, just sort of checking me out," he says.

"No bellowing, huh?" I ask.

"Not since the first night," Jason answers. "I guess they've sort of accepted me."

"That or they're quietly massing for a sneak attack," I suggest, only half joking. "I think they resent our presence here. Like maybe they're aware of the destruction we're wreaking on the rain forest all over this country."

"And worldwide," Jason adds, nodding. "Who knows how far their communications reach, what they really know."

Jason has been here a week or so and I feel a bit awkward at Christopher and I having disturbed his solitude with our Odd Couple from Hell routine. He seems not to mind, yet I don't believe he's been craving company either. Certainly not our sort of company.

"Stay at my place when you come to Puerto Viejo," Christopher says to Jason and I have a sudden rush of wanting to crack Christopher's skull. I like this kid and am quite sure he isn't in Talamanca chasing drugs. Still, I don't care to picture what might happen under Christopher's self-serving tutelage. I distract myself from the vision by asking Jason what brought him to Talamanca, and Monkey Point in particular.

"I'm trying to figure out what to do with my life," he says. "I thought maybe this would be a good place to think about it."

11.

A squall line hits the house with pelting rain and a rising sea wind sweeping through its paneless, unshuttered, unscreened windows. A candle that I've stuck with melted wax to the bed frame under the mosquito net blows out and then the darkness, the nothingness, is total, as if the world itself has puffed out.

Jason has insisted that Christopher and I take the two upstairs bedrooms. He'll crash in a hammock in the communal area, slithering nocturnal terciopelos and all. It's ten, maybe eleven o'clock, and being unable to sleep, I've started reading a novel called *The Brave Cowboy* by Edward Abbey, which I picked up at a used bookstore in Todos Santos, Baja. It's an old book, written some 40 years ago, but it's wonderful and not dated at all. Just before the weather hit, it occurred to me that the late 1950s film with Kirk Douglas, *Lonely Are the Brave,* was based upon it. The story is of a present-day cowboy's clash with the powers that be of the new west, and in the larger sense, changing times, modern times.

On the run from the law on horseback, the cowboy evades the pursuit of a posse of jeeps and aircraft by leading them into the backcountry, where he survives using the lore and skills of his antecessors. Eventually he runs out of wilderness and, trying to cross a bustling interstate, he and his horse are run down and killed by a tractor-trailer bound for California. Beneath the shock and emotion of the sudden, violent termination of his run for freedom, there is of course a grand metaphor at work, but it isn't heavy-handed; it's merely inevitable and perfect.

I light the candle again. It blows out immediately, so I read with the beam of my flashlight, but the batteries soon give up. I try reading by the intermittent pulses of sheet lightning. It's interesting the way the images jump off the page in discrete, jagged fragments like poetic apparitions, but disorienting, too. I find I'm unable to connect the story elements one to the other, so their implications are obscure and the narrative does not progress.

I put the book aside and absorb myself in the outside tumult, wondering if it will revive the lifeless reef at Salsa Brava. The weather passes, leaving in its wake a light drizzle and the sweet scents of ozone and rotting things in the jungle. The disturbance has been a local one, of insufficient intensity and duration to raise a groundswell.

Lying in the squall's dark, dense aftermath, I imagine myself tucked into the cracking green of a mean and ugly Salsa beauty, and thunder's distant grumble as the storm moves inland becomes the roar of the wave's fall onto the reef. As I drift off to sleep the image persists, becomes a dream.

12.

Shiner and I walk the beach at Monkey Point as the approaching dawn expands and assimilates the darkness, dousing starlight east to west. The night in southern latitudes dies a quick, easy death, with little fanfare. There is no diffidence in the sun's overture; it seems in a rush to rise and get on with things.

The wind is down, though as the air warms, feeble zephyrs swirl, tickling the blue-black surface of the sea, then evanesce just offshore. The early air has a heavy, uneasy feel of rainy season indecision, reflected in scattered distant clouds beyond the mottled green of the inshore island on the edge of the lagoon. An assemblage of strati lay flat and lazy aloft as if come to rest on some giant glass table; puffy cumuli scud the horizon in their own private wind stream. The clouds mill and equivocate. What to do today?

Maybe a hundred yards to the north, Padi readies his dugout for the sea, piling his net and assorted gear into the slim, frail craft. He pauses and fixes the sea horizon with his young eyes. His day's movements offshore will be directed by the predictive nuances he perceives there and elsewhere; nuances to which I, and indeed, this new-fangled system of thought called Chaos Theory, are blind: subtleties in light and shadow, color and motion; the feel of the air on his skin; scents inhaled and analyzed by his upturned nose.

The disk of the sun appears unannounced from behind a far cloud, backlighting the misty translucence of a squall falling from its gray belly with an orangey eruption that I take as indication that the day has officially, meteorologically, cosmically, begun.

I turn to walk down the beach to speak to Padi, but he has already launched his canoe and is stroking for the outside.

13.

The beach south of Monkey Point at high water is tough going, the sand being soft and steep-to, the hard flats under a couple feet of inshore Caribbean. Christopher and I bog up to our knees in the silt of an estuarine river mouth and Christopher calls the dogs back from their exploratory swim up its opaque reach.

"There are caimans in these rivers, big ones," he says, and indeed, on cue, we come across the rotting corpse of a six-footer, ghostly pale and picked clean by turkey vultures and sand crabs. The head is fairly intact, jaws clamped. This one animal is blessed with the dagger canines of a hundred timber wolves, perfectly imbricated top to bottom to make the mouth's grinning seal wholly airtight and deadly.

Christopher tells the story of a German kayaker come to grief a couple months ago, slurped down by a 12-foot behemoth like a trout taking a mayfly, a few ghastly body parts all that remained.

"From this river?" I ask.

"No, up by Tortuguero, but the same sort of water."

"Shiner! Come!" My dog is chest-deep by the bank, lapping her fill. The river is flotsamy with debris washed down by recent rains, with jagged, half-submerged logs resembling the serrated spinal columns of lurking saurians, the elevated end knots like cold unblinking eyes.

Death litters the wrack line at full flood tide, piscatorial creatures washing in, those of fur and feather, having somehow found the sea in their throes, washing out. Their remains commingle and become one in the spent white water. A plumed fish; a scaly rodent with a beak; a bird sporting a crab claw and a small porcine hoof: implied lessons in evolution's exploratory beginnings, and in inevitable individual ends. Vultures and ravens, like tourists squabbling for a cut-rate beach buffet, speckle the strand ahead.

Christopher is examining a massive chunk of high-and-dry, half-buried flotsam. He takes a long swig of sweet water, then passes over the palm nut he's hacked open.

He sets the point of my machete down in the sand by his foot, his opposite elbow akimbo. He sighs and cocks his head, leveling his straw hat—which is angled the other way—to the sea horizon. The spring sun at this latitude is directly overhead at noon, which is now, more or less, so Christopher's face is in the deep shade of the brim. Now he's tapping the machete blade against his leg and looking at me, his eyes unsquinting, bright and fiery.

My bad bush thoughts come back: Christopher is going to decapitate me with a swipe from my machete and bury my remains in the bush.

How many men did he kill as a soldier in Vietnam?

Christopher's eyes narrow as if he has sensed my brief instant of fear.

But then he sticks the machete in the sand and squats by the chunk of flotsam, which appears to be a section of the transom of a wooden vessel of good size. From its scarred, sun-bleached surface and the depth at which it is buried, this piece looks to have washed ashore here some time ago, perhaps months. A few yards down the beach a long piece of cambered timber that was probably a rib protrudes from the sand, and I'm wondering how much more of the derelict vessel lies buried under our feet.

"Remember *Windblown?*" Christopher asks. He digs around the base of the vessel's remains, probably looking for a name or home port, some clue to her identity, but most of the paint is long gone and the wood is riddled with the holes of marine boring worms.

"That was our last foreign surf trip together," I say. "Before you got busted off the Caymans."

In the early spring of 1984 Christopher and I were on the Caribbean island of Barbados. Although we had gone our separate ways careerwise since the interdiction by the Coast Guard of our pot-laden motorsailer, *Rana,* off Puerto Rico—I was spending more time on the West Coast than at Montauk—we were still close. All was theoretically well with me at the time. A movie I'd written was in production and I had just sold *Cosmic Banditos* to a publisher; and I had been one of the initial writers producer Michael Mann contacted about his new cop show, set in Miami.

The surf had been flat for the first week since our arrival, then came up fast and strong. By sundown of the second day the swell was peaking at double overhead, with some bigger sets. Christopher and I, along with a handful of locals and itinerants, were surfing a break called Duppys on the very northern tip of the island, a right-handed point that catches the brunt of swells rolling in from the North Atlantic.

Although not thick and threatening like even the average Salsa cruncher, the wave at Duppys that day was perfectly sculpted for speed. With whooshing, feathering lips kaleidoscopically backlit by the lowering sun, the surf was a marvel to experience on every level. That tranquil, mindless rush that is the be-all of wave riding—the suspension of concern with what we think of as the future—quickly faded as we stroked in at deep dusk.

That night we called a buddy back home at Montauk, a commercial fisherman and committed surfer. It had been a bad winter up north, cold and blustery, and we wanted to gloat about the day we'd had surfing big, warmwater perfect waves. Christopher called collect from a pay phone at a local bar. The place was packed and buzzing with surf jive, guys reliving their day in the water, making plans for the morning go-out. Christopher was grinning like a madman; he loved to aggravate his buddies in situations like this. But he'd barely gotten out his first sentence when he fell silent, his face going all pale and stricken. He listened for a bit, then asked a couple of questions I couldn't pick up over the barroom noise.

"*Windblown's* gone," he said, and handed me the phone.

Our friend, along with the rest of the local commercial fleet, plus Coast Guard ships and planes from all over the Northeast, had been at sea since the Montauk long-liner *Windblown* had come up overdue three days before. She'd been caught offshore in a particularly bad nor'easter. Not a trace of the boat or her crew of four had been found. Christopher, who had fished commercially on and off for most of his adult life, had been close to all four men. I knew one of them. He was a good man and a good surfer.

No distress call had been broadcast, so the prevailing theory was that a rogue wave had done the vessel in, suddenly overwhelmed her and she sank like a stone.

Christopher and I were familiar with the storm *Windblown* had gone down in; far to the south in Barbados, we'd been tracking it on the weather map. It was the same storm that had raised the groundswell we'd ridden that day. Assuming *Windblown* had come to grief during the worst of the weather, the rogue wave that had caused her founder would have arrived at our southern latitude sometime that afternoon, around the time we were surfing the peak of the swell at Duppys. Later that night, Christopher and I talked about the maybe half-dozen set waves we'd each caught that day; waves considerably bigger than their companions. Waves that likely had started their lives as rogues in the storm that spawned them.

And we talked about the fact that "Duppys" is a West Indian term meaning a corpse, a floating corpse. It was just a word, a twist of meaning, but that night we found ourselves fixated on it.

Christopher, like a crazed dog, sand flying, is still digging away at the base of the broken piece of the stranded vessel. Maybe he thinks it's a piece of *Windblown,* come to rest after more than a decade drifting around the North Atlantic in endless circles, trapped in the prevailing clockwise currents; then by a quirk of wind and weather finding its way into the eastern Caribbean, fetching up here at the leeward end of the basin.

Of course it isn't *Windblown.* But of course it could have been. Death in its many manifestations litters the beach here at high water.

14.

Padi lights a cigarette, cupping his hands around the match in the fresh late afternoon trades. He exhales contemplatively.

"My doddy comin' from Panama," he says. "When he decide to leave dere, he walkin' all de way along dis coast"—Padi sweeps his arm south to north—"from down dere to de Mosquito Coast in Nicaragua, lookin' for a good place to live. Dot a long way to walk, you know?"

Padi watches from his porch as a dugout rounds Monkey Point and disappears to the north, the high whine of the outboard fading until all is quiet again. It belongs to Sylvester, who runs boat tours and fishes out of Puerto Viejo; he lives in a tent on the beach in front of Andrés's cabinas. He picks clean and rakes the shoreline every day, from his campsite to the common in front of the Parquecita cantina, and meticulously tends to the infant palms he's planted. He is not paid for this work, but does it out of respect for the land of his birth and the sea upon which he works. He and Padi are good friends.

We talk about Padi's life here as a fisherman, how he settled at Monkey Point some 47 years ago; how, apart from the women who have loved him over the years and come to stay with him awhile, he's lived alone, as he does now.

"If a mon can't stand his own company, what use he is to other people?" Padi says. He asks me how long I've known Christopher and if all is well between us.

He's sensed the tension.

I tell Padi that I've known Christopher for more than thirty years and that I've come all this way to find he's changed, and that the changes in him have made me angry. "He's taken my money and lied to me," I say.

"You try to help Christopher with dat problem he havin'?"

I haven't mentioned anything about Christopher having a specific problem, but Padi knows, of course he knows, about Christopher's cocaine habit. Padi no doubt knows most of what goes on on the Talamanca coast. "I wanted to get him to go back to the states," I say, "where he could get help."

"Why he got to go back dere fo' help?" Padi says. "If he got a friend here."

I shake my head, thinking he doesn't understand.

"If you thinkin' he should go back to de states, then why you don't take him?"

"I tried. He wouldn't go."

"How hard you try?" Padi presses.

"What am I supposed to do, kidnap him?" I ask.

"I don't know Christopher fo' long as you," Padi says after a pause. "But I like de mon. He a friend of mine."

I feel like I've been scolded for talking about Christopher behind his back. "What would *you* do?" I ask.

Padi shrugs. "I jus' sittin' here watchin' wha' hoppen."

"I guess he's never stolen from you," I say, getting frustrated, challenging him with the essence of the matter as I see it.

Padi asks me if Christopher has stolen so much money from me that my life has been somehow changed.

I don't answer, and he sighs, looks out to sea. "We got more weather comin'," he says.

15.

Christopher and I dine alone, Jason having decided to hike out this afternoon, to do some shopping in Puerto Viejo, make a phone call, get some ointment for a boil on his leg. Night has fallen and we've lit the kerosene and gas lanterns, which swing hypnotically in a rising sea wind. The air feels ominous and heavy and jungle sounds outside are hushed under a vague, rolling grouse of thunder like a distant freight train. Lightning pulses over the sea and penetrates our gloomy landward niche, unreal and somehow rude, like bursts from a paparazzo's electronic flash on unsuspecting subjects.

Christopher and I eat in a silence that is not uneasy. We are for the moment as an old married couple, wearied of our chronic squabbling and content with wordless brooding. The dogs nap, sated after their meal of fish Padi gave us from his day's catch, along with heaps of buttered and seasoned rice; the same food Christopher and I are now eating. Sweetpea and Jumbie lurk by the doorless opening to the jungle out back, as aegis against predatory incursion. My dog, their old friend, lies snoozing at my feet.

I think to challenge Christopher on the welfare of his other three dogs, left on their own back in Puerto Viejo, but I'm suddenly struck by a recollection that brings me up short. Although I am unable to pinpoint the image's exact location in time or space, Christopher is walking the streets of Puerto Viejo, inland bound toward Hogfish Ranch. He is carrying a large sack of dry dog food, the worth of which is some 3,000 *colones*. It is a major outlay for Christopher, who is most often without funds, and represents a night of pipe-driven rapture now not to be. His five dogs are as well fed and groomed as any house pets in stateside suburbia, marked contrasts to the bony, sore-ridden street mongrels of the town, from whose ranks Christopher rescued Sweetpea and Jumbie's three adopted companions. He is often unable to feed himself, but his dogs do not go without.

Imagining him buying that sack of dog food has made me sad.

I think about Christopher's Hogfish Philosophy, his fantasies about changing the world's view of both children and the elderly. How in the new world order as he envisions it, the wisdom of the old would temper the brashness and cupidity of the young. His drug-ridden hypocrisies notwithstanding, the espousal of his philosophy does seem a fine ambition.

I think of Padi and Werner, an old man and a young boy, both of whom have declared their friendship and loyalty to Christopher, and just that quick all the others who have spoken ill of him recede to irrelevancy.

I'm on a slide, needing to feel sadder still, so I contemplate the people of my past, searching for a name or a face that might stand by me as Padi and Werner stand by Christopher, in spite of his glaring frailties. There probably are such people but at this moment I cannot picture them.

Yes, it's worked. I'm feeling sadder still.

"How hard you try?" Padi asked me, referring to my attempt to help Christopher with his cocaine problem. The answer, then left obliquely unsaid, was, of course, "Not very."

I had in fact abandoned Christopher outright and immediately when I'd moved from Hogfish Ranch that second morning. We had agreed the first day that we would cut out a space for my rig on the grounds of the ranch. My rationalization for the move—fear of nocturnal raids by neighborhood crackheads—was specious. Hemmed in by impenetrable bush and with six dogs living on the property as sentries, I would have been perfectly secure. I needed "the perspective of an ocean view campsite" all right, and that perspective excluded the effort of dealing with the desperate needs of my former comrade.

"God sent you to me, Allan," were among Christopher's first words upon my arrival, followed by, "Everything's going to be all right now." Are these not the words of a human being who knows he is in desperate straits, and who is asking for help?

Was there any excuse for my abandonment?

Christopher did not bring crack on our trek to Monkey Point. He'd come clean, as it were. But I had given no respite in my querulous, self-righteous abuse. I perceived deviltry in his motives in bringing me here, when in truth he wished only to show me his secret refuge, and perhaps to heal the wounds in our nearly lifelong friendship.

I imagine Christopher's childhood. Fatherless, forcibly taken from his mother, tossed back and forth by people who did not want him. "Shadow," they called him, hiding.

I imagine Christopher, almost a man, *almost,* cowering wounded, face shattered by shrapnel, on some jungle hilltop about to be overrun by the enemy. Christopher, sent crawling down tunnels with a knife to kill other human beings, with his own death coming, writing a note to his mother on his forearm so she might be able to read it when his body is shipped home. A note forgiving her for the traumas of his childhood.

Smug and wily in my avoidance of military service, I am meanwhile surfing off some beautiful coast and thinking about the girl I planned to seduce that night.

While Christopher hides from his childhood in some hellhole institution, I, a much-loved only child, am meanwhile camping on the cliffs of Montauk with my father.

I imagine my father kissing my forehead each night at bedtime throughout my happy youth, saying, "Good night, sweet prince."

And then I remember that my father lives in utter squalor with his cats as his only company, and that I have abandoned him.

Abandonment. *It's what I do best.*

Now, as I sit with Christopher at the dinner table in the bush at Monkey Point, I find I'm wondering something:

Who am I to judge Christopher?

16.

Unlike the squall line of last night, which hurled itself onto Monkey Point as if upon a sword, the storm tonight is taking its time in assaulting the coast. Perhaps it hesitates in the knowledge that the engine that drives it—the heat and moisture of the sea—will be left behind as it advances to the cooler, dry land. There, the hills, then the mountains, indeed the canopy of the rainforest itself, being impediments to air flow, would further weaken it. So the tempest hovers offshore and intensifies.

Dinner finished, I feel like taking a walk with Shiner down to the beach, to be nearer to Big Blue and to think about things, but my flashlight batteries died last night and you don't want to go strolling around the edge of the rain forest after dark without good light. About half the species of snakes in Talamanca are venomous, and, like terciopelos, many are nocturnal and very aggressive. Besides, a light rain has now commenced, with the sure promise of a deluge in the offing.

So I don't go anywhere, save to move from the dining table to a hammock slung nearby. I'm still feeling sad from the thoughts I had at dinner, although not unpleasantly so. Why I'm feeling this way I cannot say for sure. It's as though I've just experienced a tale of melancholy finale, yet one so well wrought as to be of perfect sense and therefore nonetheless emotionally uplifting.

I do know that I've failed in whatever was the real motive behind giving up my old life and traveling to this foreign land, and that the melancholy tale is ultimately mine. And I know that the tale does make sense, although I am hard pressed to illuminate its logic, at least in the glary light of words. Perhaps what makes sense is simply my having failed. It's so blitheringly human, so inevitable in the end.

17.

Late night now on the upstairs porch and the dazzle of bolt and sheet lightning, the booming tirade of thunder, and the pelting deluge of rain are of an intensity such as I've never before experienced on land. The offshore storm has descended upon Talamanca like Armageddon itself. Rain droplets materialize, suspended in vacant space, then splatter my face like birdshot. The air is charged, buzzing and tingly with ionic discharge seeking ground; then with blinding, brittle bolts that air erupts, illuminating like overexposed photographs the landscape and adjoining sea. Jagged pulses of lightning and simultaneous cracks of thunder have no apparent points of origin because the center of the storm, its heart and its focus, is here, right here, where I am standing.

Howlers are out bellowing in the bush, but without the edge of outrage I'd sensed in their ravings at my initial intrusion into the rain forest two days ago. On the contrary, there seems to be an exuberant harmony in their accompaniment to the tempest, contrapuntal to the thunder beats, the harsh hiss of the wind-driven rain, the low moan of the high wind vibrating the jungle itself as if it were a vast, finely tuned stringed instrument.

I'm witnessing a glimpse of violent, primordial beginnings, of far distant evolutionary causes, with the present as ultimate effect, a perfectly inevitable, sensible outcome. The center of time and the center of space in this finite yet unbounded universe merge and become one, the graceful here-and-now of the here-and-now.

I move about the porch, wanting to see it all as it is tonight, and remember it as such: The fiery sky, the feral jungle, and my old friend, keeper of my deepest, darkest fears and desires—that raging, beautiful blue vastness out there.

I turn and look through the porch window behind me, through an inner door to the back bedroom and the image flickering there in the electric air suddenly and completely narrows my vision to one specific and terrible notion, an outer manifestation of all the inner dreads I would seek to shake. All my fears merge and are instantly one: I'm looking at Christopher, lying supine, ghostly skull thrown back on the pillow, jaws agape, and his specter is so cadaverously, so hellishly still under the gauzy shroud of his mosquito net in this rip-roaring pandemonium that I know he must be dead.

It's now the darkness between lightning bursts that seems unnatural, abrupt probes from the void: a stroboscopic effulgence beyond surreal, with each brief beat of suspended time etched with awful clarity upon my senses. Like a suddenly awakened surfer who obliviously dreams on, I am unable to discriminate nightmare from reality—because there is no difference, they are one and the same.

Then, during a lull of darkness and stillness as the storm edges inland, Christopher moves. In the light of the next sky-burst he is lying sideways facing me, eyes open, and he is watching me on the porch watching him.

Christopher rolls onto his back, serenely closes his eyes and goes back to sleep, and all is once again dark and quiet.

18.

Sundown this last day finds me paddling ashore to a little beachfront space off Main Street where I've moved my little house that travels, the better to hit the road come morning at first light. As Shiner springs prancing and whining to my side, I look back out at the miracle of Salsa Brava.

I am finished with this place, and with this wave.

I bag and lash my surfboards to La Casita Viajera's roof, then do a walk-around to see that all is secure for the road.

At dusk Christopher comes by with his dogs. We talk for a while about small matters, then shake hands, and then he is gone up Main Street toward the cantina to get on with things.

Epilogue

From some distant place, we know not where.

. . . while one might, I suppose, wish for a bloom to remain in blossom, for a ripening grape to hang always on the vine—yearnings John Keats made his own, for fleeting beauty and youth, the understandably hopeless hope that we might freeze our world's better moments—the wave's plenitude is rather in the peeling of the petal, the very motion of the falling fruit.

MID-AUGUST, 1998, MONTAUK, LONG ISLAND, NEW YORK

It's been a year and three months since I left Christopher in Talamanca, time I spent largely at a place called Pavones, the adjacent end-of-the-road surfer's enclave on Costa Rica's Pacific side.

My reasons for abandoning the Down South life I was living are both complex and straightforward. There were death threats resulting from an investigation I was doing for a magazine into the murder of an American expatriate by highly organized squatters who, with covert support of certain elements of the Costa Rican government, were trying to steal land from American and European settlers in Pavones, mostly surfers.

This is the straightforward aspect and probably not the main reason I'm back in the states.

I paid Christopher a visit just before putting La Casita on a stateside-bound ship out of Puerto Limón. He seemed okay, the same, which didn't surprise me. Christopher is a survivor; in his own way, he's still fearless. He was broke but cheerful. Said his crack smoking is now under control. I gave him a of couple bucks and lent him a surf magazine containing an article I'd written. I needed the magazine back, I said, but he didn't show up the next morning at my campsite to return it and say good-bye.

I'm sure he had his reasons.

Salsa Brava was flat the two days I was there. Kurt said it hadn't been a good year; not like during my stay, which he said was the biggest, most consistent spring season in his memory.

Since my return stateside, I've been living in La Casita, which I park in a friend's yard. It's not so bad, really, being back here. Some nights I park down by the beach where I rode my first wave in 1966. Or I drive a few miles east and sleep under the loom of the lighthouse, at the same spot where my father and I camped in 1957, and where I spent that last night before leaving on my journey south.

Just across the street from where I'm staying lives the surfbuddy/commercial fisherman who assisted Christopher and me in the scuttling of our banana boat in 1977. Other friends come by and hang out with us at my buddy's garage, where he builds and repairs surfboards. We converse about board design, how poor or how crowded the surf has been lately, maybe sip some Caribbean rum. Sometimes, but not often, I talk about the waves I found in the faraway places I visited, the people I met and the experiences I had.

When I first returned, everyone wanted to hear word of Christopher. He's not doing well, I'd explain, and is broke and has a drug problem he refuses to deal with. I also try to explain that this is an oversimplification.

For a while there was talk of going down and grabbing Christopher to bring him back here to straighten him out, but it eventually died and now his name is rarely mentioned anymore.

My dog Shiner did not make it back to the states with me. She is buried in a banana grove by the house we lived in at Pavones, on the bank of El Rio Claro. It is not within my ability with words to adequately describe the grief I felt at her passing, and continue to feel now, months later.

I have a new dog, a small mixed breed female I've named Honey, for her golden-brown color and because I often called Shiner by that name, which makes the transition easier. Honey is turning out to be a good dog, although she has some big paw prints to fill.

. . .

I visited my father a couple weeks ago. In the four years since I'd last seen him, his living conditions had much deteriorated, and they were awful enough even back then. His house has not been cleaned in a decade or more and what with three dozen cats running loose the stench of their piss, shit and spray is appalling. The living areas are crammed full of cat statuary, medieval weaponry and various macabre instruments of mayhem and torture.

For all this, he was lucid, on the surface at least, and, although he was thin, he seemed physically fit. When I suggested that he sell the house, which is mortgage-free—in spite of the condition of the interior, it's probably worth upwards of $300,000—and move to a smaller place, maybe a little house or apartment near the sea, he insisted that his life is fine. When I pressed the point, he became angry and told me to mind my own business.

Neither his stove nor his refrigerator was operable so I bought him a small fridge and a microwave oven. He was dubious about the latter; he had never heard of a microwave oven. He hadn't left the house in many years, except to go food-shopping once a week.

Sitting on his porch that afternoon, a silence between us grew, and I could not help but wonder what had happened to this man, this avant-garde waterman of my childhood and young adult years; this man who was a bodybuilder/extreme-fitness advocate when these pursuits were considered oddball, and a poet whose passion for the sea was lovingly passed along to me.

And, yes, I could not help but wonder what had happened to *us*.

My father seemed glad to see me at first, but after a couple of hours it was plain that he was impatient for me to go. And it was clear that my suggestion that he leave his home had not only rankled him but frightened him. Perhaps he was afraid I'd force him to move by some legal means or even have him committed.

I did think of these options.

I also visited my mother, who lives alone in North Carolina. The breast cancer with which she was afflicted in the early 1980s has returned and in-

vaded her bones. Her condition is likely terminal, though I've been told that
with recent advances in chemotherapy and radiation she may well survive
for a long time. In a couple weeks I'll go down to stay with her and take
care of her.

Often these days I'll find myself sitting on the cliffs under the lighthouse
or taking a beach walk with Honey and thinking about things. One of my
recurring thoughts is of a particular wave I rode around this time last summer, at Pavones. The break there is amazing. It's not thick, nasty and barreling like Salsa Brava, but fast and very, very long; thought, in fact, to be
the longest point break in the Northern Hemisphere. On a well-overhead
day with a pure, long-period south swell the ride can be up to 1,000 yards
or better, well over half a mile. Rather than assaulting the land head-on,
like Salsa, and expelling its energy all in one sudden and final heave, the
Pavones wave breaks along the shore at an acute angle, which accounts for
its astounding length. It seems to be conserving itself, putting off its inevitable expiration for as long as possible. The wave at Pavones is much more
suited to me than the one at Salsa Brava, which is more of a young man's
wave.

In spite of the increasing tension of the local squatter problem, I found
myself quite taken with the area, which is much more primitive than Puerto
Viejo and very definitely has a frontier feel. (Electricity had come only a
year or so before my arrival.) There are only two structures on shore visible
to someone sitting in the lineup: a cantina at about the midpoint of the
wave and, a few hundred yards further along, a fish camp at the far northern end.

I paddled out early the day I rode this particular wave, just after sunrise.
There was only a handful of other guys in the water, well to the south of
me, surfing off the mouth of El Rio Claro. The swell was shoulder to head
high; not big enough to form those thousand-yard miracles, but, still, a
longer wave than you'll find almost anywhere on the planet.

My takeoff was just to the south of the cantina. At first the wave didn't feel like anything special—it wasn't even a set wave—but as I stepped to the nose and looked down the line ahead of me, I could see that the wave face was organizing itself perfectly for a sustained tipride.

The noseride, The Glide, is an unstable situation, not easy to maintain. This is principally due to the ephemerality of the moving niche where unbroken, green water steepens past the vertical and where the energy of the wave is released in the form of falling white water: this is the position on the wave the surfer must sustain in order to prolong the noseride. What eventually happens is that either the wave overruns the surfer or the surfer outruns the wave. In both situations a backpedal to the rear of the longboard is called for, so a change of direction and/or alteration of board speed can be accomplished; the noseride is over.

Most noserides are very brief, often no more than the time it takes to plant the front foot, or both feet, on the tip, then immediately back off. The average noseride lasts somewhere around three, maybe four seconds at most. In general, a noseride of over ten or so yards will get the attention of those lazing on shore; over 20 will have them sitting up and taking serious note; anything much over that will likely have them on their feet hooting in amazement. A noseride of 50 yards lasts about 10 seconds and is considered about the practical limit, even at extra-long breaks like Malibu and Rincon, California's two best-known points. At the World Contest in 1966, legendary tiprider David Nuuhiwa sustained a hang-five for about that length of time and distance. His ride was scored a perfect 10 and is still remembered today.

The wave in question afforded me a continuous nose position from my takeoff point to the shore break in front of the fish camp around the corner in the next bay, a distance of about 500 yards. The ride lasted upwards of one minute.

Five hundred yards, one minute, of continuous Glide time.

Imagine hitting a baseball 450 feet over the center field wall and into the seats. Imagine the sensation of the bat striking the ball. Imagine that sensation lasting *one minute.*

Imagine seeing something so beautiful that for an instant your breath is literally taken away. Imagine that emotion lasting *one minute.*

Imagine the peak of orgasm lasting *one minute*.

You don't generally paddle right back out after riding a wave at Pavones; it's too far. You hoof it along the beach or, at high tide, through the bush, then across the cantina grounds and on to your original paddle-out spot further down the shore.

Emerging from the shore break after that ride, I felt too weak in the knees to make the walk right away, so I sat down on a rock by the fish camp. There didn't seem to be anyone around, but then I noticed a guy in surf trunks on the rocky beach by the cantina. He just stood there staring at me. Shiner was trotting toward me on the beach. She'd learned to recognize me surfing and would watch me in the water from a particular spot by the cantina. When I caught a wave, she'd run along the shore and then accompany me on the walk back.

I was feeling strange, a little disoriented, as if I'd just awakened from a deep sleep and was unsure of whether I was still dreaming.

Shiner arrived and sat down on my foot. Then the other surfer walked up and said, "You didn't backpedal until the shore break, did you?"

I had to think about it. "That's right," I said. He'd watched the first couple hundred yards of my noseride from the seawall by the cantina, he said, then ran down the beach when I rounded the corner into the next bay to see how far I'd go without backpedaling.

"The wave was perfect," I said, still feeling dreamy. "It lined up perfectly."

I focused hard on the ride, trying to remember. I knew I had to remember now or I'd lose all traces of what had just happened. Something remarkable had occurred, I mean apart from the ride itself, even apart from the perfection of the wave.

I remembered the take-off and having the thought that the first section of the wave was lining up well.

I remembered making an adjustment—shifting my back foot to the inside rail to bring the board more parallel to the wave face—and barely getting through the fast section adjacent to the cantina.

I remembered having a fleeting thought that I'd been on the nose for a long time. A *really* long time. And ahead of me, the wave face continued to build and taper endlessly into the distance. It was as if each new section of the wave was self-replicating from the one before it, doing so continuously, with flawless elegance and symmetry.

I remembered that I'd made another adjustment, a slight stall—a weight shift to the outside rail—at a flattening section some distance past the threshold to the next bay; then, sensing my board accelerating as the wave steepened again in front of me, I shifted my weight back again to the inside rail for speed. What I had experienced—and adjusted for—was a tiny wrinkle in the otherwise absolute perfection of the wave.

But I could remember nothing of the final couple hundred yards of the ride, except an odd sensation, which I can only describe as one of suspension. I was flying and I was walking on water, yet it was also as if I were standing still—as if I were *stillness itself*—and *everything else* was moving past *me*.

This sort of illusion is of course a common perceptual quirk. You look out the window of a train that you thought was stationary but in reality is moving slowly, and you hallucinate that it's the scenery that's moving.

This was the difference, though: everything *but the wave itself* was moving. The water beneath my board, the sea around me, the sky above, the distant shore, maybe the earth itself, were moving past me, but not the wave.

It is not the water, not the sea itself, that is ridden when one surfs. The water is only the medium that carries the energy that *is* the wave, much as one's body is the medium, the carrier, of one's consciousness. I had perceived, in a deeply intuitive way, the seamless integration of matter and energy—without the artificial duality, the either/or-ness the human mind is prone to.

Having spent so much uninterrupted time in the place and state of mind I refer to as The Glide, I had achieved a perceptual breakthrough of some sort and was experiencing the wave on a new level of the here-and-now.

I tried to extend my understanding of this visceral insight but found I could not; I could probe no further. Then it hit me. The barrier to added insight was of a practical nature:

I did not know how surfing worked.

Walking back toward the cantina with Shiner and the other surfer, I voiced this thought aloud.

The other surfer, thinking I was speaking to him, asked me what I meant.

"I know how that wave brought me in to shore," I said to him. "But how did I ride *across* it from all the way out there?"

I looked out at the distant lineup. Someone else had paddled out and was sitting at about the same spot where I'd caught the wave. Although we'd walked nearly a hundred yards back in his direction along the shore, he still seemed very far away.

By what means *had* I traveled down the coast?

"The wave pushed you," the other surfer said, tentatively.

No, the wave didn't push me *across* it. It only pushed me toward shore.

"Gravity," the guy said. "You surfed *down* the wave."

I'd started at sea level and wound up at sea level. The concept of "down" did not apply.

The more I thought about it, the less I understood the mechanism of what I'd just done. It wasn't that I couldn't grasp the complexity of it; quite the reverse. My limitation was that some essential simplicity eluded me.

All I really knew was that I had found the perfect place on a perfect wave, and I had remained there endlessly. *Forever.*

Author's Note

A selection of color photographs about my time in Mexico and Central America is offered on my Web site, www.aweisbecker.com. My forthcoming book, the sequel to *In Search of Captain Zero*, is excerpted, as is my previous novel, *Cosmic Banditos,* which due to its still-growing cult status, is now back in print. Additional sea writings and photos are also published on the site, along with recommended readings for those interested in the activity of surfing.

Acknowledgments

My deepest gratitude to my agent, Mary Tahan of Clausen, Mays & Tahan Literary Agency, for her smarts, dogged determination, and faith from the beginning. Thanks to David Groff, who saw potential in my rough, imperfectly hewn manuscript. And thanks to my editor, Wendy Hubbert, for her determination to make this book the best it could be.

I also wish to thank the following people for their various forms of support: Patrick Abrams, David Stanford, Joe and Nikki Giannini, Eric Eastman, Beverly Rudman, Walter Iooss, Maria Lourenco, Diana Bredbenner, Linda Grant, Denise McCleod, Candice Crossley, Tony Caramanico, Jim Goldberg, Patti Goldberg, Dave and Julie Marcley, Anthony Boas, David Achong (and the Tobago surf crew), Shelley Lauzon, Mike Potts, Chuck Weimar, Mike Stewart, Jason Barlogh, Erin Lesko, Diane W. Doryland, Patti Weiss, Roland Eisenberg, Russ Drumm, Will Allison, Hank Heckel, Stewart and Madge Lester. I've saved the best for last: Lesley K. Logan.

My apologies to Peter Fried, Bill Traver and Perry Newton, for indirectly slighting them.

Thanks also to Peter Matthiessen for *Far Tortuga,* my long-ago reading of which led to the writing of this book.

And my profound gratitude to Captain David Casiles and the crew of *Atlantis II* for their courage, seamanship and deep regard for their fellow man.

About the Author

ALLAN WEISBECKER is a novelist, screenwriter, lifelong surfer, and award-winning photojournalist whose work has appeared in *Smithsonian*, *Men's Journal*, *Popular Photography*, *American Photo*, *Sailing*, *Surfer*, *Surfing*, and *The Surfer's Journal*. He is the author of *Cosmic Banditos*, a novel said by reviewers to "out-gonzo Hunter S. Thompson." Weisbecker lives in Long Island, New York.